A CICERONIAN SUNBURN

Studies in Rhetoric/Communication
Thomas W. Benson, Series Editor

A CICERONIAN SUNBURN

A Tudor Dialogue on Humanistic
Rhetoric and Civic Poetics

E. ARMSTRONG

University of South Carolina Press

© 2006 University of South Carolina

Published in Columbia, South Carolina,
by the University of South Carolina Press

Manufactured in the United States of America

10 09 08 07 06   5 4 3 2 1

Library of Congress Cataloging-in-Publication Data

Armstrong, E. (Edward), 1965–
  A Ciceronian sunburn : a Tudor dialogue on humanistic rhetoric and civic poetics / E. Armstrong.
    p. cm.—(Studies in rhetoric/communication)
  Includes bibliographical references (p.) and index.
  ISBN 1-57003-614-4 (cloth : alk. paper)
  1. English poetry—Early modern, 1500–1700—History and criticism. 2. Humanists—England.
3. Literature and society—England—History—16th century. 4. English language—Early modern,
1500–1700—Rhetoric. 5. Cicero, Marcus Tullius—Appreciation—England. 6. Sidney, Philip,
Sir, 1554–1586—Technique. 7. Spenser, Edmund, 1552?–1599—Technique. 8. Cicero, Marcus
Tullius—Influence. 9. English poetry—Roman influences. 10. Social ethics in literature. I. Title.
II. Series.
  PR525.H86A76 2006
  821'.309—dc22

005025949

For E. Aidan

Know, then, that you are a god, if a god is that which lives, feels, remembers, and foresees, and which rules, governs, and moves the body over which it is set, just as the Supreme God above us rules the universe.

—Scipio in Cicero, De Re Publica

Salute the Poet
Who saw the Sky
In a Puddle Under a Horse.

—Kenneth Burke, "Archai"

It's all social, and it's all talk, talk, talk.

—Kurt Vonnegut, TimeQuake

CONTENTS

SERIES EDITOR'S PREFACE

In *A Ciceronian Sunburn: A Tudor Dialogue on Humanistic Rhetoric and Civic Poetics,* E. Armstrong conducts an ingenious and energetic revisioning of humanist pedagogy in Tudor England. He explores a time when Cicero's *De Oratore* was read in contrast to the pedagogical doctrines of Peter Ramus, and when the relation of civic discourse and poetry was challenged. Armstrong traces humanist rhetoric through the work of Philip Sidney, Lodowick Bryskett, and, especially, Edmund Spenser. Armstrong argues that the poetry of Sidney and Spenser enacts a deeply rhetorical mode of thinking that owes much to Cicero's description of civic and prudential action in the civic world. Armstrong traces the use of dialogue in humanist pedagogy, the civic potential of poetry, the relation of rhetoric to poetry, and the influence of the contrast between Cicero and Ramus on these matters. In humanist dialogue, writes Armstrong, these Tudor poets were retaining for readers a strongly Ciceronian sense of the interdependence of sensory experience, emotion, intellect, and language.

Armstrong's original and important study will be of interest to scholars of Renaissance rhetoric and, it is hoped, to teachers and students interested in how another age responded to the threatened displacement of a civic and humanistic culture by formalism, academicism, specialist expertise, and technique, by rediscovering in Cicero and in dialogue a way to enact a civic, moral, practical, and prudential mode of thinking and acting in the world.

ACKNOWLEDGMENTS

WHAT GOOD YOU MIGHT DEEM to come of this book is largely due to the labor, patience, counsel, encouragement, and good will of others. In particular, I am grateful to Jeffrey Walker, Jack Selzer, and Rosa Eberly for their unflagging guidance and support. Thomas O. Sloane's readings and comments on early incarnations of this work were both generous and invaluable. Another kind of debt is due Professor Sloane as well, Victoria Kahn, too, for that matter, as their estimable work in the rhetorical culture of the Renaissance motivated and fed my interest in this area of inquiry. That interest was galvanized and greatly informed further through a seminar on Giambattista Vico at the Folger Library in Washington, D.C., led by Donald Philip Verene in the winter of 1994. I am also indebted to those friends and colleagues who have either read and commented on or discussed at length with me the matter of this book, especially Andrew Alexander, Janet Atwill, Don Bialostosky, Joseph Candido, Richard Cunningham, and Dominic Delli Carpini. To Barry Blose I am grateful for the careful and considerate manner in which he has brought this project to fruition. The many smart and useful insights provided by the readers Barry found have contributed greatly to this end result. The intellectual shortfalls, omissions, and errors that persist are mine alone—and they persist in spite of the sagacity and good sense proffered by those mentioned above. Thank you to those many students over the years who buoyed me with both their energy and abilities. And finally, yes, Aidan, I do think the moon and stars make music—and I can't thank you enough for asking the question.

A CICERONIAN SUNBURN

CHAPTER ONE

※

TROPING TULLY

*The best book that ever Tully wrote, by all men's judgment, and by his
own testimony too, in writing whereof he employed most care, study,
learning and judgment, is his book* De oratore ad Quintum fratrem.

—*Roger Ascham,* The Schoolmaster, *1570*

WHEN SIR PHILIP SIDNEY CONCLUDES HIS INQUIRY into "why England, the
mother of excellent minds, should be grown so hard a stepmother to poets" in his
Defence of Poetry, he seems surprised to find himself commenting on Marcus Tul-
lius Cicero's *De oratore:*[1] "But what? Methinks I deserve to be pounded for straying
from poetry to oratory. But both have such an affinity in the wordish considera-
tion, that I think this digression will make my meaning receive the fuller under-
standing" (119).

But what? Why might a good sixteenth-century humanist be taken aback at
finding any discussion of the one art complete or persuasive without some consid-
eration of the other? Every lad in grammar school knew of oratory's and poetry's
"affinity in the wordish consideration." Likewise, poetry's identification with epi-
deictic, the rhetorical genre of praise and blame, and its shared goals with oratory
to "teach, delight, and move" were commonplace knowledge. The ostensible and
utterly pedestrian point of Sidney's straying—that the spare, judicious use of simili-
tudes helps create a "sound style"—certainly does not justify such a dramatic turn.
If the digression is ironic (and it is, of course), then what circumstances might war-
rant such a posture? That is, what else might poetry and oratory share beyond
simple matters of style? And isn't the promise of a "fuller understanding" of his
"meaning" intriguing, especially when one considers that this digression concerns
the whole of his argument?[2]

Surely Sidney could depend on his readers assenting to the proposition that
poetry and oratory are bound together in their "wordish consideration." But, and

just as surely, he could count on their disagreement about what the composition, utility, value, and ends of such considerations were to be. A "fuller understanding" of the argument of Sidney's *Defence,* that is, depends on his readers' ability not only to apprehend a material similarity between oratory and poetry as rhetorical arts but also to see some likeness in their status within the current conversation on learning. And underlying that conversation is Cicero. Twice Crassus, to whom Sidney had just referred, declares that the "poet is the very near kinsman to the orator."[3] And in the *Orator,* Cicero claims that epideictic is the "nurse" and "cradle of the orator."[4] Perhaps the orator, too, nourished as he is on the milk of poetry, has found a "hard welcome in England," a land, Sidney says, that has "grown so hard a stepmother to poets."

This kinship between the orator and poet of which Crassus speaks, and on which Sidney relies for a fuller understanding of his argument, is at the heart of this inquiry. However, the dynamics and complexity of that relationship remain muted within the contemporary conversation on Tudor letters. In questioning the rhetorical turf inhabited by Tudor poets, the argument of this work seeks to extend our understanding of rhetoric within the late Tudor conversation of learning. There are at least three interrelated topics common to each of the following eight chapters. The first and most general of these topics involves the civic offices of rhetoric, the second involves an estimation of the scope and influence of Cicero / Ciceronian oratory, and the third involves, as the tableau above indicates, the role of poetic discourse within the broader conversation on learning. The matter as well as the manner in which each of these topics are addressed in this study are intended to offer a perspective on the discursive protocols and contexts dominant within the scholarship on the early modern period—and on the teaching of the same. This is to say that there are at least two rhetorical cultures with which my argument concerns itself explicitly: humanist rhetorical culture and the contemporary rhetorical culture that discovers some value in the history of ideas characteristic of that period.

In the late 1560s, Roger Ascham confidently assured his beloved Tully that "your own books, Cicero, be as well read, and your excellent eloquence is as well liked and loved, and as truly followed in England at this day, as it is now, or ever was, since your own time."[5] A generation later, Francis Bacon's efforts to advance learning beyond the "hunt . . . after words" critiques Ascham among others for deifying Cicero—and not without cause.[6] In the intervening thirty years or so, how one chose to interpret, to translate Tully into the realm of learning informed and shaped not merely the why and what of the matter but also how one chose to achieve the rhetorical aims "to teach, delight, and move." The controversies over the imitation of Cicero, controversies that themselves find authority in the competing stories of rhetoric presented by Antonius and Crassus, turned on the question

of rhetoric's capacity "to teach." In *De oratore,* both Antonius and Crassus repeat-
edly confront, as Anthony Grafton and Lisa Jardine write, the significant problem
of relating "the standard banalities of curriculum teaching to the ideals of oratori-
cal competence as an activity meshed with, and vital to the civilised status of the
community."[7] However, the conventional configuration of sixteenth-century
humanist learning is predicated on the idea that the civic offices of rhetoric were
all but discarded throughout the course of the century. These civic offices—offices
that provide rhetoric its philosophical backbone, educational imperative, genera-
tive energy, and utterly human countenance—withered away, the story goes, into
poetry and rote pedagogy. George Kennedy's influential narrative of rhetoric's
"decline," for example, charts the privileged and vital position rhetoric had among
quattrocento humanists, who recognized rhetoric to be an "intellectually demand-
ing advanced discipline" with civic priorities, to its fall into rote pedagogy and aes-
thetics in the sixteenth century.[8] Similarly, Grafton and Jardine demonstrate how
the gradual institutionalization of humanism throughout the sixteenth century
effectively reduced the ideals of an earlier humanism to pedagogical fodder.[9]
Although echoes of a civic humanism remain, the goal of preparing students for
the rough-and-tumble realm of statecraft becomes subordinated to the exigencies
of pedagogy. In this context, the "pragmatic humanism" of the late sixteenth cen-
tury strikes vaguely anti-intellectual chords in its reductive, classroom-based char-
acter, its aesthetic pretensions, and its unflinching dedication to upward social
mobility.

In many respects, of course, the story of sixteenth-century humanist rhetoric is
the story of the gradual institutionalization of Italian civic humanism. In making
education more palatable for the youths of a growing middle class, northern Euro-
pean pedagogues effectively appealed to the cultural norms, ambitions, and pre-
tensions of their clientele. But this focus on the institutional development of
humanism functions on the premise that the humanist conversation on learning
was primarily, if not only, an academic conversation held among notable peda-
gogues for the benefit of youths.[10] No doubt this institutionalized perspective con-
tributes to what Debora Kuller Shuger provocatively has argued to be the myth of
humanist orthodoxy, an orthodoxy that relies on an "oversimplified . . . 'monologi-
cal'" ideology "roughly identical to . . . the 'Elizabethan World Picture.'"[11]

In Tudor England, poets, too, sought to teach as well as delight and move their
readers. And yet poetic discourse is thought to register the loss of rhetoric's civic
debts and traditions most keenly. Ann Moss, for example, articulates an extreme
version of the conventional view when she claims that Renaissance poetics increas-
ingly "becomes above all self-referential. . . . It is not obliged to be a sign for some-
thing outside of itself. A poem signifies by reference to other poems . . . and [is]
poetic because it takes its material from a repertory of literary fictions . . . and has

entirely within its own linguistic resources the power to produce aesthetic ecstasy."[12] Poetry's alleged attempts to garner authority by cannibalizing its discursive quirks works to diminish whatever profit it might have for more socially engaged modes of discourse, including the discourse of learning.

In practice, this focus on the academic incarnations of rhetoric, although it will acknowledge the study of poetic practices, marginalizes and gladly resigns them to an attendant critical tradition predicated on and dedicated to the praise and blame of the timeless, transcendent, and ultimately private nature of poetic knowledge. Though rhetoric's ostensible decline is acknowledged to play a significant role in the great intellectual vicissitudes characteristic of the early modern period—as an embattled scholasticism, a waning Erasmian humanism, and a waxing rationalism vie for institutional and cultural legitimacy—the concomitant ascendancy of poetic discourse remains largely incidental to and merely illustrative of these changes.[13] If, however, poetic practices are removed from the periphery of *a* humanism, dislodged from the confines and peculiarities of a literary history, and viewed as *participating* within their contemporary conversations on learning, if only as a starting point, significant shortcomings attendant the conventional readings (and non-readings) of humanist poetic practices begin to appear.

Consider this example. Sidney's surprise at having strayed from poetry to oratory comes on the heels of a consideration of the similitude. He draws on Cicero's depiction of Antonius and Crassus to support his claim that the "force of a similitude" does not rest in its capacity "to prove anything to a contrary disputer, but only to explain to a willing hearer" (*Defence,* 118). Having earlier defined learning, in part, as the "enriching of memory, enabling of judgement, and enlarging of conceit," Sidney critiques those "professors of learning" who employ similitudes that tax the memory and fail to inform judgment (82, 118). He does not turn to poets or orators for productive examples of similitudes; instead, he commends those "smally learned courtiers" who effectively use similitudes, albeit unwittingly, to produce the ends of learning by "following that which by practice [they] findeth fittest to nature" (118–19).

In his *Analysis* of the *Defence,* Sidney's friend, erstwhile employee, and ardent Ramist, William Temple, faults Sidney for associating the similitude with oratory and, by extension, whatever purchase the similitude might have on a rhetorically based, "natural" process of learning. Temple maintains that a "simile [*similitudo*] . . . is not an ornament of rhetorical eloquence, but an argument of logical invention, since there is in simile a certain force for arguing and explaining something."[14] Though, in theory, Temple could be satisfied by a simile, it would be only on the grounds that its efficacy and explanatory prowess are disassociated from the vagaries of persuasion and attached to the formalities of the art of logic. In view of the subordination of rhetoric to logic implicit in this analysis (and explicit throughout the *Analysis*), Temple—a scholarly "contrary disputer," not a "willing hearer"—is unlikely to apprehend an "affinity" between oratory and poetry premised on the rhetorical arts' capacity to inform and effect learning (especially when that affinity is discovered in a comparison to Cicero, who, as Ramists were keen on pointing out, attributed more to the art of oratory than was proper). The fullness of Temple's understanding on this central point can not extend beyond what Sidney terms those "artificial rules" devised by the rhetorician and logician to "soonest prove and persuade . . . within the circle of a question according to the proposed subject matter" (*Defence,* 78).

But what is at stake here? Why is it so important for Sidney to argue that poetry be regarded as a valuable form of learning? And what role might oratory's commensurate status have in the matter? You will recall that Sidney uses learning writ large for the exigence of his argument; he feels obliged to make "a pitiful defence of poor poetry" because it "from almost the highest estimation of learning is fallen to be the laughing-stock of children" (74). He takes exception especially with those "poet haters" who, on the authority of Plato, maintain that poetry is the "nurse of abuse" and should be banished from the commonwealth (101–2).[15] Poetry, Sidney argues throughout the *Defence,* actually offers a kind of learning both essential to and conducive to civil life. Virtuous action is what the poet best teaches —and best moves one toward—and virtue can only be realized within the body politic, with the knowledge of oneself in one's "ethic and politic considerations" (83). The scholar, the pedagogue, "the philosopher, in respect to his methodical proceeding" (91) are the ones who have forgotten their civic obligations, who have forgotten that "the ending end" of knowledge is "well-doing, and not of well-knowing only" (83).

Sidney and Edmund Spenser, to whom this study devotes most of its attention, recognized the implications inscribed in academic renderings for poetry's potential to teach. In response, their poetic practices enact a deeply rhetorical mode of thinking embedded in the practical or prudential reasoning of civic life. The author of *The Faerie Queene* may seem an odd, if not perverse, choice to include in a narrative designed to argue the civic, prudential potential of poetics for both rhetorical scholars and literary critics alike. Spenser, perhaps more than any other poet of the period, is charged with a "monological" world view. Rooted in Protestant doctrine, Neoplatonism, and a rarified realm of poesy, his ethical idealism makes heroic efforts to sow moral doctrine in a corrupt, indifferent world—or so goes the critical narrative.[16] Often described as the "Prince of Poets" in reference to the inscription Ann Clifford, the countess of Dorset, set in the memorial to Spenser in Westminster Abbey, Spenser perhaps more than any other figure appears to typify humanist poetics in the conventional sense. Yet Sidney's characterization of the poet as the "right popular philosopher" (87) was neither disingenuous nor hyperbolic;

good poets did not then, as they do not now, write to be taught by pedagogues to adolescents. They wrote for a relatively small yet influential adult public whose actions as landowners, patrons of learning, diplomats, courtiers, civil servants, and trades people directly affected and reflected on Her Majesty's political body.

My inclusion of Sidney and, in particular, Spenser as *participants* within humanist discourse invested in a rhetorically inscribed moral philosophy steeped in Cicero is intended to address a persistent disconnect between students of Renaissance rhetorical culture and Renaissance literary critics. Historical inquiries into the intellectual currencies of humanist rhetoric seldom engage in the study of poetic practices in a sustained manner (though poetics in general is a recurrent topic). Cultural critiques strung together on the authority of canonical literary figures have demonstrated little use for the historical currents of rhetoric.[17] This book owes its greatest debts and seeks to contribute to the former, though I am optimistic that it might have some bearing on the practices of literary criticism (to which another kind of debt is certainly owed) as well.[18] In particular, this study is informed by Jeffrey Walker's efforts in *Rhetoric and Poetics in Antiquity* to tell a "sophist's history of 'rhetoric'" in that it "includes 'poetry' and 'poetics' as essential, central parts of 'rhetoric's' domain."[19] Sidney's straying from poetry to oratory certainly suggests such a turn of mind. And as I aim to demonstrate, Spenser's understanding might very well be characterized as "sophistic" in the sense of his understanding of the centrality of poetics to rhetoric, as well as in his grasp of the expanse of epideictic in general. Walker characterizes epideictic as

> that which shapes and cultivates the basic codes of value and belief by which a society or culture lives; it shapes the ideologies and imageries with which, and by which, the individual members of a community identify themselves; and, perhaps most significantly, it shapes the fundamental grounds . . . that will underlie and ultimately determine decision and debate in particular pragmatic forums. . . . Epideictic can also work to challenge and transform conventional beliefs. (9)

Although the real or purported efficacy of particular pieces of poesy such as Sidney's *Astrophil and Stella* or Spenser's *Shepheardes Calendar* may call into question the grandeur of Walker's vision, this consideration of epideictic is compelling. It not only offers a radically different theoretical grounding for the study of literature than that which might be gleaned from traditional, and dominant, scholarly and classroom practices but also encourages us to reconsider and address the practical effects of our own discussions of literature, as well as the forms and forums available for doing so.

This book attempts to bring some of the issues attendant to telling a(nother) "sophist's history of rhetoric" to the fore in both matter and form. That is, I have endeavored to enact my argument—*to do,* rhetorically, the understanding of rhetoric privileged in the argument. (This is why, for example, the scope, method and purpose of this work—matter typically relegated to a preface—can not be neatly separated from this introduction to it.) The aim is to perform a type of rhetorical criticism that is both demonstrative and indicative, to engage rhetoric's capacity to be a theoretical or hermeneutical art while exploiting rhetoric's power to perform practical criticism. Central to this effort is the use of rhetorical tropes to both marshal and support the argument. The title of this book, *A Ciceronian Sunburn,* is one attempt toward that end; it is a metaphor intended to offer an insight into the Tudor discourse of humanistic learning in the late sixteenth century. As a trope, as the quintessential trope, the metaphor may be conceived of simply as a "translation," an "alteration," as Thomas Wilson writes in his *Art of Rhetoric* (1560), "of a word from the proper and natural meaning to that which is not proper and yet agreeth thereunto by some likeness that appeareth to be in it" (196, 198). Or to paraphrase Paul Ricouer, metaphors extend and displace the meanings of words.[20]

The efficacy of tropes or translations such as the metaphor and its conceptual cousins the analogy and similitude does not depend entirely on their ability to conjure a likeness; they also suggest a context for that likeness. That is, their efficacy also depends on the reader's ability to sense and affirm the *propriety* of the translation. Both the likeness conjured and the aptness of that likeness are *probable* qualities contingent not only on the "proper meaning" invoked but also on the use of that invocation in a particular situation—on its rhetorical purpose. As a metaphor, thus, a *Ciceronian sunburn* is intended to capture a sense of the relationships within the Tudor discourse of learning among Antonian rhetoric and Crassus's sense of the rhetorical; it attempts to take measure of how the kinship between the poet and orator was variously translated within a particular rhetorical culture influenced by Cicero.

The original context for the title comes from a passage in the second book of Cicero's *De oratore.* The following context and meaning are what this title and this inquiry aims to displace and extend. The majority of book 2 is where the gifted and accomplished orator Antonius recounts his understanding of the matter, means, and ends of the art of oratory. While digressing into history in order to illustrate that the "orator need be only a man of some learning," Antonius seemingly betrays his thesis by demonstrating a subtle grasp of historical matter. When Caesar and Cotta point this out, he assures them that it is but the color of learning obtained while whiling away the time with some old Greek books:

> Just as, when walking in the sunshine, though perhaps for a different reason, the natural result is that I get sunburnt, even so, after perusing those books rather closely at Misenum (having little chance at Rome), I find that under their influence my discourse takes on what I may call a new complexion. (2.14.60)

In this context, one might infer that the title's metaphor proposes that the complexion of the late Tudor discourse on learning was colored by Cicero. Admittedly, this proposition is relatively uncontroversial, if not downright prosaic. There were other stars in the sky of sixteenth-century learning, to be sure, although no other figure equaled Cicero (except, perhaps, Aristotle) in magnitude, brilliance, or influence in the estimation of the most prominent participants in the late Tudor conversation on learning. Further, the identification of Cicero with "excellent eloquence," as Ascham avers repeatedly, proposes another modest, yet not insignificant, extension of the title's metaphor in that it gestures toward the privileged place of the rhetorical arts within the discourse on learning.

However true the above translations might be, they are limited insofar as they remain aligned with the story of rhetoric Antonius tells. Although well respected for his own considerable learning, Antonius proves unwilling to burden the art of oratory with the qualities and duties typically associated with the acquisition and exercise of knowledge. He maintains that "the activity of the orator has to do with opinion, not knowledge [*scientia*]"; the art of oratory itself, he says, "is founded on falsehood [*mendacio*]" (2.7.30). Although there are "some very clever rules . . . for playing upon men's feelings and making prizes of their goodwill," oratory but "wears the likeness of an art" (2.8.33). As a purveyor of opinion and manipulator of emotion, Antonius's ideal orator need only attain the semblance of learning to obtain his immediate rhetorical goals. The "clever rules" comprising this pseudo-art, complemented by whatever "learning" one might pick up, are what constitute the matter of Antonius's art of oratory.

The incidental relationship between the rhetorical arts and learning that his sunburn analogy commends is indicative of the rhetorical tradition that remains very much with us today, and it is the primacy of that tradition this work seeks to displace. In the sixteenth century, that tradition was not as firmly entrenched. Ascham understood the limitations Antonius's analogy implied for the far-reaching powers of eloquence he advocates. In fact, he appropriates it to caution teachers from using epitomes to guide their students' learning. The reliance on these brief, sententious statements to comprehend difficult matters, Ascham writes, "maketh so many seeming, and sunburnt ministers as we have, whose learning is gotten in a summer heat, and washed away, with a Christmas snow again."[21] For Ascham, the appearance of learning is no substitute for the disciplined, "orderlie study" aimed at the acquisition of true Ciceronian eloquence. In a different yet not unrelated way, Sir Philip Sidney relies on his readers' familiarity with Antonius's sunburn analogy when he recounts the process that led him to devise a poem for his beloved in the first sonnet of *Astrophil and Stella*:

> I sought fit words to paint the blackest face of woe:
> Studying inventions fine, her wits to entertaine,

> Oft turning others' leaves, to see if thence would flow
> Some fresh and fruitfull showers upon my sunne-burn'd braine.
> But words came halting forth, wanting Invention's stay.
> (5–9)[22]

Perusing books fails Astrophil; his attempts to invent a language to entertain the wits of his beloved are unstayed or unsupported by "turning others' leaves"—by walking leisurely in a lettered garden. His "sunne-burn'd braine" is left wanting for words. The muse who finally admonishes Sidney to "look in thy heart, and write" (14) commends a different kind of invention, a different kind of learning. Although the rhetorical character of this latter instance may be suspect, at the very least one might say that Sidney appropriates the kind of learning advocated by Antonius in order to point toward some alternative.

Crassus, whom Cicero offers as a dialogic counterpoint to Antonius in *De oratore* and in whom, as Ascham rightly notes, "Tully . . . maketh his example of eloquence and true judgment in learning" (*Schoolmaster*, 83), argues that the version of rhetoric advocated by Antonius greatly diminishes the purview and duties of rhetoric. In stark contrast to Antonius, Crassus confers on eloquence the power to embrace nothing less than

> the origin and operation and development of all things, all the virtues and duties, all the natural principles governing the morals and minds and life of mankind, and also determines their customs, laws, and rights, and controls the government of the state, and expresses everything that concerns whatever topic in a graceful and flowing [*ornate copioseque*] style. (*De oratore* 3.20.76)

The expanse of oratory Crassus presents is certainly difficult to grasp, though I believe it is not unlike in kind from the vision of epideictic Walker articulates. One starting point may be simply to acknowledge invention, traditionally the first of rhetoric's five canons, to be the primary issue. For Antonius, the orator ultimately relies on the knowledge invented by and demonstrated in the other arts in order to win points. Crassus, however, empowers the orator to invent, discover, and prove the origins of "all things." Crassus's orator comprehends, that is, "the origin and operation and development of all things" because he recognizes a greater role for language in *making* knowledge; he understands rhetoric's subject matter to be part and parcel of the activity of human learning itself. It is only in light of Crassus's contributions to the dialogue that the delimited version of rhetoric indicated by Antonius's sunburn analogy may be realized, and extended, to accrue additional layers of meaning. It is in view of Crassus's version of oratory that the title of this work seeks to extend the role of poetics within the late Tudor conversation on learning.

Another way in which I have tried to capture a sense of those relationships is to frame this narrative as a dialogue. There are (again) three, interrelated levels to this conversation. One level comprises the conversation among Tudor poets and scholars. Each of the Tudor authors contained herein knew, knew of, and often appropriated one another in their work. In a real way in some instances, and in a textual sense, Lodowick Bryskett, whose *Discourse of Civill Life* (1606) comprises the matter of the second chapter, Edmund Spenser, Spenser's glossarist E. K., Abraham Fraunce, Sidney, and Sir William Temple were speaking with one another.

The chapter on Bryskett's *Discourse* offers a close examination of what might be best described as humanistic or Ciceronian moral philosophy. In Bryskett's *Discourse,* a Ciceronian inflected understanding of Aristotelian *phronesis* is advanced over religious dogma, political fawning, and contemporary pedagogical practices. Bryskett, a longtime friend and colleague of Spenser, prominently figures the poet in the dialogue as the putative authority on the matter to be discussed. The third and fourth chapters offer an account of Spenser's poetic ethos through an analysis of the layers of dialogue comprising *The Shepheardes Calender:* the academic formalism that informs E. K.'s efforts to teach (the focus of chapter 3) is juxtaposed against Immeritô's rhetorical figuring forth of Colin Clout within his social circumstances in chapter 4. The fourth chapter draws on the physiological and socially inscribed moral philosophy Bryskett presents in his *Discourse* to interpret the poetry of the *Calender.*

Another level of this conversation looks to the divergent visions of learning—or Ciceronianisms—advanced by Erasmus and Peter Ramus, the two most influential figures of sixteenth-century northern humanism. Ramus, in fact, makes several appearances throughout the first few chapters, as he does via Temple above, before the section on his *Brutinae quaestiones* (*The Questions of Brutus*) in chapter 5. In that chapter, Ramus's idea of rhetoric is contrasted with that of Erasmus, whose *On the Tongue* offers an intellectual context to the previous chapters on Bryskett and Spenser as well as the analyses of Sidney, Temple, and Fraunce that follow in chapter 6. Erasmus's *On the Tongue* and Peter Ramus's *Questions of Brutus* provide another perspective on those same topics from which the rhetorical matter of the Tudor conversation are drawn, namely, ethics, aesthetics/poetry, teaching, politics, and the scope of rhetoric. A general topic comprising them all might be termed "on learning." The sixth chapter, "Making Matter for a Conceit, Making Conceit Matter," develops the significance of Ciceronian rhetoric for the discourse of Tudor humanism in general by juxtaposing poets and scholars. Focusing on Spenser's and Sidney's use of Cicero's sunburn analogy to discuss the nature and office of rhetorico-poetic invention, I show how the conscription of their poetry into the service of Ramist dialectic by Abraham Fraunce and William Temple reconfigures and diminishes the moral expanse of poetry by redefining Ciceronian eloquence in terms of form instead of human action.

Chapters 7 and 8 function as a *confirmatio* of the previous chapters by developing the political and ethical "parts" of moral philosophy with regard to what has been called Spenser's "least poetic" and most overtly political work, *A View of the Present State of Ireland* (1596), and his "most poetic" work, book 6, canto 10 of *The Faerie Queene*. Together, these works enact and advance a principled yet circumspect conception of Ciceronian *prudentia* in view of the prominent political, intellectual, and religious orthodoxies commonly used to interpret these works.

A third level of the dialogue locates these early modern disputes on learning, both historically and intellectually, in topoi discovered in Cicero's *De oratore* and *De officiis*. In the final chapter, however, I also draw on Kenneth Burke's discussion of courtesy in conjunction with Cicero in order to consider Colin Clout's musings on Mt. Acidale "from the ethical, creative, poetic point of view."[23] These sallies into Cicero are intended to either "prove" or "set-up" viable topoi I want to claim are functional in the Tudor discourse on learning. This method of proof comes piecemeal, as needed, rather than in one unified analysis "On Cicero." Again, my emphasis on the potential for Cicero to provide a kind of proof is found primarily in his authority among Tudor humanists; what matter I draw from Cicero stands thus in some proportion to or is analogous to the matter of this historical inquiry.

This principle of analogy asks one to compare at least two phenomena in order to conjure some likeness; the propriety and ultimately the sense of that matter is for the reader to judge. "The great danger of analogy," writes Kenneth Burke in *Permanence and Change*, "is that a similarity is taken as evidence of identity" (97). In James Berlin's attempt to discover a historiographic method that "foregrounds difference over identity," he disavows those such as Thomas O. Sloane and myself (albeit prospectively) "who see in Cicero's *De oratore* a discussion of an argument that 'serves as a good index to the subsequent history of rhetoric'" on the basis that we "somehow overlook the obvious differences between the violently antidemocratic Rome of Cicero and the contemporary commitment to democracy found in most Western states."[24] Berlin maintains that this "historical conception . . . sees the past and present as identical" (122). The dialectic of "identity" and "difference" Berlin posits would appear to preclude analogy as a viable and valuable form of proof. Analogies, in fact, foreground likeness, not identity; and likenesses contain differences within similarity. Analogies say "like this but not like this" in one breath: analogical proof is indicative rather than declarative, presupposing contingency by containing probabilities. Again, the focus is on the relationship of this to that, never on any one particular thing.

Indeed, Cicero's own dialogic figurations of rhetoric in Antonius and Crassus suggest that rhetorical inquiry as well as inquiries into rhetoric comprise endless possibilities—as may be evidenced by both Renaissance and contemporary debates on his work. And as poets have long known, analogical proof compels the reader to participate in and with rather than observe or follow an author in action. Of course, there are those whom "by similitudes [are] not to be satisfied." Nevertheless, in keeping with the dialogic nature of *De oratore* as well as the Tudor discourse on learning itself, my excursions into Cicero's work attempt to affirm both the poetic and what might be termed the neoscholastic (or humanistic *and* humanist) versions of rhetoric current within sixteenth-century discourse.

Some readers may find my method of organization unusual, and it does place a different set of demands on the reader. Vaguely unconventional and conceptually derivative of the dialogue genre, my method makes modest gestures toward that "disorderly order" E. K. finds troublesome in poetry. There is a cumulative effect —the voice of Bryskett in chapter 2 speaks to Spenser's in the following chapters; their voices speak to the works of Sidney, Fraunce, and Temple in later chapters. Intermittent "digressions" into Cicero are intended to point toward a "fuller understanding" of my meaning by offering a historical and intellectual context for those conversations. The rationale for this particular fiction will, I hope, become clearer in the act of reading itself. It is a dialogue of sorts, a deliberate (and so fictitious) presentation of an issue designed to move one toward a "fuller understanding" of rhetoric and poetics in humanists' efforts to teach. Perhaps delight will occur in this process, too, though I offer no guarantees. At the very least, the following chapters might shorten the distance between now and then and us and them by drawing on some shared and sharable matter of human experience. What the matter of experience is and how we might make sense of it is the subject of the second chapter. And the vitality of Bryskett's *Discourse of Civill Life* owes much to the close kinship of the poet and orator—to how he tropes Tully.

———— ❁ ————

MAKING MORALITY

Lodowick Bryskett's *Discourse of Civill Life*

Virtutis laus, actio

PERHAPS THE OBSCURITY OF LODOWICK BRYSKETT'S WORK *"A Discourse of Civill Life": Containing the Ethike Parte of Morall Philosophie* relative to the humanist texts of the English Renaissance commonly surveyed by scholars requires no explanation.[1] Its 1606 publication date comes well after the more prominent and influential statements of Renaissance humanism had been made in Latin, Italian, or English. At the time of its publication, it appears to have been absorbed quietly into what Bryskett termed in his prefatory epistle "the infintenesse of bookes, which hath introduced the distinction of good and bad, used in Commonweales." And his pledge to publish another, already prepared treatise "containing the Politike part of Morall Philosophy" on the condition that he finds "favorable acceptation hereof" remained unfulfilled. When read as a statement of humanist values, the *Discourse* appears to be utterly typical: it affirms the ideals of the active life yet appears to praise the divinity of the contemplative, it relies eclectically on the usual array of ancient sources for support, it frames its views within the well-worn conventions of the dialogue, and a full two-thirds of the text is dedicated to outlining a program of education. The *Discourse,* furthermore, admits to consisting largely of material translated from *Tre dialoghi della vita civilè,* which formed the second portion of Giovanni Battista Giraldi's (Cinthio) *De gli hecatommithi* (1565), with additional observations culled from Alessandro Piccolomini's *Della institutione morale* (1560) and Stefano Guazzo's *La civil conversatione* (1574). Intended, as the extended title declares, "for the instruction of a Gentleman in the course of a vertuous life," the *Discourse* would seem to exemplify, rather unremarkably, that curious admixture of pedagogy, pragmatics, and philosophy characteristic of Renaissance humanism.

Appropriating Bryskett

In all likelihood, both Bryskett and his *Discourse* would have been all but forgotten if it was not for the author's peripheral interest, his footnotability, as it were, to students of English poetry.[2] A fast friend of Sir Philip Sidney, Bryskett accompanied the poet on his tour of Europe in 1572–74. Under the patronage of Sidney's father, Sir Henry Sidney, then lord deputy of the kingdom of Ireland, Bryskett began his career as a civil servant for the English government in Ireland in 1569. Bryskett remained closely associated with England's Irish affairs for the rest of his life; he died in 1612, shortly after retiring to his estate outside Dublin. While serving under the elder Sidney's successor, Lord Arthur Grey (to whom the *Discourse* is addressed), Bryskett befriended the poet Edmund Spenser. It was Spenser who took over Bryskett's position as secretary to Lord Grey in 1582,when Bryskett took a self-imposed respite from his official duties, which he claims furnished the occasion for this dialogue. Bryskett figures one "Mr. Edm. Spenser" as a speaker or character, having him speak of his epic-in-progress, *The Faerie Queene.* The first edition of Spenser's 1595 pastoral *Colin Clouts Come Home Againe* included two poems by Bryskett, "The Mourning Muse of Thestylis" and "A Pastorall Æglogue upon the Death of Sir Phillip Sidney Knight"; Spenser, in all likelihood, figures Bryskett as *Thestylis* in *Colin Clouts.* And sonnet 33 of Spenser's sonnet sequence *Amoretti* (1595; in which the troubled lover laments "not finishing her Queene of faëry" [l.3]) is addressed specifically to "lodwick."

This biographical and textual evidence documenting Bryskett's and Spenser's friendship and their mutual appropriations of one another notwithstanding, scholars have been disinclined to attach much significance to Bryskett's *Discourse*. It is, by consensus, a minor work by a minor figure. Thematically consistent with other humanist works, the *Discourse* tropes English humanism—it is a literary curiosity made curious by virtue of the author's relationship and prosaic portrayal of Spenser. But the aim of this chapter is not to dispute Bryskett's status within literary history; instead, it will show that Bryskett's *Discourse* is representative of one of at least two possible, and substantively different, humanisms available in England around the turn of the century. Bryskett's *Discourse* participates within a larger debate. As such, it does not rehearse themes typical of or peculiar to humanism but addresses current issues important to late Tudor humanists; it does not repeat humanist topoi but redirects them; it does not restate humanist values but reaffirms certain humanist values and gainsays others. The following pages will focus on Bryskett's treatment of what I contend to be the crux of the contemporary debate into which he situates his dialogue—the philosophical significance of the rhetorical arts. Bryskett's close association with and appropriation of Spenser within his dialogue offers a contemporary context or, to be more precise, *conversation* within which the poet and his poetry, can be, and was, considered.

Framing Virtue

In *Spenser's Moral Allegory*, Sean Kane premises his argument on a distinction he makes between the "radically differing ways" in which Bryskett and Spenser chose to "address and organize the world."[3] Bryskett, he argues, offers his readers a "rational project" borne of the "new neoclassicism," which optimistically attempts to dominate and remake reality through the "[alarming] reassertion of the classical [or Roman] ideal of perfectibility through virtue" (4). The "dangerously mundane goal-seeking" implicit in Bryskett's project, Kane argues, would have been abhorrent to and far beneath the dignity of Spenser, whose poetry is more concerned with saving souls than civic happiness. Following the Christian Platonism of what Kane describes as "an older patristic humanism," Spenser's poetic art attempts to effect individual salvation by encouraging one to reconstitute his individual relationship with God in spite of, rather than as part of, civic happiness. Spenser's poetry, the argument goes, transcends the "goal-seeking" of earthly, human affairs by trafficking in the spiritual currency of the soul. Whatever the poet's sense of virtue might be, it ultimately relies on what one critic has termed an "aesthetic theology" for its authority.[4] Idealistic, constant, and perhaps ineffable, virtue defined in such terms is a mysterious quantity accessed and transmitted by the poet rather than a quality conditioned by circumstance and communicated by him.

Kane's narrative is worth noting because it deftly articulates some of the common critical assumptions brought to bear on Spenser's poetry: it offers Neoplatonism as the poet's philosophical umbrella, thus subordinating the temporal to the ontological; it presumes poetic discourse to be intrinsically significant; it assumes that the didactic dimension of humanist poetry is, if not opposed to, then inferior to and distinct from poetic delight; and it consecrates the poet's heroic status by placing him within the familiar battle wherein faith, will, metaphor, and feeling are used as weapons against interpretations of human history and the cold steel of reason's blade. Though Kane is right to situate Spenser's poetry within a convergence of two world views, within an emerging rationalism (for example, Bacon or Descartes) and the waning humanist discourse of an earlier generation, it is difficult to see how Bryskett's *Discourse* might actually reflect this new, "scientific" trend in philosophy. Largely a translation of Italian authors from the mid-sixteenth century, a dialogue (the literary genre of choice for many early humanists), and explicitly concerned with moral philosophy, not natural philosophy (the primary site of philosophical inquiry for the new rationalists) or divinity, the *Discourse* would seem to argue for a kind of humanism as well. That Bryskett appropriates Spenser as an authority and defender of the moral philosophy he expresses (often in terms that resonate with Spenser's own poetry) further suggests that their rhetorical goal seeking has more rather than less in common. Of course, appropriating poets was not an uncommon strategy in humanist discourse regardless of one's philosophical position, but Bryskett's use of Spenser is neither simply a kindly gesture toward a friend nor merely a rhetorical ploy designed to enhance his own credibility. Bryskett's appropriation is particularly apt because, ultimately, Bryskett self-consciously invests the *Discourse* with the power to move or persuade its readers toward virtuous action based on the authority of poetry. In fact, if it were not for the obvious generic difference, one would be hard pressed to discover significant philosophical distinctions between the *Discourse* and Spenser's body of work.

In the "Letter to Ralegh," for example, which accompanied the 1590 publication of the first three books of *The Faerie Queene,* Spenser declares that his offering represents the first portion of a (projected) twelve books that will portray "that part which they in Philosophie call Ethice, or vertues of a priuate man" in the figure of

> Arthure, before he was king, the image of a braue knight, perfected in the twelue priuate morall vertues, as Aristotle hath deuised, the which is the purpose of these first twelue books, which if I finde to be well accepted, I may be perhaps encoraged, to frame the other part of polliticke vertues in his person, after that hee came to be king.[5]

The enraged Irish, perhaps penury, and his death in 1599 conspired to prevent Spenser from publishing but six books—or one-fourth of this epic on the ethic and political considerations he proposed—to both the regret and great relief of generations of his readers.[6] In any event, here he has pointed directly to Aristotelian ethics as the area of philosophical inquiry that his surviving studies in holiness, temperance, chastity, friendship, justice, and courtesy inhabit. His "generall intention . . . to fashion a gentleman or noble person in vertuous and gentle discipline" thus attends specifically to the fashioning of the private conduct of his readers. These "twelue priuate morall vertues" are relevant to a man of action whose actions, significantly, are to be framed within, that is, complemented and completed by their civic or political consequences.[7]

Bryskett's *Discourse* not only shares the same general end as Spenser's epic, "to frame a gentleman fit for civill conversation, and to set him in the direct way that leadeth him to his civill felicitie" (5), but also presumes "the Ethike parte of Morall Philosophie" together with the "polliticke" to provide the appropriate frame of philosophical reference. And like Spenser—indeed, like all humanists writing on moral philosophy—Bryskett relies on Aristotle's technical "devising" of Moral Virtue as his ancient authority; from "his Ethikes," he says, "the rules of ciuill life are to be drawne" (74). This agreement on the general ends of Spenser's and Bryskett's work, on the authority of Aristotelian ethics, and the presence of Spenser himself as an authority in philosophy "both morall and naturall" (25) in the *Discourse* indicates that Bryskett's devising of Aristotelian ethics merits closer examination.

There are important differences in Spenser's "portraict" of the moral virtues and Bryskett's "containment" of the ethic part of moral philosophy. But I argue that the differences between Spenser's poetry and Bryskett's prose are formal differences, not differences in kind; they are the byproducts of their generic choices rather than some manifestation of the disruptive shift in the philosophical landscape. Within humanist discourse, Bryskett's dialogue and Spenser's poetry share and affirm the same rhetorical course. One generic distinction between Bryskett's prose and Spenser's poetry is, as Kane noted, that the *Discourse* does have a more formal character to it; that is, it appears to trust more in the powers of reason than the aesthetic powers of poetry to instruct its readers. The *Discourse* offers analysis and explication of ethics; it "devises" ethics as Aristotle did—the subject matter is orderly presented, comprehensively treated, and duly divided, broken down, and examined in each of its constituent parts. Another generic consequence is the scope of inquiry available. As we have seen, Spenser offered to "portraict" or figure forth the "twelve private moral virtues" in the person of Arthur; Bryskett, however, promises to "contain" ethics within a "discourse upon the morall vertues, not ommitting the intellectual [virtues]" (5). Both Spenser and Bryskett see their projects to range, in some way, over the twelve moral virtues. I want to suggest that this aspect, this canvassing of the "morall vertues," was perceived to be the poetic dimension of these texts. The addition of the intellectual virtues to Bryskett's subject matter is not insignificant. On the one hand, his discoursing on the intellectual virtues provides a theoretical frame that accounts for the more formal (that is, less poetic) character of his treatise; on the other hand, it is precisely that frame that explains or provides reasons for the poetic dimension of the text that resists the constraints of formalism. It is precisely Bryskett's addition of a theoretical frame, furthermore, that suggests why his *Discourse* might complement and augment Spenser's understanding of moral philosophy in general, ethics in particular, and the role of poetry in fashioning virtue. In the dialogue, Bryskett can explain, cogently, what and why the poet does what he does in a manner that the poet simply cannot.

Bryskett's analysis of the ethic part of moral philosophy—its origins, parts, concerns, and ends—is formal in the sense that it depends on the conventions of humanist philosophic discourse. It relies on the terms native to the subject, it would appear to eschew figurative language in its explication, it is to serve practical ends, and his analysis does not base its authority on the presumption that it will offer new knowledge or reform the wisdom of the ancients. Yet the intellectual or analytic dimension of the *Discourse* is not rigidly formal, nor does Bryskett seem to plan on inculcating moral virtue by simply providing a rational or theoretical model of it. In fact, he makes a point of declaring that his handling of ethics resists formal constraints at the very beginning of his treatise:

The course which I hold in this treatise, is by way of a dialogue (which I have chosen as best pleasing my minde). . . . Wherein though I have (I feare me) hazarded my selfe to be reprehended by such as looke after formalitie in all things: yet because my intention is to giue light as well to the meaner learned . . . as to the learneder critiques that spend their eyes to find a haire upon an egge; I haue more boldly followed my owne liking. (5)

Bryskett recognized that his decision to "contain the ethic part of moral philosophy" within a dialogue represents but one possible "course" within the contemporary debate on learning. Apparently, the proponents of another possible course, because they "looke after formalitie in all things," do not value the flexibility of the dialogue genre as a productive form of philosophical inquiry.

Throughout the *Discourse,* Bryskett regularly and directly contrasts his arguments concerning human learning and moral virtue against the arguments presented by the new formalists. The forms and formalities prized by those "learneder critiques" Bryskett later identifies more closely with the misguided practitioners of "that Logike which is vsed now a dayes most in schooles" (154). Following Roland MacIlmaine's translation of Peter Ramus's *Logike of the Moste Excellent Philosopher P. Ramus, Martyr* in 1574, the popularity of Ramist pedagogy grew rapidly throughout England, as the publishing record of Ramist texts shows.[8] Ramus's reputation as a "martyr" as a result of his rather gruesome death in the St. Bartholomew's Day Massacre in Paris in 1572 no doubt enhanced his reputation in England among religious and educational reformers alike. Ramism was especially endorsed at Cambridge, where Spenser's erstwhile mentor, Gabriel Harvey, was among one of its earliest advocates.

Ramus had developed a syllogistic method, a formal, analytical technique with which one could determine the truth or falsehood of any given proposition *unfailingly.* This method predicated its authority on two major assumptions: first, that though this method had its origins in antiquity, it represented a distilled, tidying-up, or reformation, of learning that corrected the errors of Aristotle, Cicero, and Quintilian in particular; second, that this new method imitated, or re-created, the natural machinations of one's own, divinely implanted reason. But Ramism was prized largely because it seemed to satisfy the practical, pedagogical obligations of humanist philosophy; its chief virtue was that it was easy to learn and easy to teach. Though Ramists appeared to toe the same line as earlier humanists insofar as they saw their endeavors to unite philosophy and eloquence, they premised their pedagogical theory on the assumption that eloquence was fundamentally separate and other than the pursuit of wisdom. Ramists defined the art of rhetoric solely in terms of the rules it offered for developing one's style (*elocutio*) and for the oral delivery of a speech (*pronunctatio*). Of the three remaining canons of classical rhetoric, memory (*memoria*) served as a kind of cognitive base from which all reasoning proceeded, and the discovery of matter (*inventio*) and the organization of it (*dispositio* or *iudicum*) were assigned to the art of dialectic. Philosophy for the Ramists could be found in the art of dialectic, or logic, which, when mastered, required the rules of rhetoric only for teaching. As nothing more than so many precepts and strategies to be learned by rote, the Ramist rhetorician surveyed an art of speaking well; in following the rules of rhetoric, one could speak well on any subject without regard to history, sociopolitical contexts, the passions, or other discursive contexts. Well speaking fell to the discretion of the logician; and what substantiated "well" relied on a single, formal method to assess the certain truth or certain falsehood of any given argument.

One significant result of Ramus's reconceptualization of learning thus was that both rhetoric and poetry were viewed as second-class arts designed to transmit and ornament preconceived, rational truths. Rhetoric and poetry were, at once, morally neutral and morally suspect because they employed language to affect the emotions and so were more likely to obscure rather than aid "true" reasoning. Poetry and grand displays of rhetorical *copia* were trivialized as bombast, pretty ornaments, and toys. The rhetorical arts were above suspicion only insofar as they rendered or "disposed of" the contemplated truth clearly and accurately for the benefit of instruction; and for such a purpose, it was a logical method that legislated the proper, or methodical, course of instruction. As Victoria Kahn has observed, after the arrival of Ramism, pedagogic handbooks in England "betray an anxiety about the use of figurative language—a use that requires practical judgment or discretion, and which involves an appeal to the passions."[9] It is within this broader conversation on humanist learning that Bryskett offers another course of learning by means of a dialogue that both seeks definition and discovers exigence in markedly different configurations of logic and rhetoric.[10]

Perhaps aware of those "learneder critiques" as potential members of his audience, Bryskett appears to permit the art of logic a very broad scope. Like the Ramists' claim that the art of logic was the supreme art because it alone taught men best to discover truth, Bryskett asserts that from logic "are gotten the instruments and the maner to deuide, to compound, to inuent and find out reasons and arguments; and finally to discerne and iudge of truth and falshood" (153–54). Bryskett, furthermore, appears to subordinate the art of rhetoric to the art of logic: "next to Logike is Rhetorike," for rhetoric draws its arguments from logic but employs them with "with lesse force and efficacie." But Bryskett offers important conditions on logic's primacy within the trivium that ardent Ramists would have found unacceptable.

Bryskett, for example, relies on the Aristotelian distinction between the sciences and the arts throughout his discussion, a distinction that Ramists had revised in their reformation of learning. For Aristotle, the "object of scientific knowledge exists of necessity, and is, consequently, eternal" (*NE* 1139b) and so belongs properly to theoretic wisdom, or what Bryskett generally calls speculative or theoretic knowledge.[11] The arts, however, are "concerned with the realm of coming-to-be, with contriving and studying how something which is capable both of being and not being may come into existence, a thing whose starting point is the producer and not the thing produced" (*NE* 1140a). Bryskett's characterization of logic as an art thus aligns it with practical wisdom, which "is concerned with human affairs and matters about which deliberation in possible" (*NE* 1141b). As an art, Bryskett maintains that logic is an "instrument of the sciences" rather than a science proper; as such, it must take the practical and contingent knowledge pertaining to human affairs for its subject matter. The new logicians, however, have made a "vaine science" of logic, presumably because they ascribe a divine or natural certitude to logic's truths, a certitude that denies or ignores practical contingencies.

By investing the rhetorical conventions of a liberal or humane art (described as method) with scientific certitude, these logicians have all but eliminated its more proper, productive and ethical role within probabilistic reasoning. Bryskett maintains that logic's search for truth under the aegis of the divine or natural sciences will be incomplete because that search must "as well [touch] on vertuous and civil actions, as natural and divine sciences" (154). The scientific impetus of this new logic, with its insistence on "formalitie in all things" and its presumption that it discovers divine or natural knowledge, ignores, denies, or precludes the possibility of human action to shape such knowledge; it places inordinate emphasis on the thing produced rather than the human producer of it. Instead of referring to practical contingencies, the new logicians refer their criticisms to the formal machinations of a method that then engenders questions and creates problems that have no substantive bearing on human action. The practitioners of the new logic, Bryskett says, pose "frivolous questions, seruing nought else but subtleties, and inextricable knots"; they "teacheth onely to argue and contend; they breed "dissension," and "the more they striue to be learned and subtill," he adds, "the lesse they shewe themselves to understand" (154).

Bryskett insists, however, that these misguided practioners of logic should not taint the art of logic as a whole. It is just that the "matter" they dwell on, the truth they aim for, tends to exclude questions regarding virtuous actions. Logic's office "to teache and explaine the truth" relies on a relationship with rhetoric that cannot be found in Ramist handbooks. Where the Ramists defined rhetoric as an art subordinate to dialectic that contained only those rules that taught lucid style and effective delivery, Bryskett usurps such a hierarchy by noting that "*Leontinus* did preferre [oratory] before all other, because it maketh it selfe Ladie ouer mens minds, not by force or violence, but by their owne consents and free-will." Thus the "force and efficacie" of logic's arguments suffer somewhat in their comparison to the orator's art. And though rhetoric does "not seek out the truth exactly, but only to perswade or disswade them that, which he thinketh most profitable for the speaker, or the person for whom he speaketh" (153), this job of only persuading and dissuading is no small task when placed within the realm of human affairs. "Of this Art," says Bryskett of oratory,

> have all publike and priuate actions appertaining to ciuill life need to perswade what is good and profitable, and to disswade what is hurtful and vnprofitable, to appease tumults and dissensions, to treate of leagues and peaces, to stirre vp the mindes of men to the defence of their friends, their parents, their Prince and country, and their Religion: to search out and inuestigate the truth of all things, to assist the innocent and oppressed in courts of iudgement, to accuse the faultie and offenders: and finally to giue vnto vertue her due praise and commendation; and vnto vice due blame and reproch. (153)

Whereas the logician is obligated to "find out reasons and arguments" and "discerne and judge of truth and falshood," it is the orator's task to "search out and inuestigate the truth in all things." By virtue of its contingency on human affairs—on what is and is not thought to be profitable—Bryskett's orator discovers provisional truths in actions, but especially in rhetorical actions. Such truths, moreover, take into account more than the reasons and arguments of logic; they also take into consideration the emotions associated with family, friends, prince and country, and so on. The "efficacie" of rhetoric, its ability to search out and investigate truths, lies in the fact that rhetoric touches the passions. This is not to say, however, that the orator subordinates or deemphasizes reason, but that the reason he employs cannot be abstracted or extracted from the emotions associated with any one particular situation. Rhetoric offers a form of reason that recognizes reason's relationship with the passions, that sees the two working together rather than as the separate objects of different arts. And it is the character of this relationship that binds the rhetorical with the ethical and the poetic with the politic.

Another more pointed, though less direct, attempt to argue against the new formalism arises within a digression on the merits of dueling, or "Monomachia," in civil society. Again, definitions of rhetoric play a central role as Bryskett situates his arguments within the context of those philosophers who invest reason with powers that are contrary to the social welfare. Bryskett, in no uncertain terms, considers dueling a flagrant abuse of civil law and a thing odious to nature: "These goodly defendors of this abuse say, that a man, both by order and nature, and by the opinion of Philosophers, may well repulse an iniury by his owne vertue, and not by law" (77). Those who argue the right to make judgments on the basis of their own moral sense without regard to or in spite of civil law defend their position, Bryskett tells us, by culling out of Aristotle's *Rhetoric* "namely this place, where he saith, that God helpeth those that are wronged, not understanding . . . that *Aristotle* in that place speaketh of ciuill judgments or criminall; and not of battels and combat [the antitheses of civil conduct]" (81). These men and the philosophers who support such arguments forsake

> the patterne and true rules of vertuous behaviour. . . . They take hold (forsooth) of some fragments or parcels of [Aristotle's] Rhetorikes to worke upon: as though from thence men were to take the precepts of ciuill conuersation or politike gouernment, whence onely the rules and method of well speaking are to be taken, and not of ciuille felicitie. (81)

As opposed to the "patterne and true rules of vertuous behaviour," these men offer "onely the rules and method of well speaking" (81). For Bryskett, Aristotle's orator serves too narrow an end—an end that circumscribes the orator's ken and prevents him from instructing in the matter of moral philosophy:

> It is to be understood, that onely such places in *Aristotle's* Rhetorikes are to be approved and allowed in civil or politike life, as are by him confirmed in his Ethikes and Rhetorikes. . . . For, as himselfe affirmeth, the drift of his booke of Rhetorike is to instruct a man how to frame his speech to perswade, and how to moue the minds of Iudges to anger, hatred, reuenge, compassion, and such like. . . . So as if the Orator preuaile, and attaine the end he seeketh, which is to perswade, or vse the meanes to attaine it artificially, he hath done his dutie. By which it appeareth, that Rhetorike is ordained for iudgements and controuersies, but not for instruction in ciuill life and manners. (81–82)

If the orator's sole task is to "find the available means of persuasion," his is an art committed to producing persuasion—and persuasion so conceived need not conform to nor heed the call of civic virtue.

The humanist conviction Bryskett displays regarding the orator's dominion over the ends of moral philosophy ultimately takes its authority from the Sophistic or Isocratean tradition "patterned" by Cicero in his philosophico-rhetorical treatises. Bryskett's faith in oratory's powers to inform ethical conduct suggests one reason why, though he "drawes the rules of civill life" from Aristotle, he chooses to contain them within a dialogue that his readers would have recognized as a treatise in the Ciceronian tradition.[12] The *Discourse's* similarities to Cicero's *De oratore* are many. For example, as in Cicero's dialogue, the author is recalling a conversation that occurred many years past; the conversation is occasioned by the author's retreat from his public duties; the conversation takes place in the countryside, away from the cares and constraints of city life; and each day's discussion is represented as one book of the published text. Cicero's presence in the *Discourse* is more implicit than explicit, but though his authority is more understated than is Aristotle's, it is central to Bryskett's argument.

Moral Virtue and the "Morall Vertues"

Victoria Kahn has argued persuasively that the humanists of the quattrocento defended the civic aims of their rhetorical practice by making an "implicit, and at times explicit, connection" between Cicero's articulation of rhetorical decorum and Aristotle's analysis of prudence (*phronesis*) or practical wisdom.[13] Yet Kahn's emphasis on the rational or prudential faculty cultivated by humanist rhetorical practice leads her to distance and complicate the aesthetic dimensions of their discursive deliberations; the aesthetic dimension of humanist rhetoric remains a nebulous and untrustworthy thing. Thomas O. Sloane, noting that "the rhetorical act itself . . . is, at most, one-third rational," grants the passions a somewhat broader compass within the realm of ethical instruction by accenting the orator's ability to appeal to the audience's emotions as an integral part of persuasion. "Humanists, and rhetoricians," he observes, "recognize that man is a composite of reason and emotion—that he has a body and is, essentially, imaginative."[14] My argument wants to contribute to these assessments of humanist rhetoric by asking how the body, imagination, emotion, and reason might figure into fashioning or framing virtuous conduct: When the poet and orator make an appeal to the emotions, what are they appealing to and how might their appeal effect action beyond the immediate occasion and goals of a particular speech? Bryskett's analysis of ethics offers one detailed example. Though humanist rhetoric was ideally aimed at reflection shaped and informed through the moderation of desire, it also aimed at moving bodies to act through a noncognitive, physical activity that might be considered less a habit of thought than a habit of *doing* or *feeling*. Of course, habits of doing cannot exist independently of human reason, but by the same token, human reason cannot exist apart from the "common practice, custom (*in hominum more,* or the mores of human action), and speech of mankind" (*De oratore,* 1.3.12)—the historical, sociopolitical, and linguistic contexts that inform any human action and shape the definition of what is and what is not considered reasonable. On one level, thus, the latter third of the humanist moral imperative (or Ciceronian rhetorical imperative), "to teach, move, and delight," enjoined the most fundamental, most basic elements of our being via *oratio;* but the aesthetics of humanist rhetoric can not be enjoyed, at least not fully, divorced from the practical and purposeful considerations attendant to *ratio,* or prudential deliberation. Metaphors require context, and reason provides that context. In "boldly following [his] owne liking" (5), Bryskett chooses the dialogue form because it best pleases "[his] mind" (7). He suggests thus that the aesthetics of the text are inextricable from its rationale;

and his promise to "discourse upon the morall vertues, yet not omitting the intel-
lectual" is a promise to embody or enact these separate but inseparable virtues
rhetorically.

Bryskett's Aristotelianism is, with a few significant exceptions, uncomplicated.[15]
The first and most important thing to notice is that the Aristotelian soul Bryskett
describes is not defined wholly or simply as an inviolable, eternal thing. Indeed,
whatever powers the human soul possesses do not rely on eternal necessities but
on the fact that "we [are] participants of the nature of all living things" (43). And
"nature," Bryskett later adds parenthetically, "admitteth nothing that is idle" (276).
The significance of rooting a definition of virtue in life itself cannot be overem-
phasized; human action is a biological imperative, thus any definition of virtuous
action will need to begin by considering what constitutes human life.[16] On the
most basic level, human beings do not choose rationally to act because to act is a
necessary condition of being alive. The virtue or excellence of human action is,
however, in choosing how to act—not in choosing "to be or not to be," but in
choosing *how* to be or *how* not to be. Yet the faculty governing choice, a rational
faculty that separates human beings from other animals, does not operate inde-
pendently from the baser faculties that join us to the natural world. Thus the vege-
tative part of the soul "whereby we be nourished, we grow, we sustaine life, and
receive our body and being" (50) is considered the least noble because it is the
most necessary to life and closest to nature. Bryskett describes the proper end of
this part of the soul to be "profite" only (189). It is necessary because it gives life
to and sustains the sensitive and intellective souls. Indeed, one way in which this
part of the soul nourishes itself is by reaching out, as it were, to the sensitive soul
by profiting in things delightful and by avoiding those things "that are displeas-
aunt or noisome" (55).

The sensitive (or "irascible" or "concuspible") part of the soul is the seat of desire;
it contains the appetites (or passions) and "knows" or senses only pleasure and dis-
pleasure. This is the part of the soul that Bryskett says "perfect creatures" have
because it "hath in it by nature power to feele, and to moue from place to place"
(44). The senses are "as ministers to the mind [that] receiue the images and formes
particular of things" (123). Just as the vegetative soul reaches out toward the senses
to nourish itself and to be nourished, the sensitive part of the soul can, but need
not necessarily reach out toward (that is, desire) the intellective part of the soul,
which, because it is the furthest from nature, is the most noble. This remain-
ing portion of the soul, the intellective, "is proper only to man." It has two fac-
ulties particular to it: one that uses reason to deliberate on matters of human action,
and another that uses contemplation or speculation to consider matters eternal.
This part is

that excellent and divine part of the soule, which bringeth with it the light of reason, containing in it the powers, faculties, or vertues of the other two. For it hath life which proceedeth from plants, it hath sense and feeling, & motion from place to place, proper to the second kind; and it hath besides the other part, whereby it knoweth, understandeth, discourseth, consulteth, chuseth, and giues itself to operation, and to contemplate things naturall and divine. (44)

Bryskett insists throughout the *Discourse* that this intellective part of the soul, meaning both its rational and contemplative elements, cannot be divorced from the vegetative and sensitive parts of the soul. This is a departure from Aristotle, who claimed that humans possess two kinds of reason: "desire operating through thought," which "partakes of reason insofar as it complies with reason and accepts its leadership" (*NE* 1139b 5; 1102b 30), and "pure intelligence," which is "contained within itself" (*NE* 1103a 5). Bryskett singles out Aristotle for criticism on this point: "It cannot be . . . that the Sensitive soule in man is seuered from the Intellective. And because man participateth . . . of all three faculties, I see not why these fellowes that mention two, speake not of all three as well, seeing that in man are the operations of all three" (275).

Reason ultimately determines what is and is not virtuous action, but for Bryskett, that reason always originates in the baser parts of the body. Each part of the soul builds upon a lower element, and contemplation is no different; it requires the perfection of the rational part of the soul that "understandeth, discourseth, consulteth, chuseth, and giues itself to operation."

In turn, the rational or intellective part of the soul requires the perfection of the sensitive part inhabited by desire. The senses encounter and recognize only the particular nature of things. There are, however, two kinds of things the senses may encounter: those exterior to the body that are brought in through the five senses, and those sensations within the body such as joy or pain, relief or tension. The faculty that senses those things exterior to the body Bryskett calls the *sensus communis,* or common sense; this faculty is common because it is the innate capacity human beings have to distinguish between things that lie outside of the body from those sensations made within the body: for example, the common sense can distinguish between the smell of an orange as a thing produced by the orange and the pleasure one might derive from that smell.[17] The *sensus communis,* however, only knows that such sensations are exterior to the body; it knows each momentarily and on an individual basis and cannot distinguish between some one thing smelt, heard, or seen, and so on. Yet the sensitive part of the soul does have the ability to generalize, to draw from these ultimate particulars sensed by the *sensus communis* some universals. That faculty is the imagination, or "the vertue fantastike"; it is a noncognitive virtue that makes universals on the basis of sense rather than reason.

These "imaginative universals" are "materiall" in that they are the sensory matter on which reason imposes some form;[18] that is, reason organizes, directs, and supplies purpose to this sensed matter in order to "make sense" of it.[19] The repository of these imaginative universals is the memory that, Bryskett says, has no part of the understanding (a rational virtue of the intellective soul). Memories are the body's way of generalizing about its sensed experience. Fantasy or imagination, thus, is the ability to sense similarities among disparate things without regard to an intelligible form.[20] (For example, the imagination might associate the experience of seeing the green color of an automobile, or of hearing the sound of a speeding automobile, to similar sights and sounds from previous experiences without recognizing the automobile itself as a specific thing particular to a general group of things such as "modes of transportation," "big-ticket items," or "Ford"; the car is simply perceived to be "green like grass" or "loud like rushing water.")[21]

How then, considering that the remembered experiences are noncognitive, does the understanding come to know the imaginative universals? The intellectual faculty responds to the particulars of the input from the senses and the imaginative universals of the fantasy and is able to abstract and know this sensed "matter" by inferring formal, that is, rationally imposed similarities among things:

> The intellective faculty [is] apt to apprehend the formes of things, from whence grow universalls. . . . In which respect, it is sayd, that sense is busied about things particular, and that only things universale are knowne, because they are comprehended by our understanding, without matter. (124)

Whereas the imaginative virtue of the sensitive soul is only able to sense matter, or the materiality of things, reason separates matter from form; it distinguishes between what is sensed and how it is known. Reason separates the sense that brought a particular thing to our experience from the material nature of that thing by imposing formal characteristics on it; it understands only those formal characteristics "without matter." The one mediating thing—or act—between rational understanding and memory is language, or discourse: "Memorie came from sense, insomuch as creatures wanting reason haue memorie, though they haue not rememorating as man hath: for thereto is discourse required; which according to Aristotle is nothing else but an action of the understanding in the vertue imaginative [or fantastic]" (273–74).

Discourse is another way for the understanding to impose form on sensed matter. In this respect, it is a way of understanding that matter. As "an action of the understanding in the vertue imaginative," discourse is reason's way of apprehending the matter of sensed experience. What makes discourse different from a strictly rational understanding is that, as a form of action, discourse makes a particular object understood within a particular context—meaning cannot be abstracted from its context (nor can one's feelings be abstracted from the meaning). Thus discourse is the way in which human beings come to know the sensed matter of their experience. It imposes form, but form that originates in and is contingent on human action.

The understanding, an intellectual virtue, depends on discourse; understanding "standeth in respect of the Agent understanding" (271):

> For this cause also is it said, that the understanding, and things understood, become more properly and truly one selfe same . . . that the understanding [by acting] makes itself equall with the thing understood, that they both become one. . . . And this is the very act of truth, to wit, the certain science or knowledge of any thing: which knowledge or science is in effect nought else then the thing so knowne. (125)

For Bryskett, the act of naming is the way in which the knowledge of any one thing becomes "the thing so knowne"; this is an act of both remembrance and of understanding. To speak is inherently a poetic act in the sense that meaning is made through language, and that meaning, because it is in language, conveys or transfers both the sensed matter and the (discursively) reasoned form simultaneously to the understanding. Discourse is both an act of the imagination and a rational act. It is an act that attempts to unify, and in unifying, to apprehend the sensed matter and the formal characteristics of a thing. Bryskett sees this as a process, each successive constituent drawing on the strength of its antecedent: "Nature [has] giuen us sense . . . to the end that thereby might grow in us imagination, from imagination discourse, from discourse intelligence, and from intelligence gladnesse unspeakable, which might raise us (as diuine and freed from the bands of flesh) to the knowledge of God" (277).

The intellectual or speculative virtues "are of the mind or understanding" (252). Bryskett lists five of them: understanding, science, wisdome, art, and prudence (120). He describes prudence, the intellectual virtue of the rational part of soul, as a "knot or band" of the moral virtues because it represents the "perfect operation of the mind" in deliberating about matters of human action. Prudence is the habit of thought that relieves the actions prompted by desire from responding only to "accidents" and furnishes a means to reflect and deliberate on a course of action. The understanding's comprehension of the particulars provided by discourse may be done in two ways: the "possible understanding" is the part of the intellective faculty that bends its energies toward matters of action; the "possible understanding" pertains to speculative or contemplative virtue. The passible understanding is so called because it attempts to pass beyond the affairs of this world by turning the mind's eye toward things eternal. The speculative virtue of the intellective soul, the passible understanding, Bryskett describes as "our only true forme, not drawne from the materiall power, but created and sent into us by the divine maiestie, [which] dieth not with the body, but remaineth immortal and euerlasting" (126).

Yet Bryskett does not see this to be a particularly useful virtue to cultivate while alive and on earth:

> But finding that continuall contemplation of higher things, would be profitable only to himself and to none other, in that he should thereby purchase not happiness to any but himself. And because he knoweth that he is not born to himselfe alone, but to civill societie and conversation, and to the good of others, as well as himselfe, he therefore in his endeavor with all care and diligence so to cary himself in his word and deeds, as he might be a patterne and example to others of seemly and vertuous speeches and honest actions. (208)

Indeed, the speculative virtue is something that is to be looked forward to in death, an excellence that God grants by grace to those who have sought to perfect the lesser parts of their soul while on earth. And even if one is able to access this virtue, it is impossible to sustain in a meaningful way. Contemplation is the *actus purus,* or pure understanding, which is only possible when one "is freed from the morall affectations of the body" (259); it is the "philosophy of death unto which Plato called us" (257). The possible understanding of the intellective soul thus is the most noble faculty that humans can hope to perfect as long as they are agents in this world who come to know things through the senses of their bodies. "This word *feele,*" Bryskett says, "explaneth the whole, since feeling is a propertie of the Sensitiue soul, and the understanding feeleth not. And in like manner are the words of Aristotle to be understood, where he saith, that such whose flesh is soft are apt to learn" (274).

What the flesh learns are the moral virtues. The "morall virtues" devised by Aristotle, discoursed upon by Bryskett, and figured forth in the person of Arthur before he was king by Spenser, are the products of the sensitive soul. They are the necessary, aesthetic base upon which Moral Virtue is constructed, and they are to be distinguished from it. Moral Virtue is a singular capacity, comprising excellence in the moral virtures (or natural virtues, or virtues of the flesh) and the intellectual virtues. The relationship between these noncognitive moral virtues and the intellectual virtues is reciprocal. On the one hand, reason determines what is good or what ought to be pleasurable and so offers through the help of "art and industry" what is "needfull to induce vertuous habits, to supply that wherein nature accidentally may be defective" (115). On the other hand, desire, which because it does not partake of reason on this level and so cannot see beyond the immediate gratification of itself in any given particular instance, continually revises reason's rule by responding to and acting in the moment. The moral virtues concern manners, which might be defined more broadly as actions conditioned by organized society, and are "grounded in those parts of the mind deuoide of reason" (209), that is, the vegetative and the sensitive part of the soul, which though they do not possess reason "yet [are] they guided by the light of reason" (252). Bryskett also refers to the moral virtues as the practical or active virtues.[22] Aristotle called these natural virtues because "we are by nature equipped with the ability to receive them" (*NE* 1103a). These moral or natural virtues are "formed by habit, *ethos*" (*NE* 1103a); they are the habituation of the passions to desire pleasure and avoid pain *simply* (what is good or bad is decided by the intellect). In other words, the moral virtues Spenser portrays in Arthur and the moral virtues discoursed on by Bryskett are noncognitive; they are trained rather than taught, inculcated rather than conceived of, and felt or sensed rather than known or understood. And, significantly, the particular excellences of our noncognitive moral sense both Aristotle and Bryskett locate in "the median course" relative to oneself. Propriety or ethical decorum, "choosing" the via media, thus is not necessarily a product of a rational faculty but a preference, a product of the sensitive soul's ability to sense pleasure in doing what the rational faculty judges as good.

These noncognitive moral virtues are acquired and learned most efficiently by youth, who because they have yet to develop fully their rational faculties are particularly susceptible to heed and act on the vegetative's profit seeking or, more especially, the sensitive soul's desire for pleasure. One's character or ethos is thus known by means of one's characteristic acts (*hexis*), and one's acts represent the habituation of one's appetites to desire or to avoid certain emotional states—to desire to act temperately rather than rashly, for example. These virtues are acquired through use or "long custom" and so "converted into an habite, [which] do breake and make supple those parts which by nature are rebellious to reason" (115). Habits or customs, furthermore, are cultivated by the examples set by adults; as a child, the mother, father, and the nursemaid are primarily responsible for such moral training; they are followed by tutors and others. Moral or natural virtues are formed by habit and are peculiar to the noncognitive or sensitive part of the soul. Because the sensitive part of the soul encounters only particulars, habituation itself does not rely on rational formulas for consistency but on the imagination, which stores some general feeling made of the many particulars of life experience. Where reason might construct a causal chain or note the formal similarities among things, the imaginative universals rely on metaphor or analogy to generalize—on the ability to sense, literally, the material similarities among things without regard for their particular forms. Again, Bryskett insists that the machinations of the sensitive soul can not be separated from the operations of the intellective soul, which requires the former to develop its own particular virtues. The possible understanding is the chief intellectual virtue of the philosophic mind, and central to its perfection is discourse. This understanding, furthermore, is moral in that it seeks the causes, means, and ends of human action.

The end of moral philosophy, "civil felicitie," is itself not a state of being but a manner of doing, a way of acting. The goal of civic happiness is a political construct built upon individual acts within the realm of human affairs. Human happiness is the end or goal of his project because Bryskett presumes that civil happiness will encourage and make possible the individual's potential to seek his or her own happiness within the body politic. But this "civil felicitie" is not only an end unto itself but also the beginning or cause and the effect all at once:

> The end in all things that men do in this world, is the first that is considered, though afterwards it be the last to be put into execution. And as, when it is brought to perfection, it beareth the name of effect, so is it the cause that moueth all other to bring it to effect. And therefore to treate of that end, which is the motion inducing us to discourse hereupon, we must first come to first principles which may be the causes to bring a man to this end. (32)

Though civil happiness is to be the product or effect of action, Bryskett insists that it is also the cause that propels all human action. Human happiness is not a private thing obtainable by an individual but a thing that exists because it is shared by individuals within society.

Ultimately, thus, politicians are responsible for Moral Virtue in the example they set, the customs they approve, and the laws they enforce, which dictate what is and what is not morally good. Indeed, it is because "there is no part in the whole body of law, that setteth downe, any order of thing of so great importaunce" (42) that Bryskett takes pen in hand:

> For, such as are the principles and beginnings of things, such are the proceedings. Whereupon the wisest men of the world, haue ever thought, that the way to haue cities and commonwealths furnished with vertuous and civill men, consisted in the bringing up of children commendably. But among all the lawes of our time, there is no one that treateth of any such matter. (42)

But the civic responsibility for "the bringing up of children" ultimately also rests with every individual of that society. The first principles or necessary starting points that Bryskett tenders for his discussion are the "regeneration of man" and the bringing up of (male) children:

> But because in the request made to me, I am only required to begin onely at his birthe, I thinke it shall suffice, if I declare vnto you in what maner he ought to be nourished, and brought up, and instructed, till he come to such ripe yeares

and iudgement as he may rule himselfe . . . to direct all his actions to [the nour-
ishing, bringing up, and instruction of youth], which in all humane things is the
last and best. (33)

The nourishing, bringing up, and instruction of youths is the chief moral imper-
ative incumbent on human beings as political animals;[23] the "well-bringing up of
children" is the "spring or wel-head of honest life" (42), both "needfull and requi-
site" to achieving civic or human happiness. And the training ground for civic hap-
piness begins with the habituation of the appetites to what is believed to be good
—as good is defined by a political community. Those habits, furthermore, are
acquired through action in the daily trafficking in human affairs. "It is no small
matter," says Aristotle, "whether one habit or another is inculcated in us from early
childhood; on the contrary, it makes a considerable difference, or, rather, all the
difference" (*NE*, 1103b).

In the *Nichomachean Ethics,* Aristotle points to praise to be "proper to virtue"
because it is the praise of excellence "that makes men capable of performing noble
deeds" (1101b). But he does not grant the rhetorician any particular claim to pro-
duce moral goodness because (1) the rhetor has no particular claim on the under-
standing necessary to determine what is or is not politically good (1181a), and (2)
words "do not have the capacity to turn the common run of people to goodness
and nobility" (1179b). Bryskett, as we have seen, is more optimistic and grants the
orator and oratory more expansive powers in developing the moral virtues. He
argues that the orator and, especially, the poet reign over the appetites and the rea-
son born of the appetites, and that the orator's power is based on the innate, "com-
mon" capacity of people to use words. Note how Bryskett describes the "two senses
[that] are of the most importaunce in this life," specifically, hearing and seeing:

> For that the images of things are represented to the mind by the eies, and by the
> eares do the conceits and words enter into the same. . . . The eares so much the
> more helpe us towards the learning of a civill life, as the sentences of wise men
> passe thereby into our understanding. And whereas the things which we learne
> by the eyes, are but dumbe words: so do the eares heare the liuely voices, by
> which we learn good discipline, & the true maner of well liuing. (55)

Though it is a commonplace to acknowledge the prominence of hearing and
vision in humanist writing, the significance of these senses for a humanist such as
Bryskett is lost when they are considered abstractly as gatherers of sounds and
sights. Bryskett considers their significance rhetorically, that is, in terms of their
powers to first sense, then be affected or persuaded by, then understand what is
seen and heard.

Ciceronian Oratory, Poetry,
and the Containment of Virtue

Where Aristotle seems to have seen the arguments of rhetoric to be capable of touching but not changing the passions "in all cases," Cicero maintained that only the orator could engage in ethical instruction most effectively. For our purposes here, it is important to note just two main reasons why this is the case. First, in *De officiis,* Cicero insists that speech, in conjunction with reason, is intrinsic to human beings—*ratio et oratio* are, he says, the "ultimate source" or "first principle that nature has established among men" (1.16.50). Second, he maintains that the orator surveys a much broader realm of human action. In *De oratore,* Cicero levels a defining criticism at Socrates (which is intended explicitly then to indict Socrates' disciples, Plato's Academicians and Aristotle's Peripatetics) when he has Crassus say that Socrates introduced that "absurd and unprofitable and reprehensible severance between the tongue and the heart," which leads "us to our having one set of professors to teach us to think and another to teach us to speak" (3.16.61).[24] In other words, Cicero claims that Plato and Aristotle followed Socrates in divorcing speech from that reason that originates in, or is motivated by, the appetites. In separating the tongue from the heart, Aristotle, for example, offered a rhetoric that narrowed its end to public persuasion, and because this rhetoric was defined largely in terms of (rationally conceived) *techne,* the rhetorical act could be evaluated by technical norms rather than by civic or human consequences. In stating axiomatically that speech is part of our natural being, Cicero recognizes *oratio,* in conjunction with *ratio,* to be an important form of human action that, like courage or temperance, cannot be rigidly subject to some standard. Speech is motivated by desire, too, and its virtue, eloquence, cannot be quantified.

As a faculty intrinsic to human beings, speech is both an action and a way of knowing. "The power of speech in the attainment of propriety [the moral virtues]," writes Cicero, "is great, and its function is twofold: the first is oratory; the second, conversation" (*De officiis* 1.37.132).[25] Cicero thus gives, explicitly, more powers to the orator because, unlike Aristotle's rhetor, Cicero's orator surveys both the public and more private realms of language. He renders *oratio* (or at least its conversational aspect, *sermo*) fundamental to establishing decorum or propriety—to the exercising and influencing of the moral virtues. And propriety, like Aristotle's via media, is a thing sensed rather than known: "morality," or what Cicero terms *honestum,* is the result of the intellectual virtue (prudence) and the moral virtues operating in tandem:

> Such is [decorum's] essential nature that it is inseparable from moral goodness. . . . The nature of the difference between morality [*honestum*] and propriety [*decorum*] can be more easily felt than expressed. For whatever propriety may

be, it is manifested only when there is pre-existing moral rectitude. (*De officiis* 1.37.93)

It is, furthermore, this noncognitive, physical moral sense that Cicero tells us that "the poets aim to secure" (1.38.97). For Cicero, more so than with Aristotle, words may negotiate effectively among the passions and the intellect because both *oratio* and *ratio* are natural properties of human beings, because both speech and reason have access to the sensitive part of the soul, and because both speech and reason are actions that have a stake in inculcating virtuous action.

Bryskett's effort to "contain the Ethic part of moral philosophy" presumes the conversational part of oratory (*sermo*) to be the proper place for moral instruction. As we have seen, Bryskett himself is acutely aware that choosing to treat ethics in the form of a dialogue will not appeal to the formal minded among his readers. He recognizes that dialogues resist "formalitie in all things," more so than the disreputable (by then) and arid pursuit of scholastic disputation, the fashionable "philosophic" or pedagogic harangue, or even the burgeoning essay genre. Dialogues are neither constrained by the formal conventions of "learned" argumentation nor readily perceived by formal analysis. They allow for the expression of more than one point of view, questions posed by interlocutors may cast reasonable doubt on previous statements, claims are often revised or further qualified in the course of the conversation, consensus among the denizens of the discourse on all points is rare, conclusions still rarer, and the leisured, conversational tone encourages the use of a common or popular vocabulary.[26]

Imprecise, meandering, flexible, and informal by design, dialogues are not methodical. Bryskett anticipates that his choice of genre will be perceived by some to be, in some sense, at odds or incongruous with the general ends of the work, to "frame," "direct," and "lead" a gentleman to "ciuill felicitie." It is difficult thus to point to any one spot and hold down, as it were, a particular example wherein Bryskett offers some defining representation of virtuous action because it is the conversation itself that contains ethics; and the conversation is always an action in action. Consequently, Bryskett stresses throughout the *Discourse* the importance of recognizing patterns of action rather than specific acts. Patterns are dynamic, subject to contingencies, and fluid. Patterns are things in action—or at least they are perceived to be in action when engaged by a reader. Bryskett also refers to the perfect pattern of virtuous behavior as an "idêa" (61), and he explicitly rejects Plato's notion that "the essentiall *Ideas* of all things . . . [are] separate and eternall natures remaining in the diuine mind of God" (129) to which humans might have access. On the authority of "the authors of the new Accademie" (for example, Cicero) who "said constantly, that in this world there was no certaine knowledge of any thing," Bryskett maintains that humans "know nothing so certainly as that they were not" (130); that is, humans can only understand things both for what they are and are

not. Based on this, Bryskett endorses the Protagorean position that a "learned igno-
rance" (131) can be best obtained by arguing "*pro & contra*" because

> nothing [can] be assuredly knowen to vs whiles we are here, as our soules shall
> know them whensoeuer they shall be freed from our bodies. . . . Neither shall
> [our souls] be deceiued by the senses, as in this life they are oftentimes, who
> offer vnto them the images of things uncertainly, not through default of the
> senses, but by reason of the meanes whereby they apprehend the formes of
> things. (130–31)

The means by which the sense apprehends the forms of things is, as discussed
earlier, discourse itself. Civil discourse is the ethic part of moral philosophy; as
such, it is as much the subject of Bryskett's work as it is the means by which his
readers are to arrive at some understanding of what ethical action is. For Bryskett,
the idea (as active pattern) is always subject to the understanding of a situated,
political, and inherently ethical (that is, active) "agent" or "actor." Note, for exam-
ple, in the following account of the opening of the *Discourse* that Bryskett fore-
grounds all of the contingencies particular to this conversation: its causes or
occasion, setting, ends, means, and participants.

"The occasion of the discourse," Bryskett tells us, "grew by the visitation of cer-
tain gentlemen comming to me to my little cottage which I had newly built neare
unto Dublin at such a time, as rather to prevent sicknesse, then for any present
griefe" (5). Yet it is clearly the suspicion of sickness that drew this company
together. The apothecary, Mr. Smith, who had diagnosed him with a melancholic
humor, came to see how his dose of ellebore was taking. The other gentlemen (Dr.
Long, primate of Ardmagh [Armagh]; Sir Robert Dillon Knight; Mr. Dormer, the
queen's solicitor; Captains Thomas Norreis, Christopher Carleil, Warham, and
Nicolas Dawtrey; and "*M. Edmond Spenser,* late your Lordship's Secretary" [6])
came "of their curtesie"—and their curiosity, as their line of questioning soon
makes clear. Sir Robert Dillon, welcoming the cue from the apothecary's rather
candid and unflattering assessment of the source of Bryskett's illness, declares a cer-
tain puzzlement at Bryskett's recent retirement from his official duties to Lord
Grey, the lord deputy of Ireland: "We suppose that a man of your condition and
qualities should rather seeke to be employed, and to advance himself in credit and
reputation, then to hide his talent, and withdraw himself from action, in which
the chief commendation of virtue doth consist" (8).

But it was Bryskett's physical condition, not his social and professional stand-
ing, that prompted this respite. Though hesitant to divulge in full his reasons for
resolving on this bucolic ease over the prestige and opportunity afforded him in
Her Majesty's service, he explains to his company that his late duties had produced
a "disorder of the body [that] had bred such an increase of rheume in me, and

infirmities caused thereby" that he was sure of the "certaine peril of shortening my dayes" (11) if he remained. But aware that the opportunity to converse with his friends offers its own kind of "physike," and goaded by the apothecary's imputations that his melancholia is more a product of "folly, or lacke of judgement" (13), Bryskett offers to "give [the] contents to this my resolution, grounded (as I think) upon a reasonable consideration, and an exact weighing of mine owne abilitie and disposition" (11–12).

Refusing to acknowledge his present retirement as a forfeiture of his duty to the state, Bryskett does "confesse frankly" that he has "found more quietnes and satisfaction in this small time that I haue liued to my selfe, and enioyed the conuersation of my bookes" than in all of the time he "spent in seruice about the State" (11). But this hiatus affords him the opportunity "to spend my time in reading such bookes, as I shall find fittest to increase my knowledge in the duties of a Christian man, and direct me in the right path of vertue, without tying my selfe to any particular kind" (17). And virtue, he says, paraphrasing Cicero, is to be praised in action: *"Virtutis laus, actio"* (19).[27] Though he acknowledges that "the true study of Divinitie [includes] all that knowledge, which may any way be required for the perfection of a mans life," he eschews this course of study on the basis that "there is a more speciall calling thereunto" (16) that he has not "heard." Instead, he has turned his attention specifically to

> the study of Morall Philosophie, which frameth men fittest for ciuill conversation, teaching them orderly what morall virtues are, and particularly what is the proper action of every one, and likewise what vice is, and how an unseemly thing, and how harmefull to a good mind the spot and contagion thereof is. (17–18)

Challenged still further to justify the merits of his pursuits, Bryskett asks his inquisitors why they should chafe at this line of philosophical inquiry, which "aimeth at so high a marke as humane felicitie" (22). Indignant that the moral philosopher might presume to encroach on his special province, the Archbishop of Armagh, Long, takes exception, contending that human happiness is "without, not your reach onely, but all mens, while they are here in this low and muddie world. . . . Mans felicity is placed only in heaven" (21). Bryskett further qualifies his remark by noting the philosophical distinction between "a contemplatiue felicitie (which some men haply draw near unto, but cannot perfectly attain in this life)" and an "actiue or practicke felicitie, consisting in virtuous actions, and reducing a man's passions under the rule of reason" (22), thus affirming his original claim on the strength of Long's own reasoning. It is because that contemplative felicity "cannot be obtained in this life" that Bryskett resolves, respectfully, to pursue "that humane practicke felicitie" that consists "in vertuous actions, and reducing a mans passions vnder the rule of reason" (22), and leave the contemplative life to "you Church-men and Diuines" (23).

But having resolved to "spend this time which we now have destined to familiar discourse and conuersation, in declaring . . . the great benefites which men obtaine by the knowledge of Morall Philosophie" (25), Bryskett refrains from taking the lead in the discussion. Instead, "knowing him to be not onely perfect in the Greek tongue, but also very well read in Philosophie, both morall and naturall" (25), he entreats, to everyone's satisfaction, the poet Spenser to enlarge on the subject at hand. Spenser excuses himself from this task, claiming that he has

> already vndertaken a work tending to the same effect, which is in *heroical verse,* under the title of a *Faerie Queene,* to represent all the morall vertues. . . . Which work . . . may very well serue for my excuse . . . since any discourse, that I might make thus in the sudden in such a subiect, would be but simple, and little to your satisfactions. For it would require good aduisement and premeditation for any man to vndertake the declaration of these points that you haue proposed, containing in effect the Ethike part of Morall Philosophie. (26–27)

Spenser encourages Bryskett then to deliver the contents of his ("premeditated") translations of Piccolomini, Giraldi, and Guazzo because "thereby it will appeare that he hath not withdrawne himself from seruice of the State, but hath spent some time in doing that which may greatly benefit others" (28). After everyone agrees to the subject, manner, and leader of the discussion, reproofs, indignant retorts, and resistant replies cease; everyone consents to make an effort to understand Bryskett's views. The questions by others sometimes do raise doubts and, occasionally, (seem to) digress from the topic in hand, but most often, they offer Bryskett an opportunity to investigate and expand on previous statements. Yet inasmuch as all of the preceding description might be seen as a simple strategy designed to establish and then enhance Bryskett's credibility in a rather obvious fashion (a less-than-modest pretense of modesty designed to authorize Bryskett's delivery), Bryskett's opening narrative also emphasizes the provisional status of his authority as a moral philosopher. His melancholia may bespeak a philosophic mind, but it is accompanied by poor health, retirement from his official duties, and withdrawal from social life—all of which are not praised by his company. He is, furthermore, the company's second choice in speaking in moral philosophy, as all acknowledge Spenser as the leading authority on these matters. And Bryskett's authority would appear to be compromised in that his part of the conversation is conceded to be but a disorganized account (from his "loose papers" [31]) of his translations of Italian authors.

All of the points that suggest Bryskett's particular inadequacies to lead this discourse on this particular occasion, however, underline the central point of Bryskett's humanist moral philosophy: it is not the situation itself (or fortune) that defines the man but how the man addresses the (peopled) situation that defines virtuous action. How does the virtuous man address any given situation? The virtuous man discovers his purpose for speaking within the practical and immediate exigencies of the situation, and he addresses those circumstances to the best of his abilities without the presumption of certainty and without ill will. One begins with "what is known or knowable" rather than with prescriptive formulas because the knowledge available necessarily includes, in addition to ancient philosophic or historic exempla, the particulars of the situation in hand. The imperfections and roughness of the "loose papers" of his translation, for example, are amended by memory, questions, and appeals to the common experience of his audience. He freely admits and often marks the places wherein he disagrees with his "authors"; indeed, Bryskett premises his entire part in the conversation on the claim that one should not "[tie] himselfe absolutely to follow neither *Plato* nor *Aristotle,* but gathering from both, and from excellent writers besides, so much as may yceld you the greater and fuller satisfaction" (31–32).

Within the *Discourse,* it is Bryskett's own self that best exemplifies a pattern of virtuous action. The physical ailments that prompted his retirement and his current melancholic condition thus are not insignificant. In a sense, he occasions the discourse on his own physical and mental well-being. The condition of his body is the subject that prompts the discussion, and the present condition of his mind is the subject of the discussion insofar as his retirement, and subsequent studies into moral philosophy, have brought on his melancholic attitude. The remedy for both body and mind is discovered in conversation, in understanding one's sensed experiences through a situated, timely discourse. His rhetorical performance offers a particular pattern of action that is intended to exemplify the ethic part of moral philosophy. Bryskett attempts to embody moral virtue discursively, by exemplifying the intellectual virtues he discusses. The reader experiences the "matter" of moral philosophy through the senses, through apprehending the particular actions within the conversation. On one level, then, that sensed matter is the fodder for the reader's imagination; it is the material that sparks discourse, and from discourse, understanding.

On another level, because that matter is apprehended via discourse, it already assumes a certain form. Bryskett takes advantage of that dimension of the discourse to discuss the intellectual virtues, to offer analysis and explanation. But in self-consciously offering his own self as an exemplary figure engaged in a discursive action, he also offers a pattern of behavior that grounds its authority in preparing rather than appeasing his readers' reason. His intention, "to giue light to the meaner learned (whose iudments can be content to busie itselfe rather than to learne what they know not" (5), points to these two levels. The meaner learned will content their judgments on the aesthetics of the text. Insofar as he has represented virtuous action, then, Bryskett appeals to his readers to exercise their moral sense. The learned, on the other hand, may "learne what they knowe not" by attending to the more formal (and less substantive) matter of the text.

In addition to being a participant in the *Discourse*, Bryskett is also its author, and it is in this respect that his credibility is closely allied with the poet's. The pattern of virtuous action Bryskett himself offers is finally himself as an author. As the title of his work declares, he did not intend to write on moral philosophy simply but to contain it (*"A Discourse of Civill Life": Containing the Ethike Parte of Morall Philosophie*); and toward that end, he drew on both Cicero's own "pattern" of the orator-philosopher and his "patterning of the perfect orator" in *De oratore*. In patterning virtuous action through discursive exempla, Bryskett self-consciously makes morality—and it is just that, a making, or *poeisis,* of virtue. A making that relied on the intellectual capacities of language to teach the mind and the propaideutic function of language to move the body to act by stirring the passions. A making that is invented or discovered in the world of human actions, but especially their rhetorical actions. A making that attempts to instill in others through deedful words the capacity to feel and the ability to sense, if not choose, what might bring both individual happiness and politic good. But Bryskett's making of morality is also a making in that its exigence was borne of debate and its argument bent toward some purpose. The pedagogic reforms advanced by the Ramists posed a philosophic view that for all practical purposes leveled the rhetorical playing field to matters of style and delivery. In reducing the art of oratory thus, the Ramists disengaged rhetoric from the world of ethical action, which took its substance or matter from method rather than from its capacity to effect one's moral sense.

Within the broader dynamic of humanist discourse, the humanist philosophy Bryskett advocates does hearken back to the values of an older humanism in light of Ramus's "humanist" reforms. Yet Bryskett's humanism cannot be seen as merely a rehearsal of "old-guard" principles because it embodies and enacts those values toward its own particular end. It is a form of humanism, furthermore, that looks to occasion, participation, rhetoric, and moral sense for support. The ascendancy of Ramist logic in England had already paved the way to disassociate word from deed, and word from reason. Natural philosophy, not moral philosophy, was to be the site of intellectual debate in the seventeenth century—a natural philosophy premised on the purity of a disembodied reason that, by virtue of approaching problems methodically, could isolate, analyze, and theorize on the eternal laws of the natural world with astonishing certainty. In this world, logic taught because it alone surveyed the realm of reason, rhetoric moved because it deceived people into going with the passions and against "reason," and poetry became pretty ornaments to wile away the time or inspired testimonies to arcane truths.

The dialogue genre affords Bryskett a more direct path into and through ethics that is not as "clowdily enwrapped" (LR) as is Spenser's veil of allegory. Yet it is the one course of humanism that sought to develop the potential of language to effect moral action. Bryskett maintains that discourse's power to effect moral action lies in its mediatory function, in language's power to draw from the imagination and to contain, if only provisionally, the sensed material of human experience in an intelligible, discursive, yet not wholly intellectual form. What Bryskett shows us is that the aesthetic or sensed dimension of his rhetorical practice is neither removed from nor simply a detachable dimension of persuasion; rather, it is a necessary, vital, and formative part of ethical and rhetorical decorum. It is, furthermore, that aesthetic or sensed dimension of the *Discourse* that Bryskett relies on most to effect his purpose. Spenser had "already vndertaken a work tending to the same effect"; the reputation Spenser had earned among the company gathered at Bryskett's cottage was due in no small part to his first published poem, *The Shepheardes Calender* (1579). The rhetorical challenge each author faces is to cultivate the noncognitive, moral, active, or practical virtues of the sensitive soul that, through discourse, will cultivate the ground upon which the patterning of a civic virtue might first be felt, then imagined, then spoken, and finally comprehended by an always active human understanding.

CHAPTER THREE

GLOSSING SPENSER'S HUMANISTIC POETICS (RHETORICALLY)

God bestows upon us (if indeed he does) merely reason—it is we who make it good or the reverse.

—Cotta, arguing pro the philosophic position of Cicero's Academy and contra Stoic philosophy in Cicero's De natura deorum

IN THE EPILOGUE TO *The Shepheardes Calender,* the poet known only as Immeritô (the unworthy one) articulates for his readers the aim of the whole of the preceding book:

> To teach the ruder shepheard how to feede his sheepe,
> And from the falsers fraud his folded flocke to keepe. (5–6)

I want to propose that we take the poet at his word, so to speak, and regard his intention to teach as both an honest assertion of and as an honest metaphor for his poetic goals.[1] "To teach" thus is no more declarative nor less metaphorical than any other word or phrase in this passage—or in the *Calender* as a whole. Just as "the ruder shepheard," "sheepe," and "falsers," as well as the other verbs, may accrue several layers of meaning simultaneously depending on the critical contexts emphasized (for example, biblical, courtly, literary, or religious), so too may "to teach" acquire a variety of meanings when considered within the controversies of humanism. Paul Ricoeur's preliminary yet incisive definition of metaphor as "a [rhetorical] figure" that "constitutes a displacement and extension of the meaning of words" offers a useful starting point. In choosing "to teach" to disclose the ends of his poetic efforts, Edmund Spenser (also known as Immeritô) presents the *Calender* as a displacement and extension of pedagogical possibilities—as a metaphor that negotiates the course and dis-course of the contemporary conversation on learn-ing.[2] If, at Immeritô's prompting, we consider the *Calender* within the context of, and as a participant in, its contemporary humanist discourse—the context in which the declared aim of "teaching" might be said to acquire both its metaphoric valency and philosophic vitality—then how and on what authority does Spenser's poetry contribute to, develop or advance that conversation?

A Refiguring

At the time of the *Calender*'s publication in 1579, Ramism had yet to solidify and entrench itself institutionally, as it had, for the most part, by the early seventeenth century, when Bryskett put pen to paper.[3] Yet it was not unknown to the Canta-bridgians of the 1570s (Spenser attended Cambridge c. 1572–77). Owing in no small part to the efforts of Spenser's friend, intellectual counterpart, and (briefly) praelector in rhetoric at Cambridge, Gabriel Harvey, the pedagogic and philo-sophic merits of Ramus's tidying up of Aristotle's *Organon* and the explanatory virtues of his dialectical method had been recommended favorably both to young scholars and the reading public at large. Harvey published two lectures on the art of rhetoric that, originally, he had delivered at Cambridge as praelector; both his *Ciceronianus* and *Rhetor* (1577) praise Ramus's attempts to reorganize learning by establishing hard and fast rules delimiting the extent to which each of the arts con-tributed to it.[4] Thus, as several critics have noted, Spenser would have been famil-iar with, if not very well versed in, both the theory and practical implications of Ramist pedagogical reforms while writing *The Shepheardes Calender*.[5]

The Ramist's logocentric model of learning theoretically robbed the rhetorical arts, rhetoric and poetics, of their traditional footing in moral philosophy by con-signing the rationale of all rhetorical action to the explanatory powers of a formally constant, syllogistic method. Consequently, the concept of rhetorical or poetic dis-course as a vital form of action fundamental to instruction in moral discipline is submerged in Ramism. By neutralizing the orator's capacity to discover meaning in language, Ramists effectively rendered rhetoric the obsequious transmitter of Reason's predetermined, nonverbal, and inactive "matter." Stripped of the ethical imperative grounded in human physiology, discourse, the ornaments of poesy, and rhetorical *copia* are systematically shunned and viewed with suspicion. Yet both Bryskett and the Ramists address the central question turning the changing face of humanist philosophy: Of what does learning consist and toward what ends should it be used? The participants' measured responses to this question are largely con-tingent on how they define the rhetorical arts.

The eclogues, though in poetic form, present but one facade of the *Calender*'s fiction. Yet their ability to extend poetic learning is contingent on how poetry might be displaced and rendered incidental if not inconsequential to "learning."

Like Cicero representing divergent arguments about oratory in *De oratore*, or Tacitus in his *Dialogus de oratoribus*, or Bryskett representing arguments about education in the *Discourse*, Spenser represents the course and discourse of humanism within the *Calender*. He patterns the whole of the debate (at least as it pertains to the status of poetry) by rendering both sides of the argument through exempla of rhetorical actions. For Immeritô's efforts to teach are offset and put into relief by the presence of another would-be educator within the *Calender*. The following section illustrates how Spenser shows that the eclogues' glossarist displaces and so diminishes the potential for poetry to inculcate moral or civic virtue by alienating poetry from "learning," and poetry and learning both from moral philosophy.

Displaced Poetics:
"Works of Learned Wits"

In addition to Immeritô's "Envoy," "Epilogue," and the twelve eclogues themselves, a figure known only by his initials, E. K., appends an epistle to "the most excellent and learned both Orator and Poete, Mayster Gabriel Harvey"; an essay unassumingly titled "The generall argument of the whole booke"; paragraph-length synopses (two to four sentences) of each eclogue's "Argument"; and a substantial gloss at the end of each eclogue that provides explanations and clarification of specific words, phrases, and concepts by means of historical and textual references. Though much critical attention accorded E. K. has speculated on his actual or fictive identity, the role assigned him by Spenser critics tends to assume a familiar and fairly consistent form whether he is presumed to be the obscure Edward Kirke, an obliging Gabriel Harvey, or Spenser in yet another role (as Edmund of Kent?).[6] As Michael McCanles rightly observes, "Critics quote E. K. when it suits them and ignore him when it doesn't, and in either case treat his glosses just as one would treat those of any other critic of the same text."[7] Though infamous for their inaccuracies, redundancies, inconsistencies, obtuseness, and pedantic character, the many and varied interpretive failings of E. K.'s contributions to the *Calender* have been willingly overlooked by generations of critics; in fact, he is often granted a certain prestige as "the first reader" of Spenser's text. And, indeed, many of E. K.'s observations have become familiar, if not integral, components of the contemporary critical grammar for the *Calender*. For example, his tendency to situate and evaluate the eclogues within the context of a distinctly literary history remains a common critical practice, his distribution of the eclogues into "Recreative," "Plaintive," and "Moral" is frequently employed, and many regard his claims about the poet as *vates* to be the norm for Renaissance poetics. Collectively, however, E. K.'s many citational and interpretive failings suggest that we should be suspicious of subscribing too readily to anything he has to say about the eclogues. For glossing the glossarist, whether for the sake of convenience or as a matter of critical convention, has tended to obscure the historical and intellectual consistency of the critical position E. K. exemplifies. Rather than consider his "lexical" failings and interpretive inconsistencies as evidence of just bad humanist scholarship or the prosaic counterpart to the poet, I want to suggest that his shifting and often contradictory arguments are symptomatic and representative of a unified critical position with both a historical and local resonance. That is, though E. K. may be a bad critic, he is not an unprincipled one. On the contrary, by representing, or exemplifying, current trends in learning, Spenser shows by means of E. K.'s deeply flawed evaluation of Immeritô's verse how the principles on which E. K.'s conception of learning is founded may themselves fail when brought to bear on matters beyond the realm of poetry. And for E. K., significantly, learning appears to be one of those subject matters beyond the realm of poetry. Insofar as his contributions constitute a consistent attitude toward poetry, E. K.'s prose presents an argument about how and what the reader might learn from both poetry in general, and this poet in particular; that is, E. K. presents an argument about how and what poetry can teach.

In his gloss to the (nonexistent) emblem for the *December* eclogue, E. K. declares that "all thinges perish and come to theyr last end, but workes of learned wits and monuments of Poetry abide forever" (212). His use of "and" to conjoin the work of scholars (such as himself) and the "monuments of Poetry" is but one indication of his determined effort throughout the *Calender* to define poetry as something other than learning. Consider, for example, E. K.'s opening lines to Harvey in the "Epistle": "Uncouthe unkiste, Sayde the olde famous Poete Chaucer: whom for his excellencie and wonderfull skil in making, his scholler Lidgate, a worthy scholler of so excellent a maister, calleth the Loadestarre of our Language" (13).

Both poet and scholar inhabit these lines—figuratively and "literally" (that is, through the historical analogue and within the fiction of the *Calender*). By recalling the "excellencie" of Chaucer in the words of his "worthy scholler," Lydgate, E. K. begins to establish for the reader a credible, if not indispensable, place for himself within the text. Though ostensibly directed to the credit of the poet, E. K. also prepares the reader for the important role he feels that the scholar plays in valorizing, interpreting, and making memorable or "monumentalizing" the poetry for its once and future audiences.

Indeed, E. K. imposes himself onto the pages of the eclogues of the *Calender* on the assumption that the poet's verse will require the authority and learning that a scholarly exegesis will bring to bear on the text, as the reasons he offers for adding his gloss indicate:

> Hereunto have I added a certain Glosse or scholion for thexposition of old
> wordes and harder phrases: which maner of glosing and commenting, well I
> wote, wil seme straunge and rare in our tongue: yet for somuch as I knew many
> excellent and proper devises both in wordes and matter would passe in the speedy

Ianuarie.

Colins Embleme.

Anchòra speme.

GLOSSE.

COLIN Cloute) is a name not greatly vsed, and yet haue I sene a Poesie of M. Skeltons vnder that title. But indeede the word Colin is Frenche, and vsed of the French Poete Marot (if he be worthy of the name of a Poete) in a certein Æglogue. Vnder which name this Poete secretly shadoweth himselfe, as sometime did Tityrus vnder the name of Tityrus, thinking it much fitter, then such Latine names, for the great vnlikelyhoode of the language.

vnnethes) scarcely.

couthe) commeth of the verbe Conne, that is, to know or to haue skill. As well interpreteth the same the worthy Sir Tho. Smith in his booke of gouerment: wherof I haue a perfect copie in wryting, lent me by his kinseman, and my verye singular good freend, M. Gabriel Haruey: as also of some others his most graue & excellent wrytings.

Sythe) time.

Neighbour towne) the next towne: expressing the Latine Vicina.

Stoure) a fitt.

Sere) withered.

His clownish gyfe) imitateth Virgils verse,

Rusticus es Corydon, nec munera curat Alexis.

Hobbinol) is a fained country name, whereby, it being so commune and vsall, seemeth to be hidden the person of some his very speciall & most familiar freend, whom he entirely and extraordinarily beloued, as peraduenture shall be more largely declared hereafter. In thys place seemeth to be some fauour of disorderly loue, which the learned call pæderastice: but it is gathered beside his meaning. For who that hath red Plato his dialogue called Alcybiades, Xenophon and Maximus Tyrius of Socrates opinions, may easily perceiue, that such loue is muche to be alowed and liked of, specially so meant, as Socrates vsed it: who sayth, that in deede he loued Alcybiades extremely, yet not Alcybiades person, but hys soule, which is Alcybiades owne selfe. And so is pæderastice much to be præferred before gynerastice, that is the loue whiche enflameth men with lust toward womankind. But yet let no man thinke, that herein I stand with Lucian or hys deuelish disciple Vnico Aretino, in defence of execrable and horrible sinnes of forbidden and vnlawful fleshlinesse. Whose abominable error is fully confuted of Perionius, and others.

I loue) a pretty Epanorthosis in these two verses, and withall a Paronomasia or playing with the word, where he sayth (I loue thilke lasse (alas) &c.

Rosalinde, is also a feigned name, which being wel ordered, wil bewray the very name of hys loue and mistresse, whom by that name he colowreth. So as Ouide shadoweth hys loue vnder the name of Corynna, which of some is supposed to be Iulia,

Ianuarie. fol.3

Iulia, themperor Augustus his daughter, and wyfe to Agrippa. So doth Aruncius Stella euery where call his Lady Asteris and Ianthis, albe it is yet wel knowen that her right name was Violantilla: as witnesseth Statius in his Epithalamiū. And so the famous Paragone of Italy, Madonna Cœlia in her letters enuelopeth her selfe vnder the name of Zima, and Petrona vnder the name of Bellochia. And this generally hath bene a common custome of counterfeicting the names of secret Personages.

Auisd) bring downe.

Embleme.

Ouerhaile) drawe ouer.

His Embleme or Poesye is here vnder added in Italian, Anchòra speme: the meaning wherof is, that notwithstande his extreme passion and lucklesse loue, yet kanning on hope sexe as some what recomforted.

Februarie.

Ægloga Secunda.

ARGVMENT.

THis Æglogue is rather morall and generall, then bent to any secrete or particular purpose. It specially conteyneth a discourse of old age, in the persone of Thenot an olde Shepheard, who for his crookednesse and vnlustinesse, is scorned of Cuddie an vnhappy Heardmans boye. The matter very well accordeth with the season of the moneth, the yeare now drawping to an ende. For as in this time of yeare, so ibi in our bodies

A.iii.

E. K.'s "Glosse" to Immeritô's Januarye eclogue, followed by the woodcut and E. K.'s "Argument" for Februarie.

course of reading, either as unknowen, or as not marked, and that in this kind, as in other we might be equal to the learned of other nations, I thought good to take the paines upon me for that by meanes of some acquaintance I was made privie to his counsell. (19)

Poetry, it seems, cannot communicate effectively, teach, or appear learned on its own. If the *Calender* is to be useful, valuable, memorable, or accounted as learning by anyone, it will require the "paines" of the glossarist-critic to make it so. If the reader wants to learn something from the eclogues, he will find such learning in E. K.'s "Glosse." E. K.'s explanation, furthermore, offers an initial indication as to why he believes poetry requires the glossarist's "paines." He assumes, for example, that the reader will approach poetry as he might, that is, "speedily" or inattentive to the poet's artifice. It is the formal or conventional subtleties of the poet's artifice, moreover, that he seems to assume to be worth knowing, or worth learning about for the understanding of the poem. And finally, he seems to assume that the "real" meaning or significance of the poetry is primarily associated with the author's private life.

All of which is to say, in effect, that if the poet is learned, his poetry does not appear to be accessible to his readers; what learning, if any, the poet may offer his reader will either be "unknowen," obscured ("not marked"), or autobiographical to begin with and so will need to be clarified, explained, and categorized. Thus E. K. assumes the mantle of learning and the role of teacher for himself. And throughout his contributions to the *Calender*, E. K. seldom misses an opportunity to locate his own claims within the specific context of the learned; indeed, this is perhaps the most prominent characteristic of his prose. He insists, for example, that though poetry might be "understood of the moste," it can be "judged onely of the learned" (that is, himself). He frequently associates himself with the learned with statements such as "I am of the opinion, and eke the best learned are of the lyke" (14) and "It is wel known, and stoutley mainteyned with strong reasons of the learned" (23). And at one point, he somewhat pompously notes that "in such matter of learning I am forced to use the termes of the learned" (24). He further aggrandizes his identification with the learned by castigating those who under the "colour of learning" (22) might dare challenge his erudite conclusions. E. K.'s efforts to cast his lot among the learned becomes especially important when contrasted with how he frames or characterizes the poet's efforts. Rather than "learning," he typically commends poets for their "skil," and the terms he usually employs to describe that skill are cognates of "excellence" (even "superexcellencie"), "mastery," and "worthiness."

But such grand epithets begin to ring hollow when we consider what E. K. characterizes the poet to have mastered and of what he is worthy. The most salient critical context in which E. K. develops his argument regarding the worthiness of

Immeritô's eclogues involves comparing this work to the works of previous poets, more specifically, pastoral poets. From his opening lines wherein he associates "this our new Poete" with "that good old Poete," Chaucer, and from Chaucer to "the Roman Tityrus Virgile," to his many subsequent references throughout to Homer, Hesiod, Theocritus, Ovid, Petrarch, Boccacio, Marot, Sanazarus, "and also divers other excellent both Italian and French Poetes, whose foting this Author every where followeth," E. K. attempts to validate Immeritô's poetic license by placing him among poets of renown.[9] Of course, the eclogues themselves do allude to the works of past poets, but as we shall see, there is little to suggest that E. K. and Immeritô share the same reasons for their reliance on past poets or that they define, use, and consequently value poetic tradition to the same ends.

Past pastoral poems offer E. K. a generic yardstick with which he can measure Immeritô's achievement—a known and quantifiable set of standards or conventions and themes that suggest some means for comparison. Yet having made the comparison, E. K. appears to be unclear as to exactly why or in what way the measurement he has taken may be important. Perhaps, E. K. says, the poet was moved to write a pastoral because, like previous poets, "he chose to unfold great matter of argument covertly, then professing it," or

> doubting perhaps his habilitie, which he little needed, or mynding to furnish our tongue with this kinde [that is, the pastoral], wherein it faulteth, or following the example of the best and most auncient Poetes, which devised this kind of writing being both so base for the matter, and homely for the manner, at the first to trye theyr habilities: and as young birdes . . . by little first to prove theyr tender wyngs, before they make a greater flight. So flew Theocritus . . . Virgile . . . Mantuane . . . Petrarque [etc.]. . . . So finally flyeth this our new Poete, as a bird, whose principals be scarce growen out, but yet as that in time shall be hable to keepe wing with the best. (19)

Note that the "great matter of argument" to which he referred quickly becomes "base" and "little" and its manner "homely" when cast into the narrow context of pastoral poetry. E. K.'s conclusion, that the poet in fact is testing his poetic wings in the tradition of previous poets and is presently unable to "keepe wing with the best" contradicts his initial observation that such a testing was "little needed" for one of such "habilitie." By representing pastoral poetry to be the genre of immature poets, furthermore, E. K. compromises the author's credibility in the eyes of the learned reader; Immeritô, it seems, is more the apprentice than the master. So even if one may be inclined to associate the author with the "best and most auncient Poetes," that association is based largely on the author's generic choice, the promise or pretense of future greatness, and whatever allusions E. K. may be able to cite in the poet's defense.

Setting his generic yardstick against the poet's ability to sustain what he believes to be a true-to-life portrait of "pastorall rudenesse," E. K. praises the poet for his "dewe observance of Decorum every where, in personages, in seasons, in matter, in speach, and generally in al seemly simplicitie of handeling his matter, and framing his words" (14). In this instance, E. K. seems to be relatively comfortable with the measurement he has taken; indeed, he finds the author's due observance of generic decorum to be nothing less than "morall wisenesse." Though E. K. keeps with humanist moral philosophy insofar as he recognizes decorum or propriety to be central to wisdom, his association of the poet's "morall wiseness" strictly with the conventions of the pastoral genre deprives such sagacity of any real significance. An example of what E. K. might describe as "wise" or "moral" occurs in his gloss to the *April* eclogue when Colin "abruptley" refers to Queen Elizabeth as "Elysa":

> In all this songe is not to be respected what the worthinesse of her Majestie deserveth, nor what to the highnes of a Prince is agreeable, but what is most comely for the meanesse of a shepheards witte, or to conceive, or to utter. And therefore he calleth her Elysa, as through rudenesse tripping in her name . . . it being very unfit, that a shepheards boy brought up in the shepefold, should know, or ever seme to have heard of a Queenes roialty. (78–79)

In other words, the poet's moral wiseness consists of being able to put rude words in shepherds' mouths, to make young men sound young, the elderly sound old, to observe and mark the appropriate weather condition to the month and mood, and to incorporate bucolic themes—shepherds' talk—into the text of the poem. Thus E. K.'s sense of the poet's moral responsibilities does not appear to extend beyond the generic, thematic, and lexical obligations imposed on him by a tradition of pastoral poetry and what he believes to be the real characteristics and condition of shepherds.[9]

Considering E. K.'s narrow conception of morality, it is not surprising that he never considers poetry as a means of inculcating virtue, of "moving" his readers toward virtuous action. In fact, he all but dismisses the poet's purported claim that he wrote the eclogues "to warne (as he sayth) the young shepheards .s. [*sic*] equalls and companions of his unfortunate folly" by foregrounding his own interpretation. "Onely this appeareth," he writes, "that his unstayed youngth had long wandered in the common Labyrinth of Love, in which time to mitigate and allay the heate of his passion . . . he compiled these xii. Æglogues" (19). With the potential and possibilities of moral philosophy dispensed with for the sake of formal conventions of the pastoral genre—and on the presumption that the *Calender* merely reflects the solipsistic pinings of adolescence—E. K.'s sense of the poet's "morall wisenesse" appears to have little to do with the ethical and political considerations of humanist moral philosophy.

But, more generally, E. K. dispenses with the potential and possibilities of poetry to effect moral virtue by defining poetry largely in terms of its *techne*. E. K. imposed himself on the text for fear that "many excellent and proper devises both in wordes and matter would passe." For E. K., learning constitutes not the use of but the "marking" and explaining of the poet's "devices." His glosses typically light upon a specific word, phrase, or verse that E. K. "makes significant" by explaining to the reader what it is. For example, "I love thilke lasse, (alas why do I love?) / And am forlorne, (alas why am I lornc?)" (*Januarye*, 61–62), which E. K. glosses as "a prety Epanothosis in these two verses, and withall a Paranomasia or playing with words, where he sayth (I love thilke lasse (alas etc.[)]" (34). In *Februarie*, he glosses "For Youngth is a bubble blown up with breath" as a "very moral and pithy Allegorie of youth, and the lustes thereof, compared to a wearie wayfaring man" (50); and he glosses "hoarie lockes" in the same eclogue as "metaphorically for withered leaves" (51). How consequential is it to the interpretation of the eclogue to recognize that "hoarie lockes" refers to "withered leaves," and is that the only possible meaning available? Might the rhetorical drama enacted by the inhabitants of the eclogues suggest other meanings contingent on the rhetorical situation? E. K. is only able to understand *a* possible meaning of the poet's turn of phrase in terms of its abstract, technical definition. Such definitions, furthermore, ignore the possible meanings the word or phrase might have within its rhetorical context.

Circumscribed thus by the conventions and *techne* of a poetic tradition, E. K. proceeds to search for the hair on the bucolic eggs before him. In the manner of both ancient and Renaissance style manuals, he proceeds to enlarge on diction, then composition. The greater part of the "Epistle to Harvey," for example, discusses, first, the poet's "straunge" use of antique words and, second, his "knitting of sentences" that make "the whole Periode and compasses of speache so delightsome for the roundnesse, and so grave for the straungeness" (14). His most consistent attention and praise is bestowed on the poet's language—his use of "straunge" and archaic words, his "maistery" of language, his "pithinesse in uttering." Note that such terms bespeak cleverness rather than intelligence and "wittinesse" rather than learning. Of course, such attention to the poet's language does not have to be an inappropriate critical task, but for E. K., the value of the poet's art does not seem to extend much beyond a narrow and perhaps equivocal appreciation for the poet's verbal dexterity (a virtue of his technical skill). The compass of E. K.'s argument, however, oriented as it is to praising the poet for his ability to delight (with delight conceived of as an appreciation for the poet's technical merits and without regard for any consequence beyond such "delight"), is unable to settle on a fixed direction. In his argument regarding the author's choice of "straunge" or archaic words, for example, E. K. appears uncertain as to exactly why the poet uses words that "be something hard, and of most men unused":

> Whether he useth them by such casualtye and custom, or of set purpose and choyse, as thinking them fittest for such rusticall rudeness of shepheards, eyther for that theyr rough sounde would make his rymes more ragged and rustical, or els because such olde and obsolete wordes are most used of country folke, sure I thinke, and think I think not amisse, that they bring great grace and, as one would say, auctoritee to the verse. (14)

Who appears to be responsible for the uncertainty E. K. expresses in the above passage—the "straunge" poet or the confident scholar (who surely thinks that he thinks not amiss) trying to put the best face on poetic obscurity? If the poet uses old words by "casualtye and custome," then he appears to be guilty of either an unwillingness to be understood or unconscious obfuscation; if he used them by "set purpose and choyse," then he has either succeeded in making "ragged" rhymes (no great praise, as E. K.'s later reference to the "rakehelly route of ragged rymers" suggests) or he may be considered morally wise by E. K.'s insipid standards.

Having been struck, however, with this notion that old words bring "auctoritee to the verse," E. K.'s argument takes a different direction. After implicating the poet, albeit indirectly, in one of the "faultes" of Roman historians, "that with their overmuch studie they affect antiquitie, as coveting thereby credence and credit of elder yeares," E. K. chooses to represent the poet's grave pretensions in a more positive light. Yet he is sure only temporarily that "those auncient solemne wordes are a great ornament." Citing "Tullie in that book, wherein he endeavoreth to set forth the paterne of a perfect Oratour," E. K recalls that though old words often "maketh the style seeme grave, and as it were reverend: [just as] we honour and reverence gray heares for a certain religious regard, which we have of old age," "nether every where must old words be stuffed in, nor the commen Dialecte and maner of speaking so corrupted therby, that as in old buildings it seme disorderly and ruinous" (15). But of course this poet does use old words everywhere; he in fact does "corrupt" the common dialect by stuffing in old words "unused of most." Within the one sentence thus E. K. manages to undermine the reverence first associated with old age by steeping "old" in corruption, disorder, and ruin. But, perhaps again, he continues, such ruinous disorder may be a good thing, for as he notes, "oftimes we fynde ourselves, I know not how, singularly delighted with the shewe of such naturall rudenesse, and take great pleasure in that disorderly order" (15). Yet "rudenesse," "disorderly," and E. K.'s inability to offer good reason, together with their original context, suggest that suspicion rather than praise may be a more appropriate response if one is to believe E. K.'s argument. For in the terms of E. K.'s argument, it is the poet's credibility that consistently is undermined as the grounds on which E. K. attempts to build praise for the poet are turned and turned again into reasons that more effectively question rather than confirm the poet's "excellence."

After concluding, finally, that the poet did indeed "of set purpose and choyse" employ ancient words, though largely in the (absurd) attempt "to restore, as to theyr rightfull heritage such good and naturall English words, as have ben long time out of use and almost cleare disinherited" rather than any for any of the reasons he previously offered, E. K. takes on Immeritô's "knitting of sentences" and the "compasse of his speach." Judging these qualities to be "learned without hardnes," E. K. juxtaposes this author's "well-grounded, finely framed, and strongly trussed up" sentences with the abilities of other, contemporary poets to compose solid sentences:

> In regard whereof [that is, to the poet's fine sentence structure], I scorne and spue out the rakehellye route of ragged rymers (for so themselves use to hunt the letter) which without learning boste, without judgement jangle, without reason rage and fome, as if some Poeticall spirite had newly ravished them above the meanenesse of commen capacitie. (17)

One critical aspect of this poet's "excellence," it seems, is demonstrated by his compositional skills. And this particular skill is juxtaposed against those who "rage and fome" as if divinely inspired. But the integrity of this juxtaposition, and so too the praise intended by it, becomes compromised in the course of his commentary. Most notably, in the "Argument" to the *October* eclogue, E. K. appears to tell us that the true excellence of poetry owes more to "some Poeticall spirite" than the artful composition of sentences. He says that poetry is "indede so worthy and commendable an arte: or rather no arte, but a divine gift and heavenly instinct not to bee gotten by laboure and learning, but adorned with both: and poured into the witte by a certain ἐνθουσιασμὸς. and celestiall inspiration" (170).

The poet's "skill" thus is really no skill, his well-grounded, finely framed, and trussed up sentences are not a product of art and learning but the adornments of learning wrought from rhetorical *techne*. But how then might one distinguish between the "ragged rymers" and the true poet—since inspiration cannot be quantified? Or is the use of good sentences evidence of inspiration?

E. K. chooses not to examine such questions; instead, he is content to let the poet's "skyl" and "inspiration" coexist uneasily on the presumption that both are true. In his gloss to Cuddie's emblem for the *October* eclogue ("Agitante calescimus illo etc."), E. K. appears to reaffirm the divinely inspired conception of poetry. He writes: "Hereby is meant, as also in the whole course of the Æglogue, that poetry is a divine instinct and unnatural rage passing the reache of comen reason" (183).

Yet even if we are to believe, as E. K. appears to want us to, that poetry is an art-less art and this poet a divinely inspired poet (who has "adorned" his poetry with learning as is evident in the quality of his sentences), our faith is soon shaken when we consider his other comments pertaining to the same. Based on a bogus refer-ence to Plato's "*de Legibus*," E. K. tells us in one of his glosses that "the first inven-tion of Poetry was of very vertuous intent" wherein the first poets sang "fine verses to the people, in prayse eyther of vertue or of victory or of immortality or such like" (177). The original or earlier poets, "ravished, with delight" their listeners, who, "thinking (as it was indeed) that he was inspired from above, called him vatem" (177). But again, E. K. undermines this very notion of Immeritô's poetry as "no arte" in three important ways. First, he distinguishes between the original and present poets by telling us that, in these days, poets have turned to the "lighter matter of Poesie[,] . . . some playing wyth love, some scorning at mens fashions, some powred out in Pleasures" (178). (Significantly, E. K. describes the "matter" of Immeritô's eclogues in terms that support the notion that they are in this "lighter" vein. He says that they are either "plaintive . . . or recreative, such as all those be, which conceive matter of love, or commendation of special personages, or Moral: which for the most part be mixed with some Satyrical bitternesse" [23].) At no point does E. K. associate the eclogues with a "vertuous intent," which he seems to align only with a rhetoric of praise for things ideally conceived (virtue, immortality) or demonstrably true (victory). For him, Immeritô sings with the intent to complain, for example, rather than to praise, and though the poet com-mends "special personages," his "Satyrical bitternesse" engages a rhetoric of blame that marks his intentions as different from poetry's "first invention."

Second, by continually referring to and emphasizing the poet's skill, not his "divine instinct," as a special point for praise, E. K. undercuts the notion that Immeritô's poetry is actually of the divine order. In addition to his many direct ref-erences to the author of the eclogue's poetic "skyl" throughout the *Calender*, he also reinforces that idea indirectly by characterizing Cuddie's "inspired" poetic interlude as a product of art. E. K. completes the gloss on the emblems for *Octo-ber* thus: "Whom Piers answereth Epiphonematicos as admiring the excellencye of the skyl whereof in Cuddie hee hadde already had a taste" (183). If, as E. K. would seem to want us to believe, Immeritô represents in Cuddie "the perfect paterne of a Poete" (170), he emphasizes, in addition to a vague "excellencye," the skills of a craftsman or artisan, not a poetic gift.[10] Finally, in describing these vatic powers as "divine," "unnatural," and beyond the reaches of "comen reason," E. K. contra-dicts his original assertion that Immeritô's poetry is determined to demonstrate "naturall rudenesse."

Whether poetry is a "skyl," an "artlesse arte," or some admixture of both, E. K. is quite sure that the matter of poetry is of little to no importance to the learned.

In his lengthy discourse on why the poet calls these eclogues "Æclogues" rather than "Eclogues," for example, E. K. declares the matter of poetry to be "unneccessarie." Claiming that it is "not at all impertinent to my present purposes," and on the presumption that "the word [Æclogues] . . . is unknowen to most," E. K. attempts to correct the opinions of "some of the best learned (as they think)" regarding the origins of the word "Æglogues." In addition to several more facetious remarks denigrating the learning of "most" others, E. K. learnedly seeks to set the record straight by offering an etymological argument:

> They were first of the Greekes the inventours of them called Æglogai as it were αἶγον or αἰγνόμων. λόγοι. that is Goteheards tales. For although in Virgile and others the speakers be more shepheards, then Goteherds, yet Theocritus in whom is more ground of authoritie, then in Virgile, this specially from that deriving, as from the first head and welspring the whole Invencion of his Æglogues, maketh Goteheards the persons and authors of his tales. This being, who seeth not the grossenesse of such as by colour of learning would make us beleeve that they are more rightly termed Eclogai, as they would say, extraordinary discourses of unneccessarie matter, which difinition albe in substaunce and meaning it agree with the nature of the thing, yet nowhit answereth with the ανάλυσις and interpretations of the word. For they be no termed Eclogues, but Æglogues . . . though indeede few Goteheards have to do herein, nethelesse doubteth not to cal them by the used and best knowen name. (22)

By his own admission, the issue E. K. addresses here is of little consequence because whether a proponent of "Êglogue" or "Eclogai," the object in question, in both "substaunce and meaning," contains "unneccessarie matter." And though he acknowledges that "indeede fewe Goteheards" are present in the *Calender*'s "Æglogues" (and ignoring for the time being the fact that *Shepheardes* plays a key role not only in the title but also in every dimension of the text as well—two characteristics that would seem to obliterate the substance of his argument), E. K. maintains that the poet "upon good judgement" chose the most accurate title for his work.

Similarly, in his gloss to the *December* eclogue's missing emblem referred to previously, after he declares that the "workes of learned wits and monuments of Poetry abide forever," E. K. casts his eye forward to Immeritô's "Epilogue," wherein the poet writes:

> Loe I have made a Calender for every yeare,
> That steele in strength, and time in durance shall outweare:
> And if I marked well the starres revolution,
> It shall continewe till the worlds dissolution.
> (1–4)

As if torn from the syllogistic reasoning that, perhaps, he used if not to "invent" then to marshal his criticisms, E. K.'s final comments affect the language of logical argumentation:

> And therefore Horace of his Odes a work though ful indede of great wit and learning, *yet of no so great weight and importaunce* boldly sayth:
>
>> Exegi monimentum êre perennius,
>> Quod nec imber nec aquilo vorax etc.
>
> Therefore let not be envied, that this Poete in his Epilogue sayth he hath made a Calendar, that shall endure as long as time etc. folowing the ensample of Horace and Ovid in the like.
>
>> Grande opus exegi quod nec Iovis ira nec ignis,
>> Nec ferrum poterit nec edax abolere vetustas etc.
>> (213)

Central to E. K.'s argument is the claim he articulates here (the major premise upon which his criticisms are founded) that poetry is "of no great weight and importance." Though poetry is "ful of great wit and learning," its inherent unimportance "will abide forever" only because "the work of learned wits" who take "paines" to explicate it commends it to the ages. E. K. asks the reader to "therefore" forgive the poet his boldness for claiming to have made a work that will "endure as long as time" (for he, like Horace before him, knows not of what he so boldly speaks).

E. K.'s Antonian Sunburn (an Analogy)

An insight into the set of principles guiding both the form and content of E. K.'s all-too-consistent criticisms may be gleaned from how he chooses to gloss Cicero. In his prefatory "Epistle" to Gabriel Harvey, E. K. alludes to a passage from the second book of Cicero's *De oratore* in one of his preliminary attempts to explain why this "straunge" poet uses "auncient" and "unused" words:

> I graunt they be something hard, and of most men unused, yet both English, and also used of the most excellent Authors and most famous Poets. In whom whenas this our Poet hath bene much traveiled and thoroughly redd, how could it be, (as that worthy Oratour sayde) but that walking in the sonne although for other cause he walked, yet needes he mought be sunburnt, and having the sound of those auncient Poetes still ringing in his eares, he mought needes in singing hit out some of theyr tunes. (19)

It is generally assumed that by "that worthy Oratour," E. K. is referring to Cicero himself; in all likelihood, "Tullie" is the one E. K. has in mind here. But within the fiction of *De oratore,* it is Antonius who offers this sunburn analogy in the effort to explain the relationship among oratory and the liberal and humane arts. In contrast to Crassus's claim that "the art of speaking well, that is to say, of speaking with knowledge, skill, and elegance, has no delimited territory" because "all things whatsoever, that can fall under the discussion of human beings must be aptly dealt with by him who professes [eloquence]" (3.2.1), Antonius offers a theory of oratory that operates on quite different principles. "Oratory," he postulates, "derives distinction from ability (*facultate*), but owes little to art. For while art is concerned with the things that are known, the activity of the orator has to do with opinion, not knowledge" (2.7.30).

The practical and philosophical ramifications of this view are illustrated in Antonius's treatment of history. Though he claims that histories are to be read primarily "just for pleasure" (2.14.59), Antonius concedes that, albeit indirectly, there may be "some benefit" for the orator in perusing history books:

> Just as, when walking in the sunshine, though perhaps for a different reason, the natural result is that I get sunburnt, even so, after perusing those [history] books rather closely at Misenum (having little chance at Rome), I find that under their influence my discourse takes on what I may call a new complexion.[11]

Histories, according to Antonius, in addition and quite incidentally to their capacity to amuse, may be studied by the budding orator primarily for their "fluency and diversity of diction" (*flumine orationis et varietate maximum*; 2.15.62). Second to their capacity to furnish the orator with instructive examples in verbal dexterity, historical writings also have the advantage of teaching the orator to adhere to telling the truth: "For who does not know history's first law to be that an author must not dare to tell anything but the truth?" (2.15.62). Though he does allow for some authorial bias in the telling of history by suggesting that "some intimation of what the writer approves" (2.15.63) should be evident in the narration, it is finally history's allegiance to an objective truth of sorts that recommends it to the aspiring orator. An orator's history should present history chronologically, with an "[estimation] of consequences . . . exposition of all contributary causes" that recounts the "particulars of the lives and characters of such as are outstanding in renown and dignity" (2.15.63–64). Like the historian, the orator should present an "accurate" description of the who, what, where, why, and how of history; unlike the historian, the orator manages to recommend history to the ages by presenting its truths in an ornate and flowing writing style.[13]

What significance historical *knowledge* itself, rather than certain methods of *composition,* might have for an orator, Antonius is not willing to speculate on beyond the bare notion that the orator who would embellish a history—or any other subject matter—should acquaint himself with the topic. The orator, Antonius claims, need only "be a man of some learning" who has done some listening and some reading (2.20.85), have a sound reputation and some status, and be both willing and able to speak on any subject presented him. Knowledge of history itself —or any other subject matter outside of the purview of persuasion—is useful, but not necessary to the orator. Because the orator must rely on the knowledge discovered by the methodologies of experts to make his speeches, oratory for Antonius only "wears the likeness of an art" (2.8.33). Unlike the art of history (or mathematics, astronomy, etc.), the knowledge particular to the orator "seldom attains to demonstration (*scientam*)" because oratory does not have a body of *scientia* or demonstrable knowledge particular to it; it instead deals in opinion and so is "a subject . . . founded on [falsehood] (*mendacio*) . . . which sets its snares to entrap the fancies and often the delusions of mankind" (2.7.30). The orator's "godlike excellence and power," Antonius maintains, does not lie in finding what ought to be said, but in saying it, in "his delivery of what he has to say in a style elegant (*ornate*), copious, and diversified" (2.27.120). By virtue of his command of style, who else, Antonius asks, but the orator "can entrust [history] to immortality?" (2.9.36).

While walking and reading in the garden at Misenum, Antonius acquires the complexion or color of learning by acquiring the vocabulary of the historian, and perhaps something of a historian's compulsion to explain events. This is no indication that he in fact "knows" or can demonstrate the verity of his historical knowledge, as he willingly admits. But an orator need not demonstrate history's truths, he need only appear learned for the narrow ends of persuasion in a particular instance. What the orator really "knows" or acquires by experience is a facility in swaying others by means of rhetorical *techne*. The orator does not teach; he delights in order to move others according to his will.

Antonius's emphasis on oratory as a natural ability that primarily requires practice and experience to develop leads him to eschew those "Greek professor[s]" and "rhetoricians" who proffer rules and "hackneyed axioms" (*pervulgata praecepta*) on oratory, "for they are for teaching others a thing with which they themselves are unacquainted" (2.18.76). Real oratory for Antonius is forensic oratory, and these rhetoricians teach though they have never had "experience at the Bar" themselves. For Antonius, experience with speaking, though a source of learning, is not a thing one can teach. When given the opportunity to enlarge on oratory, thus, Antonius proceeds to expound on precisely those sets of rules that the rhetoricians proffer; in fact, Crassus facetiously notes the similarity when he remarks that

> if you think it sufficient to learn the instructions drawn up by your writers on the science of rhetoric, instructions nevertheless that have been expounded by Antonius in a much more graceful and more copious form[,] . . . well, if you are content with these rules . . . you are making the orator abandon a vast immeasurable plain and confine himself to a quite narrow circle. (3.19.70)

Promising to discourse on the "matter" (*res*) of oratory, Antonius presents the conventional *techne* or artifice of rhetoric as knowledge particular to the orator—the quantifiable, prescriptive, and formal dimensions of rhetoric. He leaves only the discussion of "words" to Crassus, specifically, the "elaboration and embellishment" or ornamentation of words (2.90.366).

Where Crassus maintained that the art of oratory "has no delimited territory," Antonius claims that the orator's art is really no art at all—it is an artless art because the knowledge particular to it cannot be demonstrated, "known," or proved except by how it works in practice. If the orator does have anything important or learned to say, furthermore, it is because he has borrowed, relied on, or pilfered the methods and demonstrable matter particular to a subject discovered or "invented" by an expert in the field. Antonius perceives the rules of rhetoric to resemble the matter of other subjects because rules can be known in the sense that they can be explained, defined, quantified, and categorized. Significantly, Antonius saves the third and, in his view, basest form of oratory, panegyrics—the rhetorical genre of praise and blame that comes closest to humanist poetics—for last and treats it only summarily (2.84.345–50).

As is probably evident at this point, E. K.'s assessment of poetry is analogous to Antonius's assessment of rhetoric in some remarkable ways. E. K. wants to claim that the poet's "divine gift" (his "godlike excellence and power") lies, in part, in the pleasures or beauty derived from his ornate use of language, but (and though the effectiveness of rhetorical ebullience to instill delight cannot be denied) the ornate use of language is not to be trusted because it appeals to the emotions of the reader. Furthermore, because appeals to pathos resist rational proofs and so cannot be accounted as learning, E. K., like Antonius, searches for proof of the poet's divine gift, (his *facultate,* Aristotle's *dynamis*) in the poet's manipulation of rhetorical *techne;* and it is not the use of rhetorical skill so much as it is the marking and explanation of those skills that E. K. considers to be learning. Both E. K. and Antonius begin on the presumption that the rhetorical arts have no real stake in the pursuit of knowledge or wisdom because rhetorical and poetic discourses are but the re-forming and manipulation of a particular, codified, and known set of ideas.

Knowledge or wisdom in such a schematic is deductive; its status as knowledge relies on its demonstrable, rational, or provable character. Learning, knowledge, or wisdom in such a schematic requires, but is not contingent on, one's rhetoric. What counts as learning is instead contingent on the method of demonstration that consists of the use of rhetoric but is not itself perceived to be rhetorically constituted. To be wise in such a schematic thus depends on principles relative to a particular subject rather than principles regarding human action in general. As a result, ethics as a subject of inquiry is abstracted from human action *in general* and becomes subject to speculation provable by way of particular methodologies,

conventions, dogma, doctrine, or the pronouncements of a credible "scholar"—
any of which may or may not contribute to "civill felicitie." E. K. accounts Immer-
itô wise insofar as the poet addresses the conventions of pastoral poetry; the
"delight" he promises the reader from reading the eclogues is presented as intrin-
sically "good" by virtue of the poet's manipulation of his particular skills, not by
its capacity to affect virtuous action.

For a Tudor humanist with Protestant tendencies (as is especially evident in his
gloss to the *Maye* eclogue) who seems to associate with Cambridge fellows and
is willing to let his "present paynes" be judged by none other than "mine own
good Maister Harvey" (20), the contemporary philosophical argument that best
accounts for E. K.'s argument regarding Immeritô's verse appears to be Ramism.
Though it does not assume the more usual form of Ramist argumentation by dia-
gramming arguments or syllogizing verse, it does employ some of English Ramism's
characteristic proclivities (including Protestant zeal). E. K.'s reliance, for example,
on the language of logic, not only in his final gloss but also throughout his com-
mentary, is but one indication. More tellingly, however, is one of his glosses to the
Aprill eclogue. In *Aprill*, Hobbinoll recites a song Colin had made when he was in
love with Rosalinde. In it, Colin calls upon the epic muse, Calliope:

> I see *Calliope* speede here to the place,
> where my Goddesse shines:
> And after her the other Muses trace,
> with their Violines.
> (100–103)

E. K., incorrectly quoting Virgil, takes this opportunity to explain that Calliope is

> one of the nine Muses: to whome they assigne the honor of all Poeticall Inven-
> tion, and the first glorye of the Heroicall verse. other say, that shee is the God-
> desse of Rhetorick: but by Virgile it is manifeste, that they mystake the thyng.
> For there in hys Epigrams, that arte semeth to be attributed to Polymnia, saying:

> Signat cunta manu, loquiturque Polymnia gestu.

> which seemeth specially to be meant of Action and elocution, both special partes
> of Rhetorick: besyde that her name, which (as some construe it) importeth great
> remembraunce, conteineth another part, but I hold rather with them, which call
> her Polymnia or Polyhymnia of her good singing. (81)

Significantly, E. K. distances himself from the "they" who assign "all Poeticall
Invention" to Calliope, unwilling to affirm that the poet "invents." That unwill-
ingness is itself affirmed by E. K.'s readiness to employ the standard Ramist defini-
tion of rhetoric as consisting only of two of its five traditional canons, *pronunctatio,*

or "delivery" ("Action"), and *elocutio,* or "ornamentation."[13] Ramism maintained that all invention belongs properly to logic or dialectic. It should come as no surprise, thus, that E. K. should conflate these two muses, talking more about Polyhymnia and rhetoric while ostensibly glossing Calliope and "Poeticall Invention" even as he tries to distinguish between them. Poetry answers to the same criterion to which he holds rhetoric. E. K. "holds with them" that refer to Polyhymnia "of her good singing"; "good" here has no moral content and does not refer to virtuous action in a general sense but to the delivery and elocution of a rhetorical performance as can be accounted for or explained by the *techne* posing as learned matter conventionally associated with it.

Crassus's lament for the state of learning in his day resonates eerily with Sidney's lament for learning (and poetry's place within learning) in *A Defence of Poetry*—and, in all probability, the argument Spenser paints in defense of poetic learning in the learned figure of E. K.:

> Nowadays we are deluged not only with the notions of the vulgar but also with
> the opinions of the half-educated, who find it easier to deal with matters that
> they cannot grasp in their entirety if they split them up and take them piecemeal,
> and who separate words from thought as one might sever body from mind—
> and neither process can take place without disaster.[14] (*De oratore* 3.7.24)

E. K.'s Ramistic approach to Immeritô's eclogues repeats just such a piecemeal assault on learning. Central to that assault is the "disembodiment" of the aesthetic and invention from learning and whatever comprises the "good." Whatever comprises the good in this schema, furthermore, does not attain its quality because of the action it performs but by virtue of the (scholarly) conventions imposed on it. Rhetoric and poetry thus were more likely to obscure true, methodical reasoning than inform and guide moral action since the invention and consequences of knowledge inhabit a singular, small, detachable field of expertise.

The Logic of the Flock

Ethics or inquiry into human action is preempted by E. K.'s reliance on the conventional and the known; consequently, his narrow conception of morality, of what good or virtuous is, is constituted by the relationship between the poet and his art and is explainable in formal terms. Ethical inquiry for the quattrocento humanists, as Nancy Struever argues at length, begins from the context or drama of a particular act; as such, it serves as a constant check on the general rule because it recognizes the possible to be a condition of the probable. And what is probable is always controvertible, or controversial as Sloane argues.[15] Probability for E. K., however, is only a condition of an incontrovertible possible. This gives him the intellectual license to gloss over the probable, the controvertible, the drama of the particular act, into the realm of possibilities circumscribed by formal matters, and he does this as a matter of form. By (mis)appropriating the mantle of learning and defining knowledge in terms of its rational rather than active or ethical ends, E. K. excises "moral" from philosophy.

Without that tempering of the general afforded by ethical inquiry, the political realm becomes another, unconditionalized source of virtue (especially when contrasted to the infallibility of the ideals pronounced by various contemporary Christian doctrines). Of the three poetic ends E. K. mentions, he appears to think the recreative the most honorable, for it is the ability of the poet to commend the "worthiness and valor" of "princes and noble men" that, in part, validates poetry's "worthiness." But it is an honor conferred on the poet because he has immortalized his noble subjects:

> Achilles had never bene so famous, as he is, but for Homeres immortal verses, which is the only advantage, which he had over Hector. . . . And also Alexander the great comming to his tombe in Sigeus, with natural teares blessed him, that ever was his hap to be honoured with so excellent a Poets work . . . . Such honor have Poetes always found in the sight of Princes and noble men, which this author very well sheweth. (181)

What virtue might look like beyond implicating it in the praise of the deeds of great men, whether virtuous or no, E. K. cannot say. The poet-court relationship, for E. K., operates on a narrow quid pro quo principle: the poet immortalizes people because they are noble, and as the poet's reward, he will be esteemed and honored by great personages. E. K. attempts to fashion Spenser as a poet of the court by suggesting that the "great matter" the poet unfolds covertly has more to do with political intrigues, and he is keen on identifying possible references to the queen or her nobles in his glosses.[16] By emphasizing the political, narrowly conceived in terms of power and authority, it is appropriate then that he should deem the "Morall or generall" aspects of the eclogues as the "lighter matter of Poesie." If the recreative, in his terms, concerns itself with obsequious praise, the Moral "for the most part be mixed with Satyrical bitternesse" (23) and merely scorns at men's fashions (178). E. K. thus manages to distance poetry from the lives of ordinary, literate folk; he renders poetry an elitist, irrelevant enterprise aimed primarily at offering a "divine" pleasure unencumbered by any broad moral considerations, which is only of interest to a ruling class hungry for flattery.

The other most trusted (and plundered) theorist-critic of poetry in Spenser's day, George Puttenham, suggests in *The Arte of Englishe Poesie* (1589) that the "great matter" that E. K. says the poet "chose to unfold . . . covertly" (18) in his eclogues runs deeper than the unfortunate love life of the poet or bare political maneuvering. Puttenham notes that eclogues were not devised

for the purpose to counterfait or represent the rusticall manners of loues and
communication: but under the vaile of homely persons, and in rude speeches to
insinuate and glaunce at greater matters, and such as perchaunce had not beene
safe to haue beene disclosed in any other sort, which may be perceived by the
eclogues of *Virgill*, in which are treated by figure matter of greater importaunce
than the loues of *Titirus* and *Corydon*.[17]

Of course, E. K. says as much about Immeritô's eclogues. But Puttenham goes fur-
ther: "These Eclogues came after to containe and enforme morall discipline, for
the amendment of mans behavior, as be those of *Mantuan* and other moderne
Poets" (53). *After* Virgil and in modern times, the "matter" of pastoral appears to
have shifted in emphasis or direction from covertly "glancing" at the affairs of the
state to "containing" and "informing" "morall discipline." "Morall discipline" sig-
nifies something more general and more generalizable than, for example, the par-
ticular matters of great importance confronting Augustinian Rome or, as in the
Calender, Elizabeth's dismissal of Edmund Grindal.

The pastoral poetry of "*Mantuan* and other moderne Poets" such as Spenser
does not aim to affect the immediate circumstances (as Puttenham appears to
think Virgil intended) but takes a longer view toward political reform by aiming
more generally at "the amendment of mans behauiour." And toward that end,
modern pastoral "containe[s] and enforme[s]" the forms of behavior it advocates.
Which is to say, then, that modern pastoral exemplifies or represents virtuous
behavior and in so doing, informs, instructs, or *teaches* "morall discipline." But it
may also mean that modern pastorals "enforme" or *embody* moral discipline in the
sense that it offers exemplary patterns of virtuous (rhetorical) action. It may be
said, then that all of the eclogues are moral eclogues, and any division beyond the
acknowledgment of their most general and moral function (for example, Plaintive,
"recreative," and "Morall") is a critical technique or contrivance designed to explain
their meaning in rational terms severed from their moral considerations; such a
technique may or may not help one understand the poem.

But for E. K., learning consists of things that can be proved or demonstrated.
Consequently, the knowledge he purports to share with the reader may be easily
referred to, cited, or supported by available materials; meaning is not learned in
the act of reading, but by the act of explication. The act of explication, of analy-
sis, furthermore, is designed to show the reader how to appreciate the poet's "excel-
lence." In that process, the dimensions and texture of the poet's world of figurative
language is leveled by reason to reason: each word, each phrase, each eclogue loses
any metaphorical resonance it might have because "what this metaphor 'refers to'
or 'really' means" is either legislated for the reader or extended out toward absurd-
ity (for example, E. K.'s discussion of "Æglogues"). In this sense, we may say that

E. K.'s gloss argues for a poetics of mimesis; it is an imitation whose metaphoric making does not produce *action* so much as it reproduces *concepts*. In *Aprill*, as Thenot and Hobbinoll discuss Colin's breaking of his "Bagpype" in the penulti-mate scene in *Januarye*, Thenot asks:

> What is he for a Ladde, you so lament?
> Ys love such pinching payne to them, that prove?
> And hath he skill to make excellent,
> Yet hath so little skill to brydle love?
> (13–16)

From these lines, E. K. chooses to gloss, of all things, "to make," which, he explains, is "to rime and versifie. For in this word making, our olde Englishe Poetes were wont to comprehend all the skil of Poetrye, according to the Greeke woorde ποιεῖν to make, whence commeth the name of Poets" (77). The "skil of Poetrye" is to make rhymes and compose verse, a technical skill consisting of choosing from a predetermined set of rhetorical figures and "literary" conventions, of knitting together sound sentences, and of coloring one's insignificant matter with learning. For E. K., poetry is an art of composition; as such, it is not an art of making, but a particular form of delightful imitation.

The other side of the philosophical coin that E. K. puts into circulation offers "delight" conceived of as "unnaturall" and "divine" as an escape route from its interminable rationality. This aesthetic principle, this inclination to "monumen-talize," however, ultimately cannot be grasped substantively but only formally because its substance is derived from the formal restrictions of the ideal, the con-ventional, the traditional. The beginning point of knowledge for E. K. is not the word, or the word as metaphor or words as actions, but the "matter" anterior to and revealed by the word; the word itself carries little to no significance, but is a device or ornament designed to delight. That "matter" anterior to the word, fur-thermore, is preformed and preverbal, rational, in place, inactive or static, and immutable. Ideally, poetic delight is desirable for its own good, but only because that good has been abstracted from the natural, active world and assigned a place in the heavens. The aesthetics of the text do not inhere in the work; words per-form as rhetorical acts, but in the rhetoric they set forth in imitation of a presumed truth. As such, what is good may be explained, or not explained, innovated (tin-kered with) or accepted, enforced or submitted to, or taken on a particular faith.

If the poet is judged on his ability to manipulate language and a static set of lit-erary conventions on the presumption that such "devices" are in the service of an "unnatural reason" or supernatural *enthusiasmous,* the moral dimension of his poetry becomes responsible or answerable to a pedagogue's dogma, the pleasures of

a prince, or one particular Christian doctrine; the poet's verse is no longer a form
of (rhetorical) action but a monument of unerring truth—or falsehood. E. K.
applies such abstractions to the drama or action of eclogues in the effort to explain
them; as a result, the dramatic effect of those eclogues is lost on him. But, as we
shall see in the next chapter, it is to the *drama* of human (or rhetorical) action that
Spenser directs the reader in his effort "to teach."

※

CHAPTER FOUR

NEGOTIATING METAPHORS

On *The Shepheardes Calender*

So as the Poets were also from the beginning the best perswaders
and their eloquence the first Rhetoricke of the world.

—*George Puttenham,* The Arte of Englishe Poesie

PERHAPS THE MOST COMMON EPITHET assigned to Spenser's poetic posture regarding the various subjects, topoi, and themes discussed and allegorized throughout *The Shepheardes Calender* is "ambivalence."[1] The poet's ambivalence is sometimes associated with a profound disillusionment, sometimes with a sublime confoundment; more generally, however, it is associated with notions of a severe "complexity." The saving grace, as it were, to Spenser's persistent ambivalence would appear to be figurative language and poetic form, because both permit him to position himself without positioning himself, to communicate the complexities of an issue without advocating one side over an other, to sustain, as McCanles writes, "a continued refusal to rest conclusively in any one attitude and one perspective as irrevocably the right and true one."[2] And yet, ironically, Spenser is variously granted, excused, or commended for his resolute ambivalence on the ubiquitous critical assumption that such a posture attests to a brand of philosophic idealism characteristic of Renaissance humanism. Louis A. Montrose, for example, argues that "the poet's high calling" as a "vatic" poet, though continually frustrated by an awareness of "the constraints of social order," was "sanctioned by the artistic and ethical idealism of Renaissance Humanism" (35).[3] Though occasionally enamored, rueful, allured, indignant, pleased or frustrated by the panoply of human action, Spenser either eschews direct participation in, tempers his participation in, or condescends to participate in the rhetorical frays of his contemporaries for the sake of unobtainable "artistic and ethical" ideals.

Yet if we grant Spenser this idealism (an idealism that, as Montrose notes, is perceived to traffic among artistic form, political cabals, and, in Spenser's case, Protestant doctrine), presumptively, as a historical given, then we might well ask what Immeritô means when he claims "to teach" his readers in the Epilogue to the *Calender*. Though the notion that Spenser intends to teach his readers something has always served as a critical commonplace (insofar as humanist poets adhered to the axiom, typically ascribed to Horace, that the aims of poetry are "to teach, move, and delight" the reader),[4] the historical and philosophical (or moral) ramifications of teaching through poetry have managed to remain undeveloped and distant, if not occasionally detached altogether, from contemporary arguments regarding Spenser's poetry. For example, Montrose claims that, by means of the *Calender*'s eclogues, Spenser "proffered to readers a range of verbal strategies that could give formal expression to the complexity of an emergent generational consciousness."[5] Montrose's argument removes or abstracts both the act of teaching and the "matter" to be taught from the practical realm of human activity by claiming that Spenser offers formal matter (rhetorical *techne*) to "give expression to" a nebulous, incipient "consciousness" that may or may not have been perceived by or troubled anyone other than the poet himself. Similarly, Roland Greene's assertion that the *Calender* makes "a statement about the conditions of contemporary poetics . . . [wherein] the idea of dialogic lyric is an enigma—something to be reached for, hypothesized, but seldom realized," suggests that the "matter" of the poems owes its philosophic vitality to a form of speculation largely concerned with the complexities of literary production, absent any consideration for why or how an enigmatic lyric might teach others.[6] And S. K. Heninger's admonishment to appreciate by "discern[ing] correctly" the "frozen for all time" yet "fresh and vital" figures of the eclogues' inhabitants, represents an argument for the timelessness of Spenser's verse unencumbered by either the poem's historical circumstances or its pedagogic aims.[7] With the moral sky of Spenser's poetry surely mapped out, the practical work of poetry (to teach) becomes subordinate to, and sometimes lost among, the complexities confronted while navigating between certain fixed points.

But Immeritô's claim "to teach" his readers "how to feede his sheepe, / And from the falsers fraud his folded flocke to keepe" indicates that Spenser agrees with Sidney that "the ending end of all earthly learning" aims at "well doing and not well-knowing only"; verbs, not nouns, constitute the poet's intention. Immeritô's intention, furthermore, is not only constituted by verbs but also, more generally, self-consciously, and carefully, by *verba*, which is to say that words both enact and embody the poet's "ending end." That is, the always active and situated forms of *verba* rather than the idealized, static forms of *res* organize, guide, and embody (rather than merely "give expression to") the "ending end" of his poetic and interminably earthbound discourse. As Richard Waswo remarks, "The new meaning invoked by Sidney's and Spenser's new version of traditional didacticism is specifically between utterance and hearer, text and reader . . . they apprehended and created meaning as a dynamic function."[8] My argument in this chapter may be seen as a development of Waswo's claim with regard to the *Calender*.

We might expect a poetic education in "well doing and not well-knowing only" to privilege action over abstraction, words over ideals, and making over mimesis. For as we have seen by E. K. in the previous chapter, poetry conceived as the rational made meaningful through an alliance with the super- or extrarational (for example, the "aesthetic"), the conventional, the demonstrable, the clever, the particular and the innovative, maintains poetry to be primarily a mimetic art. When poetry is conceived primarily as a mimetic art, a poet's mastery of generic forms, conventions, and certain techniques does indeed constitute a discernible reconfiguration of (what is presumed to be) poetry's true content or "matter." It is, however, not a substantive or substantial assault because the matter re-presented or imitated is, in the final analysis, matter ossified by literary, philosophic, cultural, or theological orthodoxies abstracted from the realm of human action. The consequences of that reconfiguration, such as it is, distances poetry's capacity to teach from the reader by handing meaning over to a priestly caste of critics "in the know" about the precepts, conventions, novelties, and complexities that circumscribe and define a particular poetic theory.

A Refiguring

In this chapter, we will consider how Spenser's poetic practice represents poetry primarily as an artifice that enacts and exemplifies the action or *drama* of human making. Or perhaps I should say *the* artifice that enacts and exemplifies the drama of human making—the architectonic productive art of self-knowledge that surveys one's "ethic and politic considerations" and aims, rhetorically, toward "the end of well doing and not well-knowing only."[9] Poetry "teaches" by engaging the reader in a discovery process that persuades one to invent, feel, discern, and weigh probable and always situated or contextualized meaning*s*. Kahn, Sloane, and Waswo have identified prudential deliberation, the particular (and practical) virtue of the rational faculty of the sensitive soul, to be the chief end to this discovery process—and rightly so.[10] Sloane, especially, has argued on numerous occasions that the humanist pedagogical practice of *disputatio in utramque partem* lies at the center of inculcating a habit of thought directed toward prudential judgment.[11] This habit of thought, in other words, is invented or discovered in and cultivated through habits of rhetorical doing; exercises in reading or speaking on both sides of an argument engage, habituate, and "feed" the body in order to train or influence the rational process. Bodies *and* minds are present and engaged in the rhetorical act. It is the sensed experience of the body, the matter of learning, that makes prudence possible, and it is by means of that matter the poet appeals to "teach, move, and delight" his reader toward virtuous action.

The matter of learning is, furthermore, if not discernible, then "sensible" in the rhetorical act itself. Exercises in reading or speaking on both sides of an argument can be neither merely "academic" nor simply devices designed and employed in a moral vacuum: the act of arguing both sides of an argument inculcates habits of thought indicative of the writer's character precisely because one's ethos is physically inextricable from the rhetorical act itself; similarly, the act of reading, of weighing both sides of an argument, develops character precisely because the reader's own sensed experience is inextricable from the rhetorical act initiated by the author. How one chooses to read one's self into the rhetorical act thus is of great consequence—and because we are trafficking in the realm of human action, there is always a choice. My focus here is on metaphor as the linguistic embodiment of that choice—or *preference*.[12] As the discursive formulation of our sensed experience, metaphor negotiates between body and mind, between well-doing and well-knowing (or deliberate well-doing)—between what Aristotle recognized as the (noncongitive) moral virtues and Moral Virtue (*NE,* 1103a, 1144b). As such, metaphor may be seen as the most basic constituent of *disputatio in utramque partem:* if the ability to argue both sides of the question inculcates prudence, then the ability to "read" or interpret one's self into differing rhetorical situations requires a kind of knowledge that is both acutely self-reflexive and intensely perspicacious, a kind of knowledge that is both indicative of one's character and indicative of the sociorhetorical act in which one's character is engaged.[13] The poet makes metaphors in order to "teach, move, and delight" his readers into making metaphors themselves so that they might negotiate the possibilities of their own (habitual or characteristic) actions in any particular circumstance, and this he does rhetorically on the premise that the poetic or rhetorical invention of metaphors (rather than the imitation of categorical propositions or ideals) is the natural, active, and necessary condition of knowledge itself.

The rhetorically-poetically invented metaphor differs significantly in kind, form, and function from those metaphors designed "to give expression to" artistic and ethical ideals. In *Spenser and the Motives of Metaphor,* A. Leigh DeNeef identifies the poet's use of metaphor as a "vehicle" that transfers the poet's mimetic art to poetic making.[14] DeNeef distinguishes between a baser form of imitation that "glances occasionally at the conventional descriptions of poetry's relation to an exterior world" and what he terms poetry's "metaphoric" dimension, which he claims "is more interested in how mimesis orders and controls the internal process of poetic making" (6). This metaphoric dimension, for DeNeef, is both the poet's nonverbal "initial mimetic step" of "an abstract universal" (the Platonic "Idea") and the "verbal poem" that manifests the poet's "conceit," the "second metaphoric

imitation of the Idea" (5). But DeNeef's reason-based and reason-confined con-
ception of imitation—a conception that "orders and controls" the poet's metaphori-
cal making and disregards the physiological element of human making altogether
—subordinates the poet's use of figurative language (his rhetoric) to the realm of
abstraction, which abstractions then comprise the meaning of the text.[15] Remark-
ably, such a poet, committed as he is to nonverbal rational abstractions, "neither
teaches nor constructs Ideas; rather, he reminds the reader of Ideas latent, although
perhaps 'forgotten' through misuse or lack of use, in the [reader's] mind" (5). The
poem merely reminds readers of their potential to access rationally or know abstract
universal truths on the oft-frustrated assumption that well-knowing will elicit
well-doing; such cognitive access to the ideal, furthermore, is said to constitute
poetic delight.

One significant result of this conception of poetry is that action will only be
deemed virtuous insofar as it imitates, reveals, or expresses certain ideals; that is,
the moral or active dimension of poetic discourse is narrowly circumscribed by
particular forms of, some eminently explainable amalgamation of, or a complete
leveling of whatever might be construed as virtuous human action (including dis-
cursive or rhetorical action). Harry Berger Jr., for example, has described Spenser's
poetic project as "metadiscursive" in the sense that "his poems are discourses of
discourses. . . . They are discourses about discourses they represent." But because
the discourses Berger has in mind are primarily "literary" discourses that, as a mat-
ter of historical accident, "transgress the boundaries of literary institutions" by
implicating themselves in the "extra-literary 'texts' of social, political, and cultural
discourse," the active or ethical dimension of poetic discourse he envisions is
bound to and circumscribed by, first, the conventions inhering in the institution-
alization (or "monumentalization") of literary discourse and, second, in the some-
what less reliable conventions of "extra-literary texts."[16] The consequences of such
a view can be seen in the conclusion Berger draws in reference to a passage from
book 3 of *The Faerie Queene:* supported by the well-known principles of Neopla-
tonic discourse and protected by the "institutions" of a poetic tradition, the poet
"converts the discourse to a smokescreen [and] mystifies an appeal to political
interests as an appeal to ethical and religious aspiration" (472). What appears on a
tertiary level as a rhetorical investment in a political discourse, in other words, is
dissolved into, or absolved by an appeal to "ethical and religious aspirations" that,
by virtue of the immutable laws of Neoplatonic metaphysics, are presumed to
"ground" Renaissance humanism and the anachronistic institutionalization of
poetic forms and refuse to acknowledge even the possibility of material, meaning-
ful consequences. The poet's ability to "mystify" or disguise his aspirations with
the facade of political rhetoric, furthermore, is singled out as evidence of Spenser's
particular genius. "Complexity" and an airy yet dense discourse rather than

some useful and actionable human understanding are the result. And, significantly, "ethics"—and so virtue, presumably poetic or otherwise—obtains its meaning here by Berger's implicit association of it with Christian doctrine. Consequently, the "conspicuous ambivalence" toward all (earthly) discourse Berger and others see in Spenser's work, the "transgressive" rather than, as I want to suggest, participatory character of his work, and the principally literary concerns of his poetry lend the poet an authority that allows him to speak from a position remote from and ultimately not responsible to the rhetorical din of earthly discourses, including the discourse of humanism.

But Immeritô's re-presentation of discourse is never simply "another" representation, nor is it just a representation in poetic form. The poet *makes,* and in making he engages the reader in a process of discovery about the possibilities of language to shape both what is known and knowable (rather than to reveal or "remind" the reader of a particular category from whence meaning *ought* to be derived). George Puttenham begins *The Arte of Englishe Poesie* by drawing a distinction between the mimetic and making functions of poetry. "A poet," he writes, "may in some sort be said a follower or imitator, because he can express the true and liuily of euery thing is set before him, and which he taketh in hand to describe" (20). Principally, however, the poet is a maker; Puttenham begins his tome thus:

> A Poet is as much to say as a maker. And our English name well conformes with the Greeke word: ποιεῖν to make, they call a maker *Poeta.* Such as (by way of resemblance and reuerently) we may say of God: who without any trauell to his diuine imagination, made all the world of nought, nor also by any paterne or mould as the Platonicks with their Idees do phantastically suppose. (19)

Significantly, Puttenham rejects the Platonic notion of Ideal forms as the "mould" for making—making in this sense could only be "imitation" in the narrow sense, a recreation of some divine or speculative construct that already exists. God may have been able to create the world without exercising his "diuine imagination," but the godlike poet is not so fortunate: poets are but, and parenthetically "(in a maner of speech) as creating gods" (20), and their imaginations, like their readers, have their origins in the natural, not supernatural, world. The poet might create "a golden world," as Sidney claims, but it is a world where action, not the knowledge of abstract universals, "orders and controls" poetic making, where "a maner of speech" is a necessary, not tertiary, form of learning (*ratio et oratio*), where teaching is a moral imperative, and where the world is golden only because the poet has made it so.

Within Tudor humanist philosophy, the classical source most frequently drawn upon to authorize the humanistic philosophical position of Sidney and Spenser was Cicero.[17] We have seen how E. K.'s rather selective use of Cicero's Antonius from *De oratore* is illustrative of a critical philosophy that all but severs the (discursive) act of teaching "well-doing" from the "matter" of the text, searches for meaning in the infinite particulars of presumptive abstractions (for example, poetic form, Christian doctrine) and subjects poetic making to eminently explainable mimesis. Antonius and E. K. figure forth analogous principles of but one viable philosophic position. In an effort to show that philosophy is not comprised of positions so much as its by courses of action, however, Cicero situated Antonius's view within a dis-course and represented an alternative philosophy in the figure of Crassus. Crassus embodies an orator (whose nearest kinsman is the poet [1.16.70, 3.7.27]) who teaches, moves, and delights with a kind of learning grounded in the figurative or metaphorical rather than in the formal; it is a kind of learning that is active and *useful* rather than "knowable" (thus *probable* rather than "certain" or ascertainable by demonstration) and that moves from the particular (rhetorical) *act* to a general understanding, rather than from the presumptive to the abstract through an infinite array of particulars. Spenser offers an alternative or dis-course to E. K. analogous to Crassus in both principle and practice through Immeritô, and in so doing, Spenser shows how deeply Cicero's rhetorical pursuit of wisdom colored the whole of humanist discourse.

With an eye toward a rhetorical alternative, Berger's identification of Spenser's project as "metadiscursive" remains apt if we are willing to consider discourse in a more general sense and disregard such oppositions as "literary" and "extraliterary" that prioritize discourses. One preliminary observation we can make then about Spenser's metadiscursive project is that it self-consciously underscores the fact that it represents discourse *simply,* which is to say that it calls attention to a uniquely human activity, that is, discourse itself. For, in the most general sense, the figures that inhabit the eclogues converse: they dispute, debate, and discuss, tell stories, and sing. In this sense, then, there is nothing particularly literary about the action represented in the eclogues; the action represented is rhetorical action. And insofar as the eclogues re-present a generalized notion of discourse itself, the poet's representation of discourse may be said to contain and reconstitute the discursive possibilities that, in turn, constitute how and why and not just what we know. For Spenser, as a maker, who sees his making as a form of teaching or learning directed at "well doing," "ambivalence" thus is not a practical, exemplary, or philosophically defensible position—especially when confronted by the philosophical principles exemplified by E. K., who in practice displaces and diminishes poetic learning with definitions, demonstration, and consideration of the abstruse, trivial, and occasionally absurd subtleties more relevant to recondite debate than Spenser's figurative pedagogy. In short, the poet is everywhere deeply invested in the words he chooses—and the metaphors he invents—to make action; and because the philosophical advantage he seeks manifests itself (rhetorically) in the act of teaching that, which Bryskett noted, is essential to "civill felicitie," the metaphors he makes belong to a pragmatic and social (or humanistic) conception of morality rather than a morality defined by Platonic ideals. They are multivalent rather than ambivalent, connote a participatory rather than "transgressive" or transcendent character, and exploit their fictive and made nature rather than their real or inspired origins.

I, Me, Mine:
Colin Clout's Formal Training

"Pastoral," writes Thomas Cain, a recent editor of the *Calender*, "is essentially a literature of stasis. When something happens in pastoral it is verbal: a debate, an improvised song. When action impinges on pastoral, it is either recounted . . . or foretold" (3–4). Cain distinguishes between these lesser verbal acts that may recount and foretell real action and the somewhat more substantive acts that "impinge on" the eclogues: "The only acts that take place in the *Calender*'s present are Colin's pipe breaking in *Januarye* and his death in *December*. But, of course, even Colin's pipe breaking and pipe hanging and eventual "death" (as Cain interprets it), are verbal events, and their "happening" is no less in present time nor less an activity than Hobbinoll's recitation of Colin's song of "fayre *Elisa*, Queene of shepheardes all" (34) in *Aprill* or Perigot's and Willye's roundelay in *August*. Colin's breaking of his pipe in *Januarye* is noteworthy because Immeritô steps forward from the "Envoy" onto the bucolic stage to narrate for the audience the drama of the eclogue before and after the figure (or a figuring) of his adolescent self offers his song; he returns again at the beginning of *December* to introduce Colin's plaintive moan. The rest of the time, however, Immeritô is content to remain in the wings, the unseen but ever-present author of the artifice enacted by his characters —characters who are themselves embodied and figured discursively. But whether he writes in a part for himself or leaves the acting to others, there is no substantive difference in *what* is done because everything is said or sung; every action in the *Calender* is a verbal action.

Though eclogues were devised "long after the other *drammatick* poems" (Satyre, Comedy ["Old" and "New"], and Tragedy), Puttenham is of the opinion that the pastoral "should be the first of any other" because

> the shepheards and haywards assemblies and meetings when they kept their cattell and heards in the common fields and forests, was the first familiar conversation, and their babble and talk under bushes and shadie trees, the first disputation and contentious reasoning, and their fleshly heates growing of ease, the first idle wooings, and their songs made to their mates or paramours either upon sorrow or jolity or courage, the first amorous musicks, sometimes also they sang

and played on their pipes for wagers, striving who should get the best game, and be counted cunningest. (53)

As the "first example of honest felowship," the assembly, conversation, disputations, idle wooings, songs, and contests of shepherds are representations of the first exercises in civility because the axis on which civility turns is a discursive axis. In this sense, then, the leisure of a shepherd's country life, *otium,* long considered to be the passive, baseline condition and defining characteristic of pastoral poetry, forms a presence only in its absence. For pastoral *otium* is disturbed as the eclogues' inhabitants negotiate their sundry differences among themselves. These simple negotiations signal the absence of leisure, *negotium* (*nec*/*otium*), and point toward the most natural or basic, or "lowly" form of human activity: the necessary concourse of the discursive forms of human action. ,

An understanding of this inherently active, and so moral expanse of discourse is perhaps the most significant thing that eludes Immeritô's immature pastoral persona, Colin Clout, and distinguishes Immeritô from him. Colin admits as much in *June* when he tells a too-forgiving Hobbinoll, "I play to please myself" (72): "Enough is me to paint out my unrest, / And poore my piteous plaints out in the same" (79–80).

In fact, as one determined to please himself, Colin very much resembles the kind of poet E. K. paints in his commentary and glosses. Recall that E. K. emphasized the notion that the poet composed and compiled these eclogues "to mitigate and allay his passion" after wandering long "in the common Labrynth of Love" (19). Each of Colin's songs, whether recounted by others or sung by himself, are precisely as E. K. describes them—solipsistic and ineffectual exercises in the expression of adolescent self-indulgence.[18] In *Januarye* Colin, sitting alone, addresses "Ye Gods of love, that pitie lovers payne" (13) and bewails the unrequited love he thinks he bears for Rosalind. Frustrated that his "rurall musick" has failed to win the affections of Rosalind, and that his "dolefull dittie" has failed "to allay and mitigate" his passion (as perhaps social convention has led him to believe), Colin "broke his oaten pipe, and down dyd lye" (72). But it is Immeritô who reappears on stage at the end of the eclogue to tell us that Colin breaks his pipe; "pensife" and "half in despight" (76), Colin exits stage left as Immeritô returns to his place in the wings stage right.

In Colin's description of Rosalind's reaction to his "Shepheards devise," we see that, though her particular response probably is motivated by a city bias against country folk, it is probably not an inappropriate response. Rosalind, Colin tells us, is a lass from "the neighbour towne" (50):

> Shee deignes not my good will, but doth reprove,
> And of my rurall musick holdeth scorne,

> Shepheards devise she hateth as the snake,
> And laughes the songes, that *Colin Clout* doth make.
> (63–66)

Colin's song begins and ends with the selfishness characteristic of adolescent males; the "good will" he claims to bear for Rosalind, for example, probably does not reach far beyond ego gratification. The love for Rosalind, sprung as it was from a Petrarchan glance, Colin exploits to create a song that, significantly, reflects (though none too deeply) on his own "paine" engendered by his idealized conception of love. Indeed, Rosalind does not even figure into Colin's "pyning" as the object of his affections until near the end of his song. Colin's reference to himself in the third person underscores the self-centeredness of his song. Rosalind's reaction may not be inappropriate, then, when we consider that Colin, unlike Immeritô, uses the art of poetry self-servingly—he has no intention "to teach" others.

Immeritô's presence in the eclogue thus is not without a dramatic effect, for in addition to supplying a narrative to Colin's song, it offers a valuable context by juxtaposing the more mature poet with his younger self. Referring to Colin, Immeritô admonishes the reader not to equate Colin too readily with himself and to search for points of variance between them in his opening line: "A Shepheards boye (no better doe him call)" (1). Colin is not a poet but a country lad who happens to be skilled in versifying. One significant characteristic of Colin's songs, as we have seen, is that they are private, self-indulgent acts that do not consider the possibility of offering any end but "delight." Without social or moral action to inform his "matter," Colin then assumes the technical "devises" and dexterous manipulation of poetic form to be the mark of poetic making.

One of the tools of the trade that Colin mechanically applies in all of his songs is to observe "decorum," in E. K.'s generically prescribed definition of the word, by taking the cue for the tenor of his song from the season, or from Nature more generally. After addressing the pitiless gods of love in *Januarye,* for example, Colin turns his attention to "Thou barrein ground, whome winters wrath hath wasted, / Art made a myrrhour, to behold my plight" (19–20) in order to give expression to his forlornment. But the facility with which he employs this particular poetic device only demonstrates its dramatic inappropriateness:

> Such rage as winters, reigneth in my heart
> My life bloud friesing with unkindly cold
> Such stormy stoures do breede my balefull smart,
> As if my yeare were wast and woxen old.
> (25–28)

The youthful, ill-tempered passion Colin evinces for Rosalind does not suggest that his life's blood is freezing nor does it indicate that his "yeare" is either spent or "woxen old." And to underscore the impropriety of Colin's too-ready reliance on such a device, Immeritô locates his song at the beginning of the year and characterizes his general attitude with the emblem *"Anchôra Speme"* (still [there is] hope). Though he is unable to see past his present grief, the world has not stopped turning for Colin, and for all of his self-pitying, he breaks his pipe as much to appease Rosalind's "scorne" in the hope of her future approval as to abate his frustrated passions.

Similarly, before Hobbinoll recounts for Thenot Colin's "laye" in praise of "fayre Elisa" in *Aprill,* he tells him that Colin composed it "as by a spring he laye, / And tuned it unto the Waters fall" (35–36). Again taking his cue from Nature, Colin began his song, mechanically, by addressing "Ye dayntye Nymphs, that in this blessed Brooke / doe bathe your brest" (37). Cuddie's recital of Colin's song in *August* begins with his plea, "Ye wastefull woodes beare witnesse of my woe, / Wherein my plaints did oftentimes resound" (151–52). And in *November,* Colin refuses Thenot's request to sing either to "thy loved lasse advaunce, / Or honor *Pan* with hymnes of higher vaine" (7 8) because, in effect, Colin says that it is winter time, and "Thilke sollein season sadder plight doth aske: / And loatheth sike delightes, as thou doest prayse" (17–18). Colin's song in *December* demonstrates his mastery of this simple device as he, again alone, organizes a narrative of his life as a versifier according to the seasons. *December*'s song bears testimony to Colin's inexperience in human affairs; it shows his characteristic inability to season his songs with a practical knowledge of *human* nature. Instead, he turns to the Book of Nature void of human congress except for the presence of his own, huge, solitary, intemperate, solipsistic self to read or interpret his own experience as a glorified but failed poet. He clearly does not think of himself as just another "Shepheards boye." Colin's song in *December* bears witness to the futility of such skilled exercises in the imitation of Nature absent any consideration of human nature.

The variety and cleverness of verse forms and lavish exercises in *copie* Colin employs further testify to his facility with poetic *techne.* An example of these two traits combined occurs in *Aprill:*

> Bring Coronations, and Sops in wine,
> worne of Paramoures.
> Strowe me the ground with Daffadowndillies,
> And Cowslips, and Kingcups, and loved Lillies:
> The pretie Pawnce,
> And the Chevisaunce,
> Shall match with the fayre flowre Delice.
> (82–90)

Though clever and ephemerally pleasant, the importance of such a display is dubious when we consider its self-conscious and overt reliance on skill, and that the primary purpose of it was the mitigation of Colin's passions. E. K.'s gloss to a passage in the *December* eclogue indicates the emptiness of such an exercise: he notes that "fragraunt flowers" (109) refer to "sundry studies and laudable partes of learning, wherein how oure Poet is seene" because they bear "witnesse" to his "privie" study (211). But it is exactly the intensely personal relationship with Nature, again void of human nature, that renders such displays both curious and inherently insignificant. And though this is a song intended to praise "Elisa," a lay that we might expect thus to have a greater social end in mind, it is *morally* corrupted in the sense that Colin returns pro forma to reflecting on his own emotional state to complete the song when he turns to his love to adorn it as "a fourth grace" (113). Thenot, recognizing that Colin "hath skill to make so excellent, / Yet hath so little skill to brydle love" (19–20), grieves the misdirection of Colin's skill, aptly noting that one so taken with his own self can care for nothing else:

> Ah foolish boy, that is with love yblent
> Great pittie is, he be in such taking,
> For naught caren, that bene so lewdly bent.
> (155–57)

In Immeritô's idiom, and as one who wants to "teach the ruder shepheard how to feede his sheepe," Colin's incapacity to care for "naught" but himself suggests that he has much more to experience and learn than the skills of poetry.

Another device Colin presumptuously employs is the topos of humility. Colin vacillates between boastful claims of pleasing "rude" Gods, as in *Januarye*, and facile displays of extreme self-centeredness, such as when he brings the frozen ground, the bare trees, the "feeble flock" (43) and sundry meteorogical events particular to winter to bear on the state of his pervasive "I." (The predominance of the latter suggests, then, what the other half of Colin's "half in despight" might be when he breaks his pipe, namely, wounded pride. Proud of his "rurall musick," and supported in that pride by most of the inhabitants of the eclogue, that pride is deflated when Rosalind "laughes" at his songs.) In *June,* Colin humbly admits to Hobbinoll after the latter has heaped praise on the delight his verse offers: "Of Muses Hobbinoll, I conne no skill" (65), and he then claims that he "never lyst presume to *Parnasse* hyll" (70) and concedes that his rhymes are "rough, and rudely drest" (77) and his manner "homely" (82). But again, feigning humility proves to be a trick of the trade when we realize that Colin is still the same selfish self we met in *Januarye*. He begins his conversation with Hobbinoll by blaming his unhappiness on "cruell fate, / And angry Gods" (14–15) that relentlessy "pursue" him— as if raining misfortune on his "lucklesse pate" (16) is the top priority of the gods. He ends that conversation by again returning to reflecting on the pain of his own unrequited love for Rosalind by separating himself from "Ye gentle shep-heardes, which your flock do feede" (106) with the claim that his heart is nothing less than "the truest shepheards hart . . . / That lyves on earth" (111).

Having lost all hope in winning Rosalind, all hope in moving the fate or gods to bend to his will—of changing his persistent bad luck—Colin seeks refuge in a metaphysical strain of versifying in *November*. After persuading Thenot that the time of year is best suited to a sadder song than he can devise, Colin agrees for the prize of "yond Corsett" (42) to sing of the drowned "Dido the great sheapherde his daughter sheene" (38). Humbly, Colin offers a brief apology to Thenot for his "rugged and unkempt" rhymes, but again, his humility is proven a facade as he audaciously begins his dirge by calling:

> Up *Melpomene* thou mournefulst muse of nyne,
> Such cause of mourning never hadst afore:
> Up grieslie ghostes and up my rufull rhyme,
> Matter of myrth now shalt thou have no more.
> (53–56)

Colin is confident that not only will Melpomene answer his call but also that his "humble vaine" (50) will rise "up" as occasion demands. The irony is, however, that the lost life of Dido that occasions Colin's technically sophisticated and emotion-filled song appears to be somewhat less deserving than the exalted praise Colin heaps on her. E. K.'s claim that "Dido is unknowen and closely buried in the Authors conceipt" (196) has led critics to speculate on Dido's real or historic referent; within the drama of the eclogue, however, perhaps it is enough to know why Colin laments her loss so:

> She while she was, (that was, a woful word to sayne)
> For beauties prayse and plesaunce had no pere:
> So well she couth the shepherds entertayne,
> With cakes and cracknells and such country chere.
> Ne would she scorne the simple shepheards swaine,
> For she would cal hem often heme
> And give hem curds and clouted Creame.
> O heavie hearse,
> Als *Colin cloute* she would not once disdayne.
> O carefull verse.
> (93–102)

A kindly country dame who kept the lads cheery and sated and never once disdained poor, "lucklesse" Colin has met her untimely end in a nearby pond. The emptiness of Colin's formal devices are mirrored in the parochial and obsequious lament for a lady who, as Colin's subsequent musings on life and death indicate, had led an intrinsically meaningless life. Colin takes this occasion, prodded by the reward of "yond Corsett," to construct "carefully" (that is, both full of care or woe and with great care or skill—as the first ten of his song's fifteen stanzas remind the reader, repeating "O carefull verse") a song to express his own anxiety about life and death in general.

The same frustrated idealism that Colin bestowed on Rosalind in *Januarye,* which led to his loss of all hope in *June,* now compels Colin to cast his eye heavenward for comfort; and so he supplants the fickle and intervening gods of *June* with indifferent, yet blithe gods in *November.* But whichever narrative of the gods he chooses to believe, the practical effects remain the same as in previous songs. Colin turns Dido's death into something resembling a rustic passion play; offering her the role of a Christ figure, Colin says that, in spite of death, fate,

> And gates of hel, and fyrie furies forse:
> She hath the bonds broke of eternall night,
> Her soule unbodied of the burdenous corpse.
> (164–66)

Concluding, then, that "Dido nis dead, but into heaven hent" (169), Colin looks to her for relief from the futility of life on earth, where human kind "swincke and sweate for nought, / And shooting wide, doe misse the marked scope" (154–55). Human kind may miss the mark, but Colin, owing largely to his glimpse of Dido in her glorified state ("I see thee blessed soule, I see, / Walke in *Elisian* fields so free" [178–79]), presumes to have hit the mark. In hitting the mark, he is filled with a contempt for all earthly things, and claims, in stark contrast to Immeritô's pedagogical efforts, that they are but "Unwise and wretched men to weete whats good or ill" (183). Thus the youthful Colin condemns Immeritô's poetic efforts.

The contempt Colin displays for all earthly things is essentially no different from the scorn that prevents him from seeking social intercourse both earlier in the eclogues and in *December,* except for the sychophantic Hobbinoll in *June* or the prize-bearing Thenot of *November.* Even on those occasions, Colin is not a pleasant person with whom to keep company. In *November,* for example, after Thenot's first request to sing a song in praise of Pan or Rosalind, Colin haughtily replies:

> But if thou algate lust light virelayes,
> And looser songs of love to underfong
> Who but thyself deserves sike Poetes prayse?
> Relieve thy Oaten pypes, that sleepen long.
> (21–24)

Though Thenot accepts his secondary status as a lesser and "looser" poet (that is, one whose verse is not as "carefull"), he so desires a song from Colin that he offers him reward for his pains and then humbly begs, "Let not my small demaund be so contempt" (48). Contemptuous, yet tempted, Colin accepts the deal. At the end of the song, Thenot is greatly moved in the sense that he feels some emotion well up, with "doolful pleasaunce, so as I ne wotte, / Whether rejoyce or weepe for great constrainte?" (204–5). Significantly, however, Thenot has learned nothing from Colin and does not know what action to take. And the ephemeral and inconsequential character of the emotions resulting from Colin's carefully wrought song are almost immediately forgotten. Thenot hurriedly bestows the "cossette" on Colin as a parting gift and urges him homeward, now that the effects of the "mizzle" (208) have supplanted the "doolful pleasaunce" wrought by Colin's song.

The Poet's Second Act:
On Immeritô

The contrast between Colin Clout and Immeritô is immediately and dramatically underscored at the beginning of the *Januarye* eclogue, when both figures cross the pastoral stage. Colin begins and ends the eclogues singing to himself, first from hope, then from a tempered despair (*November*), followed by utter despondency in *December;* if he has grown or matured within the calendar year, it is a limited development, the minor shifts in emphasis of a consistent set of principles—variations on a theme. Those principles alternately privilege fate, fortune, acts of Nature, and God's imperious will over human action, and they disregard language's instrinsically social function, are marked by an underlying contempt of others, and value private, narcissistic, and ephemeral delight over goals that look to a broader social end. Furthermore, these principles in practice embody the presumption that the matter of verse is in no way contingent on its mode of representation; consequently, either the meaning *refers* to the formal and technical proficiency of Colin's exercises in *copie* and verse (for example, *August*), or meaning *refers* to the "authenticity" of the poet's (self-serving) passions as can be seen in Nature (*Januarye, December*), or the meaning is validated by virtue of obsequious praise for a noble's virtue (*Aprill*) or the verity of Dido's "*Elisian* fields" (*November*). Insofar as these principles resemble those valorized by E. K., Colin may be said to represent the versed, or well-versed, form of E. K.'s prose. And inasmuch as Colin is the darling of the pastoral's universe by consensus of all its inhabitants, we might say then that the values he represents are *representative* of that world, a versified and delightful representation, but a (mimetic) representation nonetheless. In other words, Colin's particular talent lies in his imitation of the values, beliefs, ideals, and expectations of his rustic society; as such, Colin does not teach but reminds and appeases, and in so doing, he reaffirms the parochial conventions of his social milieu and is duly rewarded for his efforts. Colin thus might be considered a rhetorician or sophist in the conventional and narrow sense—or in E. K.'s sense of those terms.

Yet Colin's story is a story *told.* In this section, we will look at how the ways that story is told informs the what of its telling before considering in the next section

why telling the story so may be important. Toward that end, Immeritô's represen-
tation of how tales are told within the drama of the eclogues proves instructive; for
in telling or retelling (or telling at one, fictive remove from) those tales, Immeritô
gestures toward the principles that organize and guide his own poetic practice. Per-
haps the most significant way that Immeritô activates or puts Colin's story to work
is by situating that story within its "ethic and politic considerations." This not only
shows the failings of Colin's version of poetry but also shows us something about
the society in which he participates. Or, as Bryskett might say, Immeritô locates
Colin with a "civill conversation"; for in the most general sense, the society the poet
presents is knowable by and through the words it uses to represent itself. The *Feb-
ruarie* eclogue, for example, casts Colin's facile analogy between the season and his
"life bloud friesing with unkindly cold" from *Januarye* into a conversation between
Thenot and Cuddie—figures that enact a drama that negotiates the *topos* of age
and youth, experience and inexperience.

The idyllic ease of country life is disturbed by young Cuddie's complaints about
the weather to Thenot, who "thrise threttie yeares" (17) has borne the vagaries
of the seasons; Cuddie, a less pretentious yet baser figuring of Colin, complains:

> Ah for pittie, wil rancke Winters rage,
> These bitter blasts never ginne tasswage?
> The kene cold blowes through my beaten hyde,
> All as I were through the body gryde.
> (1–4)

Thenot, perhaps too eagerly, takes the youth's protest as an excuse to forego his
shepherdly duties; and waxing philosophic for a moment, he gravely counters the
lad's idle remarks with the pessimism that underlies the Stoic's world view of man
reacting to Fortune's whim:

> Lewdlie complainest thou laesie ladde,
> Of Winters wracke, for making thee sadde.
> Must not the world wend in his commun course,
> From good to bad, and from badde to worse
> From worse unto that is worst of all,
> And then returne to his former fall?
> (9–14)

Thenot's morose and excessive musings are not without a point, however; as one
who never "was to Fortune foeman" (21) and has always "gently tooke, that un-
gently came" (22), he exhorts Cuddie not to dwell on Nature's doings but to tend
to the business in hand, the keeping of his sheep.

The disputation that ensues, however, proves futile. Thenot's contempt for the youth is evident in his sententious moralizing, condescension, and general truculence, and Cuddie's scorn for the old man that "wouldest me, my springing youngth to spil" (52) results in charges of senility. Thenot, recognizing that such disputation is ineffectual, lures the boy in with a promise of a story "I cond of *Tityrus* in my youth" (92). Cuddie immediately agrees, though he feigns his youthful enthusiasm for a story by aping the conventional wisdom of his elders:

> To nought more *Thenot*, my mind is bent,
> Then to heare novells of his devise:
> They bene so well thewed, and so wise,
> What ever the good man bespake.
> (94–97)

Thenot, claiming that of the many "meete tales" Tityrus told, there is "none fitter then this to applie" (100), urges Cuddie to listen all the way to the end of the tale.

Thenot proceeds to tell Aesop's fable of the Oak and the Briar, though in this telling, the tale undergoes some significant revision. In Aesop's tale, the old Oak scorns the young Briar growing near, but even as he boasts how the wind can never harm him, a hurricane comes and pulls him out from the roots. The Briar, however, remains standing after the storm has passed over. Thenot's immediate purpose, however, is not Aesop's, and consequently, he remakes the tale to "applie" or suit his needs. He does this by refiguring the "goodly Oak" (103) as the victim of the young shrub's pride or, as he charged Cuddie with earlier, "carelesse corage" (47). The "bragging brere" (115) resolves on asking the "Husbandman" to cut the Oak down because, in effect, he believes the old Oak to "spil" his "springing youngth." Because Cuddie is young and inexperienced, Thenot has the young briar rely on rhetorical artifice to advance his cause:

> With painted words tho gan this proude weede,
> (As most usen Ambitious folke:)
> His colowred crime with craft to cloke.
> (160–62)

For Thenot, his experience grants his point of view a "truthfulness," and because his tale reveals that truth (that is, is the mimetic representation of that truth), any argument to the contrary would have to employ the deceits of rhetoric. The old Oak, unable to muster an argument in defence of his position because of the "coles of displeasure" (191) kindled by the briar's scorn, remains silent and is soon chopped down, "pitied of none" (221). But as Thenot proceeds to narrate at some length the demise of the briar in the following winter for "scorning Eld" (238),

Cuddie cuts the old man short, as it were, maintaining, "But little ease of thy lewd tale I tasted" (245).

Immeritô's telling of the tale of Cuddie and Thenot is markedly different from Thenot's telling of his tale. To begin with, Immeritô's representation is overtly a fictive representation or, we might say, an "honest" fiction in the sense that it pretends to be nothing else but a fiction. This does not empty "fiction" of meaning; on the contrary, the poet draws the reader's attention to the inherently fictitious nature of the stories people tell to make sense of the world. For Thenot's tale is not a fiction by virtue of the fact that it employs a well-known fable, but a fiction in the sense that it mirrors his own attitude toward life. Thenot too colors or cloaks his advice to Cuddie with rhetorical ornament as well, specifically, with a narrative. His condescending sense of morality derives its authority on the basis of his experience alone, and it is on that authority that he attempts to persuade Cuddie. But because the story he tells is simply a restatement of his earlier argument—the transparent and mimetic conversion of his particular and self-interested view into a familiar fable—his willingness to grant it the status of truth is suspect. In short, his tale is too moralistic in the sense that it uncompromisingly supports his own position—"Youngth are a bubble blowne up with breath, / Whose witt is weakenesse, whose wage is death" (87–88)—without the slightest consideration or empathy for Cuddie's position. Even Cuddie's "weak wit" discerns the resemblance.

From Thenot's point of view, he has not made the tale so much as he has "applie[d]" it to his purposes. Though there may be formal differences in Thenot's presentation of himself between the outset of the eclogue and his re-presentation of himself in the fable, there is no substantive difference between his tellings because all his discourse refers back to himself for meaning and shares the same purpose. Thenot has made a tale to suit his purposes, but his is a making designed to imitate a knowable (at least in aphoristic form) but intrinsically meaningless kind of knowledge for an inexperienced youth. And because his tale is not bent toward his audience such that it addresses Cuddie's point of view in a conciliatory manner, it represents the rhetorical failure of mimetic representation. The meaning, his moral, moreover, is a narrow and self interested meaning as is shown in his complete unwillingness to consider or empathize with the troubles of a Cuddie, all of which understandably stem from his youthfulness and inexperience. That inability to understand another's perspective leads Thenot to his scorn and condescension for anyone unlike his own sage self.

The practical consequences of Thenot's attitude are manifest in a form of pedantry that feigns good will and relies on an appeal to his authority by virtue of his experience, which is to say that Thenot's argument constitutes a form of teaching. So confident is he in the sagacity of his own position, and so scornful of others, that he forgoes the niceties of civil conversation, of presenting his case to others of a different mind in a productive manner; instead, he rules by aphorism. Consequently, when he passes from this earth or is hewn down, he is "pitied of none" because others have only the rule and the scorn that accompanied it to recall him by. Cuddie's statement that he found no "ease" in the tale suggests that he agreed to listen not because Tityrus's stories are "so thewed and so wise" as he claimed, but because he expected "delight" from it; instead, he was condescended to by a didact.

This points to another quality of how Immeritô represents acts of representation. For the poet, meaning is always controversial, that is, it is contingent not only on the speaker and his aim but also on the interests or experiences of the listener / reader. Of course, each of the eclogues employs this rhetorical device of arguing both sides of the question (even *Januarye* and *December* when we consider the juxtaposition of Immeritô and Colin Clout); we might say that Immeritô's poetic form has its origins in rhetorical form. Sloane has argued that, more than just a rhetorical device, the ability to argue both sides of the question is indicative of the skepticism at the heart of both Ciceronian and humanist oratory: the practice of *disputatio in utramque partem* "provokes a challenge to dogmatism" and is "aimed at judgment [and] is predicated less on the immutability of truth than on the possibility of human concord."[19] When we consider thus that Colin's story is imitative of his world, and that neither Thenot nor Cuddie, for example, are representative of laudable, civil, or exemplary discursive action, then Immeritô's representation of the controversy asks the reader to question whether aligning oneself with one view over another is desirable. Rather than exemplifying the poet's ambivalence, the poet's use of arguing both sides of the question persuades the reader to seek or invent topoi other than those either presented by the actors themselves or by E. K.—to discover "the possibility of human concord" in its absence. This suggests, furthermore, that the poet has an active interest in dissuading the reader from basing their actions in the attitudes he represents.

Yet whatever the judgment one might arrive at based on commonplaces of literary, political, or theoretical exigencies, the moral character of the eclogues' inhabitants are perceived in their flawed and failed attempts to represent themselves in a manner conducive to civility *in general*. Those failings, furthermore, are evident by Immeritô's own representation of the modes of discourse employed by the eclogues' actors; in this way, the poet draws the reader's attention to the act of representation itself. Thenot makes himself through the words he chooses and the stories he tells, but, and by virtue of his experience, he is not prepared to acknowledge his representation of himself as a making, nor is he able to consider Cuddie's side. For Thenot, human will is subject to the whims of Fortune; consequently, his social relations are circumscribed by the very narrowness of his experience as he defines it in his relationship with "Fate." By representing Thenot's tale as a social failing made and circumscribed by Thenot's own self, Immeritô compels the reader to recognize and judge the poet's representation. As an "honest fiction," it offers an alternative to the "sincere" narratives of both Thenot and Cuddie by announcing its own *madeness* with every word. And in offering a distinct alternative, Immeritô directs the reader's attention to the controversial essence of meaning itself—controversial because meaning can be known only in action and the way humans make meaning can be found only in the concourse of human action.

Just as the relative innocence of Cuddie's remarks are offered further qualification by the conversation between Willye and Thomalin in *March,* Thenot's heavy-handed moralism is put into a different context in the *Maye* eclogue, where, again, a narrative is enlisted in the service of interested speakers. Piers and Palinode, two men of "elder witt" (18), come together to discuss the "jollity" of youths. Palinode takes pleasure in the celebrations of the month: "To see those folkes make such joyousaunce, / Made my heart after to the pype to daunce" (25–26). Piers, a God-fearing and self-righteous shepherd, is "so farre . . . from envie, / That their fondness inly I pitie." Condemning those who merry make as "shepheardes for the Devils stedde" (43), Piers contends that a "true" shepheard "muste walke another way, / Sike worldly sovenaunce he must foresay" (81–82). Palinode, however, as a "worldes childe" (73), operates on the premise that "concord" and "felowship" rather than invective and intransigent moralizing should characterize men's speech. But Piers wants no part of "concorde," declaring, "I list non accordaunce make / With shepheard, that does the right way forsake" (164–65). And forsaking the right way for Piers is less a matter of doing the right thing or choosing the right path than it is learning how to stay out of the way of those "Wolves, ful of fraude and guile" (127) that abound in the countryside, and in that effort, "chaunce" rather than providence dictates events. Evil for Piers is never the fault of someone who has chosen the right path.

Yet so sure is he that he knows the proverbial light, he offers to tell Palinode a story of the fox and the kid in order to teach him the right way. Like Thenot's story before him, Piers's story is the transparent representation of his narrow view of the world. And the practical or pedagogical consequences are the same, though in this case, those consequences are also embedded in the tale itself. The good mother goat goes abroad for "good reason" (177), but before she leaves, she schools her "wanton sonne" (227) thus:

> Kiddie (quoth shee) thou kenst the great care,
> I have of thy health and thy welfare,
> Which many wyld beastes liggen in waite
> For to entrap in thy tender state:
> But most the Foxe, maister of colusion:
> For he has vowed thy last confusion.
> For thy my Kiddie be ruld by mee,

And never give trust to his trecheree.
(215–22)

She teaches as Piers might—declaratively and by precept, for the story he tells but barely clothes his intent. Piers's dogmatic teaching is notably countered by the absence of any pretension of teaching on Palinode's part. But just as Cuddie's view of the world was not exemplary, though it did not deserve Thenot's harsh treatment, so too is Palinode's attitude blemished by his blithe indifference to the possibility of evil.

In the interest of social concord, Palinode is not willing to make waves; his is a "go along, get along" attitude. For example, after cogently defending the youngsters' merry making against Piers's rehearsal of his faith's doctrine, Palinode agrees for the sake of "felowship" to hear the other's tale anyway: "Now *Piers,* of felowship, tell us that saying: / For the Ladde can keepe both our flocks from straying" (172–73). That he delegates his duty to the "Ladde" to keep their flocks from straying is but one indication that Palinode is perhaps too willing to forego his social responsibilities for the sake of concord. After Piers's tale, Palinode declares his dissatisfaction with the "matter" of the fable: "Truly Piers, thou art beside thy wit, / Furthest fro the marke, weening it to hit" (306–7). His dissatisfaction, however, does not prevent him from wanting to share the tale with others:

Now I pray thee, lette me thy tale borrowe
For our sir John, to say to morrowe
At the Kerke, when it is holliday:
For well he meanes, but little can say.
But and if Foxes bene so crafty, as so,
Much needeth all shepheards hem to knowe.
(308–13)

Indifferent, Palinode is as willing to grant Piers a modicum of good will as he is "sir John," and on that basis, he is then completely unconcerned with what they say. "But and if" there are people who will lead you astray, then perhaps the story is worth telling. Uncommitted to what is taught, Palinode appears more taken with its mode of representation, with the story itself—or perhaps he is more taken with the length of the story, which will supply Sir John with more to say. In this case, Piers's argument is not only controversial but also eminently convertible.

More than showing the reader a subtle and "covert" allegory, the poet shows that the stories people accept, choose to believe, or make are themselves fictions by situating those stories within a broader social frame or conversation. What those fictions mean, or are intended to mean, are subject to the vagaries of rhetoric: to the speaker, audience, occasion, and purpose. By showing the inherently controversial and convertible character of the stories people tell about themselves, the poet also shows that, inevitably, some form of teaching results. That is, rhetorical action will have some effect on others regardless of the "sincerity," naïveté, or indifference one might grant one's intentions. In offering a window into the personal investments and blind spots of the figures telling the story by representing those stories as but one side of an always controversial issue, the poet shows that not only what one chooses to tell but also how one chooses to tell it are representative of the speaker's self.

Palinode thus presents a significant problem. He appears willing to accept the fictiveness of any and all stories and thus is indifferent to how they are used; he is willing to disregard or employ any story that will keep the peace. In other words, his indifference to how stories are used is indicative of his indifference to what people *do*—so long as they are happy. If, as I have argued, Immeritô aims to emphasize the inherently fictive or representational nature of the stories we construct for ourselves, tell to each other, and use to teach, how then does he address the problem of moral relativism raised by Palinode? Puttenham claimed that it was because the pastoral represented the first form of "honest felowship" that it was to be first among others, but Palinode, too, seeks "felowship."

An answer lies in the body of the poet's work, that is, in the place where the how and the what of the story told intersect—in what Puttenham called "stile." In "The Third Booke, Of Ornament," he writes: "Stile is a constant and continual phrase or tenour of speaking and writing, extending to the whole tale or processe . . . and not properly to any peece or member of the tale" (160). He later associates a person's style in his daily maner of speech and ordinary writing to his *"Phisiognomy"* as the one "certaine" point wherein one can "judge a mans manners" (161).[20] Puttenham looks to the style of the speech for "certaine" proof of a man's character or ethos, in their patterning of discursive action; what a man's character is, is how he represents himself to others on a regular basis. In this sense, the what and the how of the narrative, the *res* and *verba,* dissolve into each other, creating one insoluble poetic character. Immeritô "proves" the character, and the character flaws of the eclogues' inhabitants, by showing them rhetorically in action. But Immeritô also proves his own character, his own story, his own fiction discursively, and that proof is in the proverbial pudding—in the metaphors he invents to enact and embody an *ethos* that figures then refigures itself in the act of discourse.

If, as I have argued, Immeritô persuades the reader to judge the drama he has put into action primarily based on the (always active) rhetorical patterning of the moral character of the persons speaking, then the philosophic origins from whence the means and standards for proving his argument advance differ significantly in kind not only from E. K.'s but also from most of the critical machinery currently used to farm Spenser's poetic fields. At the heart of this difference lies the question "what do metaphors (or simply 'words') *do?*" As I indicated in the opening pages to this chapter with specific reference to DeNeef, metaphor defined primarily as a mimetic act subordinates the notion of the poet as maker by rendering his poetical invention an "expression of" and responsible to the theoretical exigencies of formal matters (for example, "artistic and ethical idealism," poetic form, rhetorical *techne,* or religious doctrine). In that process, the "character" of Colin and other characters, Immeritô, E. K., and ultimately Spenser himself become detached from the human action, circumstances, occasions, and words comprising their moral universes; "character" becomes yet another representation of an eminently rational construct known because it refers to something else other than the rhetorical act itself. [21] A rhetorico-poetic metaphor, however, invents rather than imitates and enacts human understanding rather than gives expression to it.

Extending Metaphors:
Inventing Poetic Proof (an Analogy)

After claiming to have enlarged on the *res,* or "matter" of oratory, Antonius gives leave to Crassus to discuss the "embellishment and elaboration" of words—what appears to be the superficial and insignificant part of the orator's art, *elocutio,* or "ornamentation." Crassus, unwilling to accept Antonius's facile division of oratory into *res* and *verba,* remarks that he "seemed to me to be discussing both of the two subjects conjointly" (*De oratore* 2.90.366). Nevertheless, Crassus provisionally accepts Antonius's division, noting that though "one has to begin by accumulating a supply of matter, a department that Antonius has dealt with[,] . . . the matter has to receive shape (*forma*) from the general texture and style of the speech"; "any speaker," he observes, "no matter how defective, could apply [Antonius's technical matter]" (3.16.103). In other words, the technical matter only really matters when formed toward some useful purpose in the act of speaking. Because "all oratory is made up of words" (3.37.149), Crassus argues that "the highest distinction of eloquence consists in amplification by means of ornament, which can be used to make one's speech not only increase the importance of a subject and raise it to a higher level, but also to diminish and disparage it" (3.26.104). Implicitly thus, at this point, Crassus associates "the highest distinction of oratory" with the aim of the poet—"laudation and censure," to praise and blame (3.27.105). Of the three kinds of words Crassus claims the orator uses to ornament, and so teach and move his audience, "rare words, new coinages, and words used metaphorically" (3.38.152), Crassus elaborates most fully on metaphorical words, as they might appear either singly or in combinations with other metaphors (as allegory).

Crassus notes two distinct kinds of metaphors: the first "sprang from necessity due to the pressure and poverty and deficiency" of language-thought and "was brought into common use for the sake of entertainment" (3.38.155); the second kind of metaphor is "somewhat bolder" and does "not indicate poverty but convey[s] some degree of brilliance to the style" (3.38.156). The first kind of metaphor is the sort Antonius discusses with less admiration while considering "jesting" in book 2 (65.261). It is based on resemblance or likeness, may be used for brevity, and is used to make something more clearly understood. Such metaphors, Crassus says, "are a sort of borrowing" (3.38.156); they transpose or carry over a meaning of a thing from one context to another, and they are a source of great pleasure, either because one delights in the "cleverness" (*ingenium*) required

> to jump over things that are obvious and choose other things that are far fetched . . . or because a single word in each case suggests the thing and a picture of the whole; or because every metaphor, provided it be a good one, has a direct appeal to the senses, especially, the sense of sight. (3.40.160)

In any case, the "highest merit" of such metaphors, he claims, are "when the metaphorical expression directly hits our senses" (3.41.163).

Ernesto Grassi has termed this kind of metaphor a "literary" metaphor. The literary metaphor itself may be understood in at least two different ways. "Some authors," he writes, "limit the function of the metaphor to the transposition of words, that is, of a word from its 'own' field to another."[22] As "borrowings" detached from any consideration of their sensory effects, this first kind of literary metaphor relies on available or known fields of reference for meaning or significance. Such metaphors thus lend themselves to being explained in rational terms, as E. K. so devoutly demonstrates; a metaphorical meaning may be readily *referred to* for the sake of *explanation*. In this sense, the paragraph-length "Argument" E. K. contributes before each eclogue may be seen as supplying the topic of the following poem. The "Argument" directs the reader to the locus or general area of accessible matter that the reader might draw from to apprehend, understand, and then judge the eclogue. Thus, the meaning for *Februarie* can be determined if the reader recognizes that, according to E. K., the poet intended it as a means to talk about the differences in age and youth primarily, or that *Aprill* stems from the poet's desire to praise (Elizabeth), or that *August* is understandable when we realize that the poet made it "in imitation of that ["controversie"] in Theocritus: whereto also Virgile fashioned his third and seventh Æglogue" (137). Similarly, the whole of the *Calender*'s eclogues may be understood when the reader recognizes that their general aim is either "Recreative," "Plaintive," or "Morall." The topics E. K. locates as the source of meaning for the eclogues, in other words, are formal, cognitive matter that lend the eclogues their significance. In this limited understanding of the metaphor, the visual or sensory affects Crassus alludes to are either significantly diminished (as ephemeral delight) or altogether neglected.[23]

On the grounds, however, that the chief power of literary metaphor lies in its ability to "hit the senses," Grassi rejects the strictly rationally based understanding of the metaphorical process. Emphasizing the literary metaphor's visual nature (as does Crassus), Grassi identifies another way of apprehending it:

> The "literary" metaphor already is based on the "discovery" of a *similar nature;* its function is to make visible a "common" quality between fields. It presupposes a "vision" of something hitherto concealed; it shows to the reader or to the spectator a "common" quality which is not rationally deducible. (*Rhetoric as Philosophy,* 33)

Literary metaphors offer up their own kind of Heraclitean proof that cannot be explained to be known (as is the case with E. K.) but only "seen" to be known. The metaphor offers an "immediate insight" into similar phenomena from different fields or contexts. (E. K.'s argument and gloss thus may be considered cousins to an explanation of a joke; offering reasons for why something should be humorous is never an adequate substitute for the pleasure one gets in "seeing" the humor in something immediately—similarly, one takes little pleasure in E. K.'s erudition.) As borrowings, this second kind of literary metaphor also relies on available or known fields of reference for meaning or significance, though that meaning is conditioned by the senses. As such, they indicate the "poverty" of language and thought to adequately convey an understanding of something by "hitting," and so exploiting the formative powers of the senses to make understanding possible. Grassi chooses to call this kind of metaphor "literary" as opposed to "poetic" (or rhetorical or philosophical) because such metaphors, as borrowings, are inherently mimetic insofar as they derive the significance from and may be referred to concepts or things. In this respect, Immeritô's eclogues comprise literary metaphors invented to affect his readers: Thenot's aged, scornful, stoic attitude is *similar to* attitudes the reader is probably familiar with, Piers and Palinode's attitudes *resemble* attitudes prevalent in the religious controversies of the day, and Colin's poetic efforts *correspond to* current poetic practices, and so on.

Crassus, however, mentioned a second kind of metaphor, "another somewhat bolder kind that [does] not indicate poverty but convey[s] some degree of brilliance to the style." He adds, cryptically, that "there is no need for me to give you a lecture on the method of inventing these or on their classification" (3.38.156). Bryskett's discussion of language in the *Discourse* suggests why there is no "need" to give a "lecture" on or categorize this latter kind of metaphor. Recall that Bryskett's discussion characterized discourse itself to be fundamentally a poetic or metaphorical act based on discourse's mediatory function between the senses and the intellect. The infinite particulars of our sensed experience are generalized in the Imagination, the "highest" part of the sensitive soul, and collected (or re-collected) by Memory; this is a nonrational process. Discourse mediates or negotiates between the sensitive and intellectual parts of the soul; it makes these "imaginative universals," these generalized *feelings* intelligible by placing (socially determined) discursive form on them. Discourse (language, speech) "transfers" or "carries over" our sensed experience to the rational understanding.[24] This metaphorical process, furthermore, does not arise out of "poverty and for the sake of entertainment" but *naturally,* which is to say, out of *necessity.* But the necessity that provides the impetus for this kind of metaphor is not of the "necessity due to the pressure and poverty and deficiency" of language or thought but from the biologically conditioned *activity* of human beings (as political animals). "Nature," as Bryskett noted, "admitteth nothing that is idle" (*Discourse,* 276). The quintessential or intrinsic human activities prescribed by nature are reason and speech, *ratio et oratio,* and the quintessential action that represents the essence, nature, or necessity of human activity is this transference of our sensed experience to an active understanding via speech or metaphor. This latter kind of "bold" metaphor does not hit the senses but originates in, is drawn from, and negotiates between our sensed experience (the matter of knowledge) and the necessary or natural human compulsion to ratiocinate about the world.

The central difference between the literary and the rhetorico-poetic metaphor may be located where the meaning of the metaphor originates—the topoi from which each kind is drawn. The literary metaphor presumes a shared body of knowledge—shared field of reference, and is known or seen by a reader or auditor

The December *woodcut shows a broken oaten or reed pipe, though in the eclogue Colin ruefully hangs his pipe up on a tree. Immeritô takes Colin's pipe from the tree, so to speak, to reinvent himself; E. K. leaves Colin's broken pipe where it lay to become a "scholler" of poetry, rather than its maker.*

The Januarye *woodcut shows a broken bagpipe instead of the "oaten pipe" (72) that Immeritô tells us Colin "broke" near the end of the eclogue.*

*The woodcut functions as a metaphor that is apprehended by and appeals directly to the reader's sensed experience of it. The "Argument," eclogue, and gloss that follow the woodcut represent two ways in which poetry may be interpreted as a "speaking picture" (*Defence, *82).*

Immeritô refigures the woodcut in discursive form in his eclogues in order to "make sense" of his sensed experience for and with the reader in his efforts "to teach"; E. K. ignores the woodcut altogether, offering an "Argument" and "Glosse" that refer to "matter" detached from the drama represented in order to explain it, or explain it away.

insofar as it immediately brings together concepts or things that are perceived to share a similar nature or function. The literary metaphor hits the senses because it originates in and takes its meaning from an "insight" into things exterior to the body. Thus, for example, Spenser's title, *The Shepheardes Calender,* may be understood in terms of previous pastorals, the poet's later work, calendars in general (as in E. K.'s lengthy discussion regarding whether January or March marks the new year in the "generall Argument"), politico-religious debates, literary disputes, sundry ideals, and so on. Though they may hit the senses, the topoi from which the metaphor originates are propositional and depend on the reader's tacit assent. The second kind of metaphor originates in the senses and is made in order to "make sense of" the body's sensed experience. Such metaphors are the site for the invention or discovery of knowledge because they enact and embody the human *need,* as prescribed by nature, to understand the matter of knowledge (our sensed experience). The invention of metaphor is the act in which the (always active) nature of being human is known, and that action embodies the making of knowledge—the invention of knowledge—rather than the revelation of a knowledge already extant; it is, as Grassi notes, "a continual task and an uncontrollable possibility."[25] Without drawing on the humanist or rhetorical traditions directly, Mark Johnson describes metaphor as the fundamental act of human knowledge in terms similar to Grassi. He describes metaphor as

> a pervasive mode of understanding by which we project patterns from one domain of experience in order to structure another domain of a different kind. So conceived, metaphor is not merely a linguistic mode of expression; rather, it is one of the chief cognitive structures by which we are able to have coherent, ordered experiences that we can reason about and make sense of. Through metaphor, we make use of patterns that obtain in our physical experience to organize our more abstract understanding.[26]

Because the making of that metaphorical or poetic knowledge, furthermore, has its origins in human physiology, its meaning *for* other human bodies cannot depend on propositional topoi developed for or perceivable to the mind's eye. The poet's art of persuasion instead depends on his ability to appeal to the feelings of the reader, to draw on sensory topoi, the loci or "commonplaces" of sensed experience by which the sensed matter of a body's feelings may be experienced by others.[27] "This word *feele*," says Bryskett (to Spenser), "explaneth the whole" (*Discourse*, 274), for these sensory loci form the basis of human knowledge, and the metaphors —the arguments—that enact and embody the desire to make the sensed matter of our experience known, are discovered in the feelings humans share. Unlike the literary metaphor, which originates in the apprehension of the similar nature among things exterior to the body, the poetic metaphor is invented in the natural ability of human bodies to sense or feel the matter of experience common to all human beings. In this respect, metaphors enact the fundamental interpretative act of human nature, and so embody the "richness" of being human as opposed to the "poverty" of propositional or dialectical reason. The poetic metaphor "proves" itself at the moment of its invention, for it is invented in and discovered by the reader's physical or experiential response to it.

With this in mind, we might think of the woodcuts before each of E. K.'s "Arguments" and the eclogue that follows as metaphors designed to appeal to the senses without the aid of propositional language. Unlike E. K.'s "Argument," which offers a rational topos to the reader in order to guide his understanding of the eclogue, the woodcut urges the reader forward by "referring" them back to their own sensory experience in the vision of the picture. Each woodcut offers its own particular sensed experience that draws on a sensory topos (though what feelings the visual experience might be intended to appeal to, I cannot say) that will form the basis of the poet's metaphorical language and the reader's understanding of it. That understanding is intuitive and gestures toward what experiences one may "expect" to discover discursively in the eclogue: for example, *Januarye*'s woodcut, with its barren trees, bony sheep, and a "sheapherds boye" pining for the city, are indicative of experiences such as loneliness, emptiness, yearning, dissatisfaction, and so on. And just as each woodcut might be considered the topos of the poet's "Argument," it may also be considered the poet's gloss. Unlike E. K.'s gloss, which always refers back to the poem (both in the physical construction of the book and conceptually) in order to explain it, the woodcuts look forward to the following eclogue but with "reference" to the reader's own sense of things rather than E. K.'s. The woodcut does not explain the eclogue; the eclogue offers in narrative, discursive, or dramatic form a re-presentation or refiguring of the scene. The first indication the reader has as to what matter the eclogue contains is captured in the experience of looking at the woodcut. E. K. explains what matter the eclogue really contains in his gloss. Where the poet's eclogue makes sense of sensed experience, E. K.'s gloss makes the eclogue conform to a learning barren of sense.

Sidney claimed that "only the poet . . . lifted up by the vigour of his own invention, doth grow in effect another nature, in making things either better that nature bringeth forth, or, quite anew . . . so as he goeth hand in hand with nature, not inclosed within the narrow warrants of her gifts, but freely [ranges] only within the zodiac of his own wit" (*Defence*, 78). The poet's other or second nature is a distinctly human nature insofar as it recognizes the necessity of humans to make sense of their lives via metaphor. It is a human nature, for example, that can refigure and control the movement of time itself by making a calendar that reinterprets the passing of the months in terms of one's own (socialized) experience. It is a human nature that recognizes that the reckoning of time itself is a thing made for and by humans. That making begins in the senses, in the particular sensed experiences of a particular individual's body; but the significance of that experience can only be realized in the act of human concourse. Immeritô characterizes human concord as discourse, what Bryskett termed "ciuill conuersation." This is to say that neither concord nor discord alone lies at the root of "felowship" but that human action always contains the possibility for both. The possibility of concord or discord is not controlled by Nature but by the human nature that both participates in yet is distinguishable from Nature. And the means by which human nature is made distinct, the means by which it may negotiate human possibilities, is the making or invention of the poetic metaphor.

The Poet's Ethos:
On Spenser

The poetic metaphor responds to the problem of moral relativism raised by Palinode, who, you will recall, is complacent and indifferent to what people do so long as they are happy, by locating the possibility of "honest felowship" in what people *do,* naturally, instead of in a glib optimism regarding human nature in general. Similarly, the moral blind spots of each of the eclogues' denizens may be understood in their disregard for or their inability to appreciate fully the *human* or physiological causes of the narratives they construct for themselves and the consequences those narratives might have on others. Collectively, their moral blind spots are the result of a self-interest that may be self-absorbed, scornful of, or indifferent to others. Colin's verse is representative of and approved by his social milieu precisely because his unmitigated interest in himself reflects the general values of his auditors.

The proof for this argument is enacted in the *ethos* of Immeritô, in the rhetorical actions that pattern or figure his character as he patterns a world wherein "character" is defined in terms of what one believes, thinks, or *ought* to do rather than in terms of what one *does* in order to know within the discourses of human action. The proof lies in what Crassus called the "general style and texture of a speech," which gives matter its "shape" or form. The "matter" of Immeritô's speech, too, originates in self-interest. For it is Immeritô's interest in himself that compels him to invent Colin Clout. But Immeritô makes sense of his sensed experience by *making* Colin a civic poet in spite of the latter's self; that is, the self-knowledge resulting from Immeritô's self-interest is invented or discovered in the invention of himself, refigured as Colin Clout, as a political, rhetorical animal. Unlike Colin, who attempts to define himself in terms of Nature, poetic form, his fashionable love for Rosalinde, and an equally fashionable heavenly vision, Immeritô discovers himself by situating Colin within his ethic and politic—or moral—considerations. Indeed, when we mark Immeritô's socially inscribed self-knowledge as the defining point of difference between him and Colin, it is E. K. who emerges as the adult version of Colin more so than Immeritô. E. K. is the Colin who has broken rather than hung up his pipes. He is the figure who, having forsaken the "toyes" of poetry, moves on to more "serious" study.

Youthful and inexperienced, Colin represents the possibility of both Immeritô and E. K. He is the figure who both is and is not the poet, the metaphor that gestures toward both the possibility of poetic knowledge and the elimination of that possibility. Colin, one might say, is Immeritô's fundamental interpretive act in the effort to "make sense" of his experience. But, and as is the essence of interpretive acts, they are subject always to another interpretation; metaphor contains the possibility of both interpretations. For just as Immeritô discovers the meaning of Colin's story by setting it in its social milieu, E. K. offers another interpretation by setting poetry among and subordinating it to learning. Spenser's poetic ethos is available to the reader in his patterning of the conversation between Immeritô and E. K.—in his refiguring of the discourse of humanism by engaging the reader in it. That conversation turns on the issue of whether the poet has anything to teach, and if so, what does he teach and how does he teach it? E. K. responds to that question by appropriating the task of instructing the reader by revealing what, in particular, is worth knowing about the eclogues. Immeritô responds to this issue by self-consciously making his character known by representing it as an invented figure that is discernible to the reader in the act of representation itself. In that act, in any act, it is the reader's sensed experience that constitutes the "matter" of knowledge, and it is on and from that matter that the poet seeks to connect with his reader. By inventing himself in action through a process that can only be known (that is, experienced or felt, then spoken, then thought) in the metaphorical making of one's self as a social being, Immeritô exemplifies a form of learning that appeals to the reader's self-interest as a speaking, social animal to invent himself in his discursive acts.

Insofar as Immeritô's example, furthermore, argues for a form of learning that originates in and *transfers* a knowledge of himself in his moral consideration to a reader such that the reader is moved to invent or interpret, or reinvent and reinterpret, their own selves, the poet's metaphor may be said to contain the possibilities of learning. Thus Immeritô's extraordinary claim in the epilogue proclaims one viable pedagogic possibility:

> Loe I have made a Calender for every yeare,
> That steele in strength, and time in durance shall outweare:
> And if I marked well the starres revolution,
> It shall continewe till the worlds dissolution.
> (1–4)

It is a calendar for every year because it grounds itself in a fiction of the self that, if he "marked well" or patterned the course of Nature in such a manner that only an "I" invented in its moral considerations could be invented—that is, figuratively —then it "shall continewe till the worlds dissolution" insofar as it patterns not only what but also why we come to know the world. And that figuring enacts the possibilities of human knowledge because, at the same time that it enacts a moral understanding of the self among selves, it does so as it re-presents selves that are rhetorically ineffectual, narrowly self-interested, scornful, and unwitting imitators of the good and ill woven into the social fabric. Thus Immeritô's teaching can become the fodder of E. K.'s learning rather than teach the reader of his intrinsic usefulness to others in how he chooses to make himself, rhetorically.

Spenser's *Calender*, replete with Immeritô and E. K., argues for poetry's ability to teach "well-doing and not well-knowing only" by patterning a figure of the poet in conversation with a figure of learning, a patterning that shows Spenser's ethos in a refiguring of the contemporary debate on learning.

CHAPTER FIVE

———— ❉ ————

WHOLE/SOMENESS

On This Book as a Whole

THE CRUX OF THE MATTER IS CREDIBILITY—the ethos of the orator or poet attempting to teach, move, and delight the audience. Young Colin Clout's credibility among his peers rests largely in his ability to delight. E. K. almost desperately seeks credibility by claiming a seat among the learned. Immeritô patterns a poetic counterpoint to E. K. that finds its authority in presenting Colin's songs and E. K.'s scholarship to be forms of community action in action. Spenser's moral authority is inextricably linked to how effective he proves to be in making his fiction a fair yet principled representation of the (whole) controversy over what might best teach, move, and delight, and how one might best achieve those ends. The aim of this chapter is twofold. First, it asks you to take some measure of Bryskett's moral philosophy and Spenser's poetic ethos with reference to Cicero's attempts to "contain" the whole story of rhetoric through Antonius and Crassus in *De oratore*. Again, this discussion of Cicero is analogous or stands in some proportion to the arguments of the preceding chapters in that it suggests a conceptual framework and perspective on the potential of the rhetorical arts central to the late Tudor conversation on learning. And, looking forward, the considerations of Erasmus and Ramus also offered herein are intended to aver and develop the propriety of Cicero's presence insofar as they are indicative of a larger conversation on learning within the sixteenth century. The appropriateness of Eramus's and Ramus's appearance here (via Cicero and their historical currency) are developed further in the next chapter, in which Spenser's contemporaries rub shoulders, as it were, in the effort to displace and extend rhetoric's capacity to teach, delight, and to move. Though they are but a small "some" of this book, together these two chapters comprise the whole of both the matter and means of its argument.

Cicero's Figuring of the Whole

Cicero tells his brother Quintus in the introductory pages to *De oratore* that "the whole art of oratory . . . is concerned in some measure with the common practice, customs, and speech of mankind" (1.3.12).[1] In the dialogue that follows, Cicero takes historical, theoretical, and practical (or moral) measurements of the art of oratory through his speaking figures of speech, Antonius and Crassus.

You will recall from the introduction that Antonius takes the position that, unlike history and the other liberal arts, oratory is "founded upon [falsehood] (*mendacio*)" (2.7.30) and only "wears the likeness of an art" (2.8.33) because its matter is best learned through experience and practice and cannot be demonstrated satisfactorily by rational methods. Proposing to leave the lesser matters of style or *verba* to Crassus, Antonius proffers a rhetorical theory that largely sees the *techne* of rhetoric to be its matter (*res*), which matter constitutes more the disposition rather than the invention of knowledge. As a purveyor of opinion and parasite of learning, Antonius's orator need only attain the semblance of learning, and such learning is gained largely by chance, developed with practice, and is to be employed when propitious (2.39).

The theoretically narrow and morally ambiguous version of rhetoric advocated by Antonius is made known as such by and through Crassus, who, in stark contrast to Antonius, argues that eloquence "embraces the origin and operation and development of all things" (3.20.76). Although Antonius also offers the orator considerable power to encourage virtuous and discourage vicious conduct (see, for example, 2.9.35), the orator ultimately relies on the knowledge invented, and demonstrated in the other arts. Crassus, however, allows the orator the ability to invent, discover, and prove the origins of "all things" because he affirms *verba* to be elemental to the *res* of human knowledge itself. An orator embraces "the origin and operation and development of all things" *because* he embraces "the natural principles governing the morals and minds and life of mankind." And chief among those principles is the understanding that knowledge originates from our natural abilities to reason and speak (*ratio et oratio*), and that knowledge operates and develops discursively. This cognitive process, furthermore, is understood to be "natural" (or natural to humans) in that the sensed or "feelable" stuff of a body's experience comprises the matter of knowledge from and upon which reason (discursively) makes formal distinctions.

The foremost characteristic of eloquence for Crassus, significantly, is that an eloquent or wise speech be ornate: the "highest distinction of eloquence consists in amplification by means of ornament" (3.26.104). Cicero says as much in *De partitione oratoria,* when he tells his son that "eloquence is nothing else but wisdom speaking copiously" (23.79). Cicero, furthermore, associates this phrase with "the same class of virtue . . . [that] is more closely adapted to the emotions and to the feelings of the common [people] (*ad motus animorum vulgique sensus accommodatior*)."[2] Ernesto Grassi explains Cicero's emphasis on ornateness (or copiousness) to be a necessary condition of eloquent speaking by recalling that "*ornatus* originally came from the Greek word *kosmos,* which refers in an ontological perspective to the 'relationship' between particular parts and a whole and names the particular order that holds them together."[3] "The *ornatus,*" he continues, "is never something that belongs to particulars in isolation; only in relationship to something else, a whole, does the particular receive its essential meaning and become part of an interconnected arrangement." Crassus appropriates this ontological or cosmic perspective when he invokes the assertions of the "great men of the past" who claimed that

> all this universe above and below us is one single whole, and is held together by a single force and harmony in nature; for there exists no class of things which can stand by itself, severed from the rest, or which the rest can dispense with and yet be able to preserve their own force and everlasting existence. (3.5.20)

The eloquent or ornate speech is a speech of the whole in the sense that the subject matter of the speech is indicative of "the world," which, significantly, Cicero portrays as a world originating from and made by human action in which "the whole art of oratory . . . is concerned in some measure." *Eloquentia* as such is not merely "the expression of" wisdom but inseparable from wisdom itself.

One ornament or figure of speech Antonius uses to clarify the limits of rhetorical invention is his sunburn analogy. What influence the matter of history might have on his ability to speak on the subject is not well founded and likely to fade over time:

> Just as, when walking in the sunshine, though perhaps for a different reason, the natural result is that I get sunburnt, even so, after perusing those books rather closely at Misenum (having little chance at Rome), I find that under their influence my discourse takes on what I may call a new complexion. (2.14.60)

This trope receives its meaning (as far as Antonius is concerned) in its relationship to *his* entire speech on oratory. The analogy functions synecdochially to name the relationship of oratory to other learned pursuits, and it is in (or through or by means of) this trope that the nature of Antonian rhetorical invention is made known at the outset of his discourse on the second day of the dialogue; the analogy "names the particular order that holds [oratory and learning] together."

However, Crassus's speech forces Antonius's sunburn analogy to do double duty: his exposition on the all-encompassing character of eloquence situates Antonius's particular ordering of learning and oratory within a broader frame of reference. Instead of subordinating oratory to history, for example, Crassus argues that, because the orator "has gained profound insight into the characters of men, and the whole range of human nature, and those motives whereby our souls are spurred on or turned back" (3.12.53–54), "the orator will speak about ['all the other branches of study'] far better than even the men who are masters of these arts" (3.15.65). From Crassus's viewpoint, then, Antonius's analogy is indicative of a theoretically limited and inventionally impoverished knowledge available to *an* orator, rather than to *the* orator, because Antonius dismisses the sensible matter of human experience as a form of knowledge.

Still more generally, however, the relationship between Antonius and Crassus points toward an argument on oratory that suggests that Ciceronian rhetoric is neither wholly Antonian nor solely Crassian. For it is important to remember that inasmuch as Crassus's philosophical rhetoric appears to correspond with Cicero's own,[4] Cicero himself is unwilling to reject Antonius's somewhat less capacious view of rhetoric's matter.[5] Indeed, Cicero's extensive portrayal or figuring forth of Antonius's views in book 2 bears testimony to the fact that Antonius's technically oriented and theoretically narrow approach to oratory represents not only one historically sanctioned view but also a view that is eminently viable and need not be detrimental to an orator's character and effectiveness.[6] Cicero's own argument on oratory thus resists the confines of an either/or proposition; instead, we might think of it as taking a both/and form.[7] Cicero's discourse comprises both Antonius's argument and Crassus's argument: both Antonius and Crassus are *ornati* embellishing a historically sound, remarkably practicable, and very probable argument regarding oratory; *both* comprise one conversation, one dialogue—Cicero's "On Oratory." This does not suggest, however, that Cicero is either indifferent to or ambivalent about how people measure oratory against "the common practice, custom, and speech of mankind." Cicero enacts a "cosmic" or philosophic perspective (what Grassi calls "an ontological perspective") in order to "name"—or, more appropriately, figure—"the particular order that holds [Antonian and Crassian oratory] together." It is a "cosmic" perspective that is rooted in a deep, abiding, and historically situated interest in "the world" and in what can be, and might be made of it, rhetorically.

The philosophical proof or "demonstration" of knowledge for Ciceronian oratory ultimately lies precisely in this act of embracing or, to use Bryskett's term, "containing" both sides of the argument. Neither Antonius nor Crassus alone can offer a complete account of what the art of oratory is because the art of oratory becomes something different in each of their speeches. Oratory becomes something different because what it is *depends;* specifically, it depends on who "takes measure." What is made of the art of oratory, furthermore, depends not only on who but also on the demands of occasion: For whom is it made thus? to what end? and when? where? And, significantly, the form Cicero uses in order to "prove" his argument is not simply "a dialogue" but Cicero's "present-day" telling of a dialogue, a narrative that is itself "an old story" told him as a youth. In choosing to recollect and tell "an old story" (1.2.4) in dialogue form as opposed to recalling "from the cradle of our boyish learning of days gone by, a long string of precepts" (1.6.23), Cicero responds to his brother's exhortation to discourse on the education of an orator with a narrative.[8] In doing so, he chooses to "contain" the art of oratory within a discursive form that is only knowable in action—as a story or tale told wherein any given (rhetorical) action depends on every other action. Or, more specifically, the art of oratory becomes a form of discursive action that is only knowable as the action embodied in a narrative—for it is only in Cicero's telling that Antonius's and Crassus's rhetoric can become two different "things" at once, and still be *made* to be neither of those "things" at the same time.

It is this allegiance to the contingent and made nature of oratory, ironically, that proves to be Cicero's still point of the turning world. It is a point toward which perhaps Protagoras's axiom best gestures: "Of all things the measure is man, of things that are that they are, and of things that are not that they are not."[9] Historically, Cicero argues, what "man" has made of the art of oratory has to do primarily with how one "measures" the pursuit of wisdom against "the common practice, custom, and speech of mankind." Antonius associates the common practice and so on with deception (*mendacio*), opinion, and emotion and creates a "semblance of an art" that has no real or true recourse to rational demonstration. Crassus, on the other hand, associates what humans do as political animals with the "natural principles [that govern] the morals and minds and life of mankind." Cicero neither wholly affirms Crassus's oration nor wholly disavows Antonius's oration so much as he shows or proves *oratio* (and its conversational aspect, *sermo*) to be inextricable from the natural imperative of humans to make things discursively, including the art of oratory itself (as it is and as it is not). Insofar as Crassus's contributions in books 1 and 3 tend toward the same end, we might say that Crassus tropes Ciceronian oratory; more particularly, Crassus enacts Ciceronian oratory synecdochially. (Keeping in mind the traditional definition of synecdoche, which Kenneth Burke renders as "the figure of speech wherein the part is used for the whole, the whole for the part, the container and the thing contained.")[10]

What people make will depend; how people make things (that is, discursively) remains, in the most general sense, constant. Crassus *enacts* a making of oratory that encompasses Antonius's what by arguing that what things are and what things are not cannot exist independently of one another—such is the essence of action in the natural world that any action taken is indicative of at least one other action not taken.

ELOQUENTIA · LOGICA

Zeno's hand

In "measuring" how "the whole art of oratory . . . is concerned . . . with the common practice, custom, and speech" or actions "of mankind" within a narrative "ornamented" by Antonius and Crassus, Cicero enacts eloquence as an ornate speech "of the whole." This act, in Sidney's words, "nothing affirms"—or affirms "no thing" (*Defence,* 102). What is affirmed, however, is the natural human action of rhetorico-poetic invention—of making—itself. These wordish measurements, these rhetorical makings, these discursive acts gesture toward and are indicative of the *characters* of their human creators; and what makes that character human is that it is situated in a (speaking) body within time and space, and among other humans.[11]

Or instead of pointing toward the classically "philosophic" statement of Protagoras as the warrant for Ciceronian oratory, perhaps a more appropriate axiom for Ciceronian rhetoric might be Zeno's more visual, and so "sense-able," depiction of rhetoric as an open hand and logic as a closed fist.[12]

Noting that "over and over again in logical and rhetorical treatises of the English Renaissance" humanists used the metaphor of Zeno's hand "to explain" the proclivities of "philosophic" and "rhetorical" discourse, Wilbur S. Howell maintained:

> The fact that this metaphor gives both arts the same flesh and blood, the same defensive and offensive function, and the same skeletal structure, is merely an indication of the conviction of Renaissance learning that logic and rhetoric are the two great arts of communication, and that the complete theory of communication is largely identified, not with one, not with the other, but with both.[13]

But by converting the "flesh and blood" of this metaphor into one "theory of communication," Howell's explication loses the physical or material, the *made* or poetic and active qualities of Renaissance Ciceronianism.[14] In fact, Howell's use of Zeno's hand metaphor is a modern-day example of Antonius's sunburn analogy: both offer the metaphor as something intended to "explicate" a "theory of communication." As an "art of communication," rhetoric in this schematic becomes fact-bound and fiction-less, and its figures are subordinate to a literal meaning. But just as hands make things, so too do *verba*. Zeno's metaphor does not explain or explicate the relationship, but it shows, proves, or demonstrates what the relationship is *analogically;* it is a picture that tells a story by containing both sides. What story one tells will depend. How one tells the story, and why, will remain constant in the most general sense.

Ironically (and I do not use that term lightly), Antonius's sunburn analogy is not, as far as I know, a "borrowing," or what Grassi has called a "literary metaphor," but an honest invention "he" discovers in order to make sense of, to ornament, his experience as an orator. Yet according to the theory of rhetoric Antonius puts forth, that invention can offer no true knowledge; for Antonius, metaphors (similitudes, analogies) are merely pleasant, witty devices that may be useful in winning an audience.[15] As we saw in the previous chapter, however, the similitude or metaphor is fundamental to Crassus's account of rhetoric. And the power of Antonius's sunburn analogy ultimately lies not in what relationship it names between oratory and learning but in how it names that relationship, that is, analogically or metaphorically rather than through explication. And the significance or meaning of that metaphor must be assessed, then reassessed, then reassessed again as the parts or ornaments of Antonius's speech are brought into relationship with Crassus's—and within Cicero's whole discourse "On Oratory."

Dialogic Figurings

The controversies over the imitation / emulation of Cicero that flourished among Renaissance humanists are but one indication of the extraordinary hold the Roman orator sustained in the hearts and minds of several generations of Europe's foremost scholars—and poets.[16] The controversy on oratory that Cicero figures in *De oratore* was refigured over and over again among Renaissance humanists. But where Cicero invents a controversy by recalling, or remaking, the words of Antonius and Crassus, Renaissance humanists invented their controversies by reinterpreting, or remaking, Cicero himself. In a general sense, and though I suspect that it is not quite fair to Antonius, the two dominant interpretations of Cicero recurring throughout the Renaissance might be termed "Antonian" and "Ciceronian." The Antonian version of rhetoric would be more likely to see Cicero's writing on rhetoric merely as an elaboration of his youthful *De inventione*. The Ciceronian version of rhetoric would be more likely to recognize the school-art version of rhetoric as one viable, yet considerably less interesting, and less *useful,* interpretation of rhetoric.

Erasmus's contribution to these controversies, *Dialogus Ciceronianus* (1529), reads like a "who's who" of European humanism. In addition to Erasmus's self-effacing comments on himself as "the Dutch word spinner," Agricola, Pontano, More, Bembo, Melancthon, Vives, and many others are discussed within the dialogue.[17] After Erasmus, only Ramus's several treatises on Ciceronian rhetoric appear to have made a significant contribution to the controversy; not incidentally, it is to Ramus that most scholars point as making the last significant contribution to humanism itself. For though controversies over Cicero appear to have dissipated as a genre among scholars after Ramus (with Harvey's *Ciceronianus* being one exception),[18] how one conceived of the art of rhetoric within the learning process was decisive in how one approached and discoursed on the subject of human learning itself: whether eloquence remained strictly a stylistic virtue or elemental to the inculcation of prudence, and whether one wrote Ramist handbooks or poetry, it was the authority of Cicero as either "a mere rhetorician" or philosopher toward which humanists turned to support their positions.

A consideration of the two most influential figures of northern humanism will help to develop a context for the late Tudor conversation on learning by considering the works of the two most influential figures of northern humanism. In view of both the preceding chapters and the following chapter, my thesis might be stated thus: Bryskett and Immeritô are to Erasmus as E. K. is to Ramus. There is much wanting in the above analogy, to be sure. I can make no claim to its accuracy in terms of the vast differences extant regarding theological doctrines, political bents, social circumstances, temperaments, or any number of personal, professional, and cultural particularities that might be drawn. Still, I offer it as on the grounds that important similarities exist among their thinking and practices of rhetoric.

In practice, and in a general sense, Erasmus and Ramus may be seen as figurings of Crassus and Antonius respectively insofar as the differing rhetorics they promote enact the age-old dispute between philosophy and rhetoric—between rhetoric as a primary form of knowing and rhetoric as primarily a form of communication, between rhetoric as a way of life and rhetoric as so many rules for persuading, between poetic wisdom and theoretic or contemplative knowledge.

Of course, the humanisms of Erasmus and Ramus are indicative of their own rhetorical cultures.[19] Erasmus, "the schoolmaster of Europe," recognized his reforms of learning to be inextricable from the reform of the Holy Catholic Church in Rome in that the predominant mode of learning, scholasticism, perpetuated the divinely guided order, mores, and ends of the church in matters both spiritual and political. But perhaps the most revealing aspect of Erasmus's learning is that, when confronted with the choice between contributing to a schism within the church that could (and did) raise hell, so to speak, throughout all of Europe, Erasmus, whose incessant calls for reform had made him a genuine thorn in Rome's side for many years, chose to continue his reforms under the aegis of Rome on *humanistic* grounds rather than risk abetting Luther's dogmatism. Ramus's pedagogical reforms, however, have a more academic—or scholastic—cast than Erasmus's rhetorically based humanism, as Ong persuasively shows (though Ramus himself considered his reforms to be antischolastic).[20] Beyond effecting the curricular reform of learning itself, Ramus appears to have been notably unconcerned with either the civic or religious implications of his work for the greater part of his life. Though the English Ramists used Ramus's supposed "martyrdom" in the St. Bartholomew's Day massacre in 1572 to promote the Ramist method as anti-Catholic, Ramus's own Protestant leanings appear to have developed well after the seeds of his intellectual life had borne most of their fruit.[21]

The following section develops Erasmus's understanding of rhetoric as a virtue of the senses by focusing on the aesthetic dimension of Erasmus's rhetorical praxis, the physiological dimension of rhetoric that informs and tempers prudent deliberation. In contrast, the section on Ramus focuses on his understanding of rhetorical and prudential virtue as a virtue of the mind or intelligence.

On the Tip of Erasmus's Tongue

Echoing many of the critical commonplaces of modern scholarship on Erasmus, Bruce Kimball in *Orators and Philosophers* characterizes Erasmus's writings as "often platitudinous." Designed to teach an idealized conception of virtue, Erasmus's brand of humanism "skews" philosophy from the speculative tradition, fosters an "epistemological dogmatism" based on elitist appeals "to the authority of the Bible and classical authors" (most notably, Cicero), and encourages good, though highly "ornate" Latin. Erasmus, writes Kimball, attempts to impose "definite standards for personality formation" through his work.[22] Of course, it would be disingenuous for any educator to claim that his or her teaching might somehow escape offering "standards for personality formation" (though, as we shall see, Ramus certainly tried). Kimball objects to what he sees to be the definiteness of the particular standards he associates with Erasmus, standards that are considered to be elitist, non-speculative (too practical?), dogmatic, prescriptive, and excessively ornate. Nancy Struever's description of Erasmian humanism as "a depressing kind of Whiggery" that bears unfavorable similarities to the humanism of this century perhaps captures the conventional interpretation of Erasmus most succinctly.[23] Victoria Kahn, Thomas Sloane, and Richard Waswo have been more forgiving; they see that

Ciceronian skepticism rather than an elitist idealism informs Erasmus's rhetorical-philosophical-literary-educational endeavors.[24] Consequently, they characterize the "habit of thought" that Erasmus attempts to teach as an always rhetorical, always situated figuring of some sociopolitical act. For though Erasmus does not shy away from offering advice about the "best" kind of authors, and so on, his conception of decorum as an action relative to the subject in-hand, the circumstances, place, and people involved serves as a practical corrective to the rigidities of theory.[25]

Nowhere is the physiology of rhetoric more fully developed by Erasmus than in his 1525 treatise *De lingua* (punningly, *On the Tongue* or *On Language*).[26] Indeed, Margaret Mann Phillips has described *On the Tongue* as "a complete example of the Erasmian approach." "All of his work," she claims, "is reflected in it."[27] Or, given the gravity of the circumstances surrounding its publication, we might say that *On the Tongue* is indicative of rather than "reflective" of the "whole" Erasmian approach. Occasioned by the calumny that followed his public disavowal of Luther's program of reforms in *On the Freedom of the Will,* and in anticipation of Luther's reply, *On the Bondage of the Will,* which appeared some months after its publication, *On the Tongue* permitted Erasmus to articulate, represent, and defend himself in a genre better suited to his philosophical temperament. He disapproved of the scholastic nitpicking requisite to theological debates and expressed dissatisfaction with the generic constraints of his *On the Freedom of the Will* soon after publication; in *On the Tongue,* he was able to forgo much of the formal or specialized niceties customary to theological disputation for a more flexible and more persuasive style—at least he hoped that it would be more persuasive.[28]

Erasmus realized that his theological wrangling with Luther was inseparable from his own educational reforms. He characterizes the general problem he addresses in *On the Tongue* thus:

> Today we see the schools of the philosophers disputing with so many opinions, and all Christians battling to the death with so many conflicting dogmas. Are we not repeating the construction of the tower of Babel? What harmony can exist among those carried away by vanity, when no man yields to another? (406)

Both the babbling philosopher and intransigent Christian share the same foundation: vanity. Both use the same material, words, and contribute to building the same edifice. These linguistic erections, as it were, Erasmus says, constitute an abuse of language, and it is the use and abuse of language, as the extended title of the work indicates (*de linguæ usu atque abusu*) with which this treatise, and all of Erasmus's writing, are concerned.[29]

The foundation for the abuse of language, vanity and its attendant vices such as envy, avarice, anger, hatred, and ambition are not, however, the source of the problem, at least not directly. In the dedicatory epistle, Erasmus observes:

> Since man being composed of body and soul, is troubled by two kinds of afflic-
> tion, wise men have always sought to know whether the ailments of the body or
> those of the soul are worse, and the answer they have given is that ailments of
> the soul have more terrible consequences. . . . Physical illnesses only make men
> sick, but diseases of the soul make us evil and wretched as well, because they
> come from within ourselves. (257)

Given Erasmus's emphasis on the evils of the mind or soul, we might be tempted to focus on a rational remedy, an intellectual cure, a theoretical corrective or method that might heal those vices. We might be inclined to analyze the diseases of the soul that come from within ourselves in terms of their intellectual or spiritual or psychological properties. Erasmus, however, appears to be unwilling to do just that—or *just* that—for throughout the treatise, he insists on referring to the afflictions of the soul in terms of their physical analogues. That is, the vices are not errors in judgment (though they are that too, of course) but "diseases," "ailments," and "afflictions" that require "cures" and "remedies." Though "the mind can pass judgment on the ailments of the body," he writes, "this is impossible in the case of illnesses of the mind, because we are damaged in the very part which enables us to judge." "What remedy then," he asks, "could you apply to help [the avaricious, vain, or envious man]" (258), the man whose view of the world is blinded by rigid opinion or dogma?

Erasmus's insistence on the rhetoric of the physician rather than philosophical or theological rhetoric is based on the simple notion that we are comprised of body and soul. "Being composed of body and soul," the afflictions or diseases of the intellect are not inseparable from what the human body does; indeed, as the physical location of the mind or soul, what the body does or is trained to do is of great consequence. And Erasmus leaves little doubt as to what is the most important thing that a body does: it speaks. He begins his treatise with an extensive analysis of the tongue as a physical thing that inhabits "a central position as spokesman for the heart and mind." "Nature," he writes, gave the tongue a place beneath the brain, but not far from the heart, keeping the organs of all the perceptions—eyes, ears, and nostrils—above but near at hand" (265). The tongue does not simply address the affairs of the heart or express the ruminations of the brain but makes intelligible to others some admixture of the body and mind together. This recalls Cicero's central and defining criticism of Socrates (which is intended explicitly then to indict Socrates' followers, Plato's Academicians, and Aristotle's Peripatet-ics) when he has Crassus say in *De oratore* that Socrates introduced that "absurd

and unprofitable and reprehensible severance between the tongue and the [heart]"
that leads "us to our having one set of professors to teach us to think and another
to teach us to speak" (3.16.61).

Both Erasmus and Cicero avoid this "unprofitable" severance by insisting that
speech and reason conjoined are intrinsic to human beings—*ratio et oratio.* "When
the forethought of Nature," writes Erasmus, "granted the tongue its place in the
highest part of the body, she made quite clear to us the importance of this organ"
(266). In *On the Method of Study,* Erasmus tells us what that importance is: "Since
things are learnt only by the sounds we attach to them, a person who is not skilled
in the force of language is, of necessity, shortsighted, deluded, and unbalanced in
his judgment of things as well."[30] As a faculty intrinsic to human beings, speech is
both a form of action and a way of knowing. The tongue and the actions or words
that emanate from it point to both the physical, sensed, and noncognitive begin-
nings of knowledge, and the intellectual or rational and always social qualities that
circumscribe and condition that knowledge. Thus, Erasmus posits language as a
mediator between the matter of knowledge—the infinite particulars of our sensed
experience—and the discursive form that knowledge takes in order to be under-
stood by the reason.

Erasmus follows Cicero's example for inculcating prudence by claiming that
language is necessary rather than incidental to the formation of character; rhetori-
cal practice habituates the body to act, to speak:

> Now the evils that descend on us from stars or forces of nature cannot be com-
> pletely averted, but human effort can ensure that their harm is reduced. We have
> derived medicines from the most poisonous of creatures; we tame wild animals
> and monstrous beasts, we can make land which was rough with brambles and
> overgrown with poisonous weeds productive and adapted to the needs of men.
> This is how we train colts, converting their natural spirit and mettle into a docil-
> ity responsive to our needs. By training, we can take the proud, unbending spirit
> of young men, with its potential destructiveness, and convert it to good citizen-
> ship. Why then can we not achieve the same success in taming the force of the
> tongue? (264)

In this way, Erasmus articulates his resistance to speculative or religious idealism:
human nature can reduce the harm brought about by both Nature and human
nature by our actions; humans thus are responsible for the moral universe they
make because it is just that, of our own making. And in that enterprise, Erasmus
chooses to be involved by declaring not only his interest in morality but also by
laying the groundwork for defining what morality might be: whether to leave it to
the opinionated philosopher or to the dogmatic and no doubt sincere theologian,
or to the orator-poet who looks to language as a material form of action and the

primary way of knowing, that is, to the person that recognizes that "the first merit of speech is that it should be appropriate, taking into account the case, circumstances, place and people involved" (294), to the person who is able to temper his conception of prudence with reference to socially situated praxis.

As the speaker of the heart and mind, the tongue mediates the body's sensed experience and makes it intelligible and so meaningful to others by placing discursive form on it. Language is a way of negotiating the infinite particulars of our sensed experience as the tongue "makes sense" of the body's perceptions through discursive action, both literally and figuratively. Language is both sensed and known; it is a sensation gathered through the senses of the eyes and ears, and a form of knowing. Words are felt as much as they are understood; in fact, they are understood because they are felt. The play on meanings in the title of the work, *Lingua,* is not wordplay alone but a pointed and particularly apt metaphor.

The argument of *On the Tongue* addresses both the body and the mind or soul. Its more formal dimension rehearses the argument I have just sketched out. It posits language (rather than nondiscursive ideals) as an important form of human action and knowing. It argues that the abuses of the tongue may cause the most destruction, and that the prudent use of the tongue may cause great benefit. It argues for the aesthetic effect of language by locating the tongue in the body and claiming that it responds to, addresses, and interprets the body's experience to and for our rational faculties. It repeats on several occasions the concept that "pleasant speech, shrewd and serious, will adapt itself to the occasion in-hand; it will take into consideration the subject, circumstances, and persons involved" (271). It argues for the essentially participatory, hence essentially moral, nature of any human action, rhetorical or otherwise, on the basis that morality is a social construct rather than a preformed and static rational construct.

Yet this formal or rational dimension of Erasmus's argument is not considered particularly effective by most modern scholars; critics generally describe (or dismiss) *On the Tongue* and most of Erasmus's writings as "literary" (which means, as far as I can tell, that its argument is not linear but "disordered").[31] Erasmus's *Lingua* is abrupt and peppered with digressions, it employs an eclectic array of both classical and biblical exempla characteristic of Erasmus's other works, and, as the most recent editor notes, it leaves "relatively short [the] development of positive recommendations to Christians to use their speech to restrain malice, to reconcile" (255). In terms of its intellectual or rational teeth, as it were, *On the Tongue* appears to leave something wanting, and in terms of articulating definite correctives to the abuses it enumerates, it does appear to expound disproportionately on the abuses rather than virtuous uses of language. In short, it does not "teach" in as clear or concise or methodical a manner as some might expect.

This so-called literary handling of a philosophic problem, however, is precisely what makes this so typical of Erasmian, humanistic rhetorical praxis; rather than looking for its intellectual coordinates, we might look to the form of actions it embodies rhetorically. *On the Tongue* does not promulgate but enacts or embodies its philosophical principles; it is intended to engage both the senses and intellect, the body and mind of the reader. Prudent deliberation, the ability to judge with reference to the time, place, and people involved in a given matter, will be the result of reading his text, of experiencing the written word rhetorically. But Erasmus knew that bodies will act both with and without the luxury of reflection; consequently, and in addition to articulating the formal argument, Erasmus appeals to the senses by patterning the form of actions he wants to inculcate within a narrative that speaks to a particular and momentous dialogue between himself and Luther. Yet Christian dogma plays no major or defining role in that narrative; the actions one takes as a Christian within society does. In this respect, the morality of one's action is to be measured in humanistic rather than doctrinal terms. Christ and Paul are offered up as examples for imitation (or emulation) in the latter third of the text just as Cicero, Homer, Horace, and Virgil were offered in the previous two-thirds. Whether Christ or "St. Cicero," as Erasmus dubbed the orator, persons, times, place, circumstances, and actions are the matter of knowledge: interpreta*tions* rather than any one interpretation thus must be considered. Furthermore, Erasmus chooses the narrative form over the rigors of scholastic *disputatio* because his aim, "personality formation," seeks to appeal to the reader's noncognitive, sensed experience. Erasmus wants to "delight and move" the reader to act, to speak, following the example he sets. And part of the "proof" of his argument will be his reader's sensed experience of the text's matter, that is, the activity of engaging words as physical or material forms of action. Erasmus's narrative thus embodies a process similar to that found in Bryskett's *Discourse:* from delight comes the motives of speech, and from speech the possibility of reason, the possibility of teaching. In this activity or process of learning, rhetorical habits may be instilled in a reader, and from these rhetorical habits, and primarily from these rhetorical habits, will the mind learn to habituate itself to the example set by the speaking tongue.

"Let Us Do Away with Human Opinion": On Ramus and Ramism

Though Ramus is reputed to have opened his long and tumultuous academic career with a dissertation arguing the that "everything that Aristotle taught was wrong," Cicero was the classical figure whose authority he challenged most frequently. Between 1546 and 1557, Ramus penned no less than ten treatises on Cicero and

Ciceronianism, recognizing that it was Cicero, more than any other ancient figure, who sparked then continued to fan the flames of humanistic learning among his more "unreasonable"—or poetically inclined—contemporaries.[32]

The "object of our search," Ramus notes in *The Questions of Brutus* (1549)—in response to his question "For what is wisdom?"—is "decorum":

> Decorum advises us on what is needed in each case, on what is suitable, and on what is fitting. Although its advice is necessary in every art, indeed, in every word and deed, nevertheless in practice and theory, if it has any proper practice and theory, it belongs properly to dialectical invention and arrangement.[33]

Ramus's art of dialectic "owns" decorum, and it "owns" decorum by virtue of its power to invent and arrange arguments. Ramus's art of dialectic thus "owns" wisdom, since dialectical decorum appears to answer, if not solve, the question "What is wisdom?" Furthermore, whatever decorum may advise as to what is suitable or fitting in each case—whatever wisdom is—appears to have nothing to do with moral philosophy and the knowledge of human affairs. For Ramus first answers the question "What is wisdom?" by telling his readers what it is most assuredly not:

> Is it moral philosophy? Not at all. . . . Do you mean wisdom in human affairs such as your Aristotle defined in his *Ethics*? Not even this can be said, since we are not after a choice of good and useful things (*nullus enim delectus bonorum & utilium quaeritur*). (73–74)

Though decorum (wisdom, dialectic) "advises," it does not pursue matters concerning "choice," nor does it involve matters concerning "good and useful things." Nor, he continues, does wisdom (dialectic, decorum) have anything to do with "the philosophy of nature and arcane subjects" (for example, astronomy). Somewhere between pragmatics and the arcane lies Ramistic wisdom. Or, perhaps I should say, somewhere above and outside of the realm of human affairs and arcane subjects lies a philosophy Ramus believed to be "universal," obscure, and certainly true.

Ramus's claim that his art of dialectic does not involve "good and useful things" is particularly remarkable when we consider that the enduring hallmark of Ramism is its "usefulness" or "practicality."[34] Ramus himself maintained repeatedly throughout his career that the separation of dialectic and rhetoric is a "theoretical" distinction worth making for practical purposes: "I teach that the arts must be separated according to their precepts and rules, but I want them to be joined in use. For as a result of this separation, they will be more easily learned, and in a shorter time they will be put to use" (18). We may well ask, however, what kind of "use" one might expect from this theoretical or formal distinction between the arts in general and rhetoric and dialectic in particular, especially as this distinction is a priori and necessary to whatever learning might follow from it: Practical and useful to what end? And for whom?

Both Sidney (à la Cicero) and Ramus, of course, might answer that the matter taught by their poetic and methodical modes of learning (respectively) would be practical and useful to any and all comers. Indeed, Sidney argues in the *Defence* that the power of poetry is founded on its ability "to teach, delight, and move" the populace. It is the poet, he claims, who "is indeed the right popular philosopher" (87), who first led the philosopher and historiographer "into the gates of popular judgements" (75). And before noting that he deserves "to be pounded for straying from poetry to oratory" (119), Sidney notes that "Antonius and Crassus, the great forefathers of Cicero in eloquence . . . [attempted] with a plain sensibleness [to] win the credit of popular ears (which credit is the nearest step of persuasion, which persuasion is the chief mark of oratory)" (118). For Bryskett, Spenser, and Sidney, furthermore, it is precisely this power to engage "popular opinion" toward the end of "well-doing" that suffuses the rhetorical arts in a moral philosophy concerned with "human affairs"—ethical and political inquiry. Since the "supreme knowledge" of poetic wisdom is "men's manners," a rhetorical or poetic "practicality" resists formal or theoretical strictures because it is subject to the rhetorical activity that comprises man's "second nature."

However, as indicated by Ramus's recurrent remarks about the falseness and error of "human opinion" and his complete disregard for what humans might regard as useful or good, human nature is for him something to be overcome rather than studied. Nor, as his remarks about natural philosophy indicate, will the study of the natural world prove particularly useful. Instead, Ramus speaks of a "nature" that is not defined by the biological imperatives of action but by its immutable consistency and rational (or formal) constancy. As Walter Ong observes, "natura" for Ramus signifies "its older, more elemental sense of origin and birth." And the art of dialectic, which Ramus claims to be more perfect than the innate abilities of humans to perceive things (albeit dialectically or rationally) is, as Ong notes, "style[d] in the Platonic fashion [as] aptitude, reason, mind, the image of God, the light rivalling the eternal light."[35] The dialectical artifice is something that imitates the natural reasoning powers of a human being; it, too, is a "second nature" of sorts. For Ramus, however, the power of this second nature does not lie in its ability to promote moral discipline, but to determine what is certain, static, and indisputably true.

And the art of all arts, the science of sciences by which one learns how to separate the precepts and rules of the arts—or anything, for that matter—is Ramus's art of dialectic and its one true method (to be distinguished most notably from any method that smacks of Aristotle or scholasticism). The most obvious and perhaps compelling use of Ramus's dialectic is, of course, that it was so easily learned

by the young boys who populated the growing number of schools. But the bene-
fits were appreciated not only by students but also, as Ong emphasizes, by teachers
as well. Teachers could now discover and easily formulate the truthfulness or false-
ness about art because it was the methodical disposition or arrangement taught by
the art of logic through which each art could be explicated, adjudged, and so
known. Ramus's method had the advantage of parceling out "alien matter" (43)
from the subject matter of the arts by virtue of its "universal" and certain method:

> If one is looking for a means of teaching clearly, then method is the arrangement
> of subjects from their universal, general principles down to their subdivided par-
> ticular parts. . . . Method is the light of universal order by which subjects accord-
> ingly arranged are taught more clearly and understood more easily. (56)

As a pedagogical tool closely connected to the business of the classroom, Ramism
sustains its useful character. Though there appears to be a general presumption that
his method might be useful to those outside of the academy's walls as well, Ramus
seldom takes the opportunity to explore what they might be. One of the few exam-
ples of his explicit attempts to make his method applicable outside the classroom
occurs in the dedicatory epistle of *The Questions of Brutus* to "Henry Valois, most
Christian king of France":

> I am confident that knowledge of this art, and indeed of all reputable branches
> of learning . . . is proper for kings. And what is more fitting for kings to study
> than the subjects which the greatest kings have explored for the glory of every
> kingdom and have left to posterity in the eternal monuments of literature
> (*aeternis literarum monumentis*). (3)

Significantly, "the subjects" explored by the greatest kings—including rhetoric but
also, more importantly, dialectic—are glorious chiefly in their distinct separation
from the king's human subjects:

> All outstanding political leaders have believed that their teachings about human
> life and customs were at all times appropriate to their distinguished positions.
> Yet when they attributed their laws to specific divinities . . . they acknowledged
> that these teachings were worthy of more glory and distinction than earthly
> kingdoms and rulers. (4)

Kings are not to learn from the "customs, manners, and speech" of their average
subjects but from academic subjects. And these subjects, according to Ramus, teach
according to divine laws. Ramus's aim is to teach his king of those heavenly laws
"worthy of more glory" than the land he owns and the people he rules. Such is the
kind of "statesmanship" Ramus proposes to teach by explicating "the debate be-
tween the great republican leaders, Cicero and Brutus[,] . . . the most distinguished

and brilliant men in Rome [who], in addition to excelling in wisdom and elo-
quence, also engaged in a serious controversy about the best kind of eloquence" (6).

Disturbingly, beyond the satisfaction one undoubtedly receives in attributing,
with certainty, the laws to their "proper" place in the heavens, Ramus says precious
little as to what the substantial benefits of "statesmanship" might be beyond the
vague and dubious end of "obtaining the highest honors." There is no talk, for
example, of securing or providing for the common good or, as in Bryskett, pursu-
ing "civil felicite." In addition to obtaining honors, Ramus mentions two other
advantages. First, the learned statesman may "set afire with an incredible love of
letters" "many senators, and many men from all walks of life" (5). Second, in "prop-
erly" understanding "the serious controversy about the best kind of eloquence," a
debate that, as Ramus was well aware, bears striking similarities to the contempo-
rary debates he had sparked in his own books and teachings—the well-taught
statesman will then patronize and protect his right-minded inferiors. In Ramus's
idiom, such protection will cause even "the Aristotelians [to] rejoice" in the good
king's continued support of one Peter Ramus, the "object of [the Aristotelians']
fierce and bitter persecution" (6).[36] As blatantly self-interested as this latter reason
may be, the former reason, that many men will be "set afire with an incredible love
of letters," displays the common humanist presumption that education and good
letters (*boné litteré*) will be efficacious in achieving some end. For Ramus, what
makes letters good, and toward what end their apparent goodness might be turned,
will not acquire meaning or significance within the realm of human action but
according to his method.

In order to understand "the best kind of eloquence," Ramus knew to invoke
Cicero, though unlike Erasmus, his main aim was to critique, correct, and revise
rather than emulate. Though he still accounted Cicero beneficial or useful, Ramus
knew that the benefits would depend entirely on *how* and toward what end Cicero
might be read. This last observation is precisely the point that the poetry of
Spenser and Sidney attempts to teach. But where Spenser and Sidney point to feel-
ing, active, and socially inscribed (and so moral) bodies as the starting point for
the invention of reasonable speech, Ramus offers "reason" attributable to some-
thing more or other than "human opinion" and the earthly affairs of human kind.

That is, Ramus offers a form of reason simply. Though he grants that "reason
and speech are the two universal gifts the gods granted to men, and the source of
almost all the others," he is adamant in denying speech any part of the cognitive
process, declaring: "Dialectic is the theory of reason. Therefore whatever is the
property of reason and mental ability and can be handled and practised without
speech, attribute this by right to the art of dialectic" (16). And, significantly, the
properties he attributes to "reason and mental ability" are the first, second, and
fifth canons of classical rhetoric: invention, "arrangement," and memory.[37] "I am

convinced," Ramus writes (while faulting Cicero for holding to "Aristotle's decep-
tive and fallacious opinion"), "that Invention, Arrangement, and Memory belong
to the dialectical art, because they entirely concern reason, and because without
any use of speech they can be self-sufficient" (40).

Whatever benefits devolve from his program of education, whatever makes the
litterê "good," thus will have no material bearing on their rhetorical embodiment.
Since a distinctly nondiscursive form of reasoning invents, arranges, and remem-
bers the really important matter of knowledge, "an incredible love for letters" is
but a means to a contemplative end. Ultimately, a love for letters and the letters
themselves are useless without Ramus's method. When he praises Alexander the
Great for studying those books written by "men skilled in the ways of nature" (4),
it is a nature of "obscure matters" not accessible through discourse—yet eminently
knowable and indisputably certain or truthful once known. What is the useful-
ness or practicality of an "incredible love of letters" to the state? It appears that
such a love will bend one's mind toward matters more obscure, more complex, and
truer than any political matters and any other matter derived from "human opin-
ion"—the antitheses to and bugbears of "true judgment" derived methodically,
through the art of dialectic.

"An incredible love for letters," if read just so, affirms the values and conven-
tions of the educated teachers of method. Academic conventions and scholarly
conceits become the backbone of knowledge. Wisdom or decorum is not prized
for the actions it promotes so much as it is valued for the methods it invariably
demonstrates to be valid. The virtue of rhetoric for Ramus thus is not a moral
virtue but an intellectual virtue. Virtue is not to be praised in action (*virtutis laus
actio*) but is instead a function of a theory privileged for its ability to resist the
demands of occasion, to dismiss the interests and involvement of an audience
(wherein differing views, "opinions," might surface), and to repress the material of
sensed matter of human experience entirely.[38]

Briefly Recalling Spenser

E. K.'s endorsement of Antonian-Ciceronian rhetoric through his use of the sun-
burn analogy underlies his efforts to teach readers what, according to him, Immer-
itô cannot teach. But Spenser's dialogue, that is, his narration or telling of the
dialogue between E. K. and Immeritô, gestures toward a telling of the whole. In
Hobbinoll's recitation of Colin's song of "fayre Elisa" (46) in *Aprill*, for example,
Colin (facilely and perfunctorily) makes a comparison between Elisa and "Phoe-
bus," who "thrust out his golden hedde, / upon her to gaze" (73–74) only to blush
"to see another Sunne below" (77). This hyperbolic, and hackneyed, comparison
of the brightness of Elisa's magisterial rays to the sun, however, appears to leave

Colin at a loss for poetic invention; promising to give his "goddesse plaine" the finest fruits of his labor, he notes that he makes this offer under adverse conditions: To her will I offer a milkwhite Lambe:

> Shee is my goddesse plaine,
> And I her shepherds swayne,
> Albee forswonck and forswatt I am.
> (96–99)

Though "forswonck and forswatt," which E. K. glosses as "overlaboured and sun-neburnt" (83),[39] Colin indicates in his very next breath that he might overcome his want of invention in a vision of Calliope: "I see *Calliope* speede her to the place, / where my Goddesse shines" (100–101).[40]

Colin's reference to Calliope, coming as it does on the heels of his confessed for-swonckness and forswattness, prompts E. K.'s commentary on Calliope as the one "to whome they assigne the honor of all Poeticall Invention, and the first glorye of the Heroicall verse. other say, that shee is the Goddesse of Rhetorick" (81). By defining rhetoric Ramistically as only "action [or delivery] and elocution" (81), E. K. effectively denies the poet the capacity to invent knowledge by virtue of this belittled and vague association of rhetoric with poetics.[41]

But by situating Colin's song within the *drama* of its "ethic and politic" consid-erations, Immeritô shows Colin's "forswonck and forswatt" self to be the naïve expression of a technically proficient but morally irresponsible "shepheardes boye." Similarly, by situating Immeritô within a dialogue with his glossarist, Spenser shows the paucity of E. K.'s efforts by casting his use, then interpretation of the sunburn analogy into the (inherently moral) realm of human or rhetorical action. Spenser, that is, embraces or *contains* both sides of the argument within a *narra-tive,* showing his readers that the matter of poetry has to do with how they come to know the world, and how they come to know the world is itself "contained" or "embraced" or embodied in the dialogic process itself. Spenser models his poetics, and his poetic ethos, on the Ciceronian ideal of eloquence: in terms of rhetorico-poetic invention, E. K. is Spenser's figure for an Antonius-like reader of poetry, whereas Immeritô figures a Crassus-like poet. Together they "ornament" the whole of the contemporary conversation on poetry. And insofar as Spenser persuades his readers that poetic learning embraces the whole of human action, and that, as Sid-ney claimed, "well-doing not well-knowing only" comprises the "ending end" of such learning, his *Calender* is a rhetorical embodiment or *enactment* of Ciceron-ian eloquence.

The controversies of over rhetoric (including poetics) and logic among Spenser's contemporaries will help flesh out the question. In the next chapter, we will see how Spenser's and Sidney's poetic *ethe* were appropriated to serve in efforts designed to further instruction in humanism's new learning, Ramism, by men of good will who, like E. K., demonstrate or prove poetry's ability to teach a form of reason. In those efforts, the possibility of the poetic metaphor to enact and embody a necessary form of reasoning itself is precluded on the presumption that the true matter of knowledge is transmitted to the human mind from Nature rather than transferred from the body to the mind in the natural process of human—or humanistic —learning.

CHAPTER SIX

———— ❀ ————

MAKING MATTER FOR A CONCEIT, MAKING CONCEIT MATTER

As both a sometime scholar and late arrival to the Bar, Abraham Fraunce presents *The Lawiers Logike* to the "Learned Lawyers of England" by likening himself to "Tully," who, "at the earnest request of Trebatius, a towardly Lawyer of Rome . . . eloquently put downe the first part of Logike in his *Topikes,* to the præcepts whereof he applyeth Law-like examples, for the better instruction of Trebatius and helpe of other Lawyers."[1] Fraunce, however, intends to go Cicero one better. Cicero, who "put downe the first part of Logike in his *Topikes,*" discourses on those topics he claims belong to the art of invention. Fraunce (guided by Ramus) records inventional topics, too, but more important, he "puts downe" those topics belonging to "judgement," or logic.

An Exemplary Ramist:
"Let Passe the Learned Poets and Orators"

Fraunce tells his readers that his *Lawiers Logike* underwent no less than six revisions in the seven years before its publication, acquiring its present title only in its "last alteration"; this "new name of the Booke," he writes, "proceeded from the chaunge of my profession" (¶v). As a relative newcomer to the Inns of Court, Fraunce attempts to establish himself as something of an authority on the theory of law in his introductory epistle by emphasizing the arduousness of his earlier philosophical or scholarly pursuits. Though he offers no explanation for his "sodayne departure from Philosophy to Lawe" (¶v), he does stress his university origins to his professional audience, expanding on his "eight yeares labour at Cambridge" at some length (¶v, ¶2v). Those heady days as a "Vniveristie man," he says, "did yet so racke my raunging head, and bring low my [creased] body, that I felt at last when it was too late, the perpetuall vexation of Spirite, and continuall consumption of body, incident to euery scholler" (¶2v). Wanting to spare the lawyers of England similar, physical hardships in their studies, to spare them from "the continuall beating of their braynes about endles controuersies" that, to Fraunce, smacks of Catholicism (¶2r), he offers them the *certain,* unwavering "light" (¶3v) of the Ramist method. But "because many loue Logike, that neuer learne Lawe," Fraunce tells his reader that he has retained "those ould examples of the new Shepheards Kalender" (¶v) that he first collected for the six previous, apparently more philosophically bent or scholarly drafts of the *Lawiers Logike* titled *The Sheapheardes Logike,* wherein he drew exclusively from the twelve eclogues of Spenser's *Calender* to accomplish his primary aim, "the easie explication of Ramus his Logike" (¶r, ¶3v).[2]

But why did Fraunce consider examples from the English Common Law and Immeritô's verse to be useful in the "easie explication" of Ramus's logic? And why are examples from poetry in particular "fit" to aid Fraunce in his efforts to explicate the virtues of logic (though not "most fit" or as fit as "Law-like" examples)? Tamara A. Goeglein has argued that English Ramists such as Fraunce employed examples from poetry by calling our attention to the fact that Ramists knew their art of logic to be, like poetry, an artifice.[3] Ramus and his disciples, she argues, were well aware that their much touted method relied on "artificial" or "unnatural" rules and precepts; thus "regardless but not in spite of what the Ramists themselves may have intended," Ramus's logic actually underscores the "representational" or "metaphorical" function of "all language" ("Wherein Hath Ramus," 100). Goeglein's contention, that Ramism is not dissimilar to contemporary notions of poetry, warrants scrutiny. To be sure, Fraunce notes that "Logike is an Art, to distinguish artificiall Logike from naturall reason" (2r), and he does describe the aim of logic to be "to reason well and artificially" (4r). Moreover, he even recognizes his use of the word "method" to be "artificiall," a metaphor applicable "to any orderly proceeding" whatsoever (114v). For Fraunce, however, all arts are methodical. Unfortunately, Goeglein's argument largely depends on the theoretical currency of semiotics rather than the historical currents of discourse that constituted humanistic philosophy; consequently, she presumes that the Ramists' use of "metaphor" as an "artificial" or "unnatural" mode of representing remained a constant *thing* within the "humanist discourse of reason."[4]

Yet Fraunce's Ramistic use of poetry to ornament and exemplify Ramus's logic marks a significant reconfiguration of learning and poetry, the matter that constitutes them, the ends toward which they are directed, and the relationship of each to each.

The magnitude of this reconfiguration, however, is not always easy to discern given the *thematic* similarities apparent in various treatments of "invention," "poetry," "decorum," "matter and words," "rhetoric," "reason"—or even "Cicero." That is, if it is presumed or granted that figures such as Sidney and Fraunce are speaking, in essence, about the same thing, "poetry," or if Spenser and the Ramists

THE FIRST CHAPTER
OF THE FIRST BOOKE.

What Logike is.

Logike is an Art of Reasoning.

Annotations.

Lthough this woord, *Logike*, bée generally receaued of Englishmen, and vsed euen of them that know no Logike at all, yet for that it was a stranger at the first, I thinke it not impertinent to séeke from whence it came, and what it doth betoken: λόγε, therefore in Gréeke signifieth Reason, of λόγε is deriued this word, λόγικά, that is to say, Reasonable, or belonging to Reason, which although it bée an adiectiue, and must haue some such like word, as Arte, Science, or Facultie, to be adioyned vnto it as his substantiue, yet is it substantiuely taken and vsed in Latine, as also in our English tongue.

Sturmius and some others, deriue this word Logike from λόγε as λόγε betokeneth spéech or talke: whose opinion, although the other name of this Art (which is διαλεκτική, of διαλέγεσθαι, to speake or talke) doe in some respect séeme to confirme, yet for that the whole force and vertue of Logike consisteth in reasoning, not in talking: and because reasoning may be without talking, as in solitary meditations and deliberations with a mans selfe, some holde the first deriuation as most significant.

Dialectica & Logica, saith *Hotoman*, dictæ sunt a sermone siue oratione, sed illa proprie ab eo genere sermonis, qui cùm altero interrogando & respondendo commiscetur. Fictum enim verbum est παρὰ τὸ διαλέγεσθαι quod est, verba cum altero commutare, colloqui, disputare, sermocinari, sermones cædere. Nam cùm philosophorū consuetudo hæc esset, vt de rebus ad artes suas pertinentibus sæpè inter se commentarentur, eruditas illas collocutiones, διαλόγους (vt Laertius in Platone scribit) apellarunt, earumq; habendarum artem, Dialecticam, qua de causa eandem Laertius

B.   codem

The first page of Abraham Fraunce's explication of Ramistic dialectic in The Lawiers Logike *(1588). The sentence "Logike is an Art of Reasoning" is an "argument" that functions as an axiom for the whole of the text. The "Annotations" that follow are not argumentative, but expository for Fraunce, technically speaking, in that they make known the truthfulness of the proposition that "Logike is an Art of Reasoning."*

are talking about the same thing, "reason," then these things tend to become generalized under recurrent themes comprising "humanist discourse." Of course, in such a scenario, even humanist discourse is a thing in that it encompasses the many themes consistent throughout certain authors in certain times. These themes are broached differently by different authors, to be sure—some methodically or logically, some poetically, but of a certain philosophical consistency nonetheless. Consequently, the term "humanist" functions either as a false substantive or an adjective. In both instances, "humanist" derives its meaning with reference to a thing for its meaning, a scholarly conceit—"humanism"—and in this formulation, it is the -ism that ultimately substantiates whatever might be "human" about "humanism." What is humanism? It is a philosophical genus or class or species that is definable by certain things that may be thematized. As opposed to a humanistic philosophy, in which "humanistic" functions as a "true" adjective in that its substantive form, "human," qualifies "philosophy": a humanistic philosophy thus is a pursuit of wisdom invented for humans, by humans. Or we could say that a humanistic philosophy is a rhetorical philosophy inasmuch as it acknowledges itself to be something rhetorically constructed. A humanistic philosophy thus would encompass any given humanism. For example, of "art [or 'artificall rules'], imitation, and exercise," Sidney claims, the poet only really concerns himself with exercise, though even in the exercise of his wit, the poet does act as one might expect—he proceeds "forebackwardly":

> For where we should exercise to know, we exercise as having known; and so is our brain delivered of much matter which was never begotten by knowledge. For there being two principal parts, matter to be expressed by words and words to express the matter, in neither we use art or imitation rightly . . . . never marshalling [our matter] into any assured rank, that almost the readers cannot tell where to find themselves. (*Defence*, 112)

On the face of it, Sidney's insistence on the poet's possession of a "fore-conceit, or *Idea* of a work" that allows the poet "to exercise as having known," together with his separation of words and matter looks very much like a Neoplatonic—or, more specifically, a Ramistic—approach to both poetry and knowledge, an approach presumed to be characteristic of humanism. First, the matter of a poem is invented, conceived of, or known, then words are attached to express what is known. But if a conceit conceived of in strictly rationalistic terms as a form of knowledge is the poet's beginning point, then how does a brain deliver "much matter which was never begotten by knowledge"? The matter of the poetry is not a conceit but the act or process of conceiving itself (a rhetorical process), and neither "artificiall rules" nor the "right" imitation can embody that process.

Consider the proximity of Sidney's articulation of the poetic process with these lines from Abraham Fraunce's dedicatory poem to Sir Philip Sidney's brother-in-law, Henry Earle of Pembroke, at the outset of *The Lawiers Logike* (1588):

> I say no more then what I saw, I saw that which I sought,
> I sought for Logike in our Law, and found it as I thought.
> (7–8)

Fraunce, too, appears to have written his logic "forebackwardly"; he "exercises" as one who knows rather than for the sake of knowing. Unlike Sidney, however, Fraunce is keen to "use art and imitation rightly" and to marshal his matter into an assured rank. But this difference appears to be only a difference in "method"—a formal difference that may be used to distinguish between poetic discourse and logical discourse—as the matter each expresses is born of the same inventional process. They just choose to make their way through that matter differently.

Fraunce, at least, thought such to be the case. Following from what appears to be a similar definition of art as Sidney, namely, that an art consists of "artificiall rules" or precepts that prescribe how a thing is to be produced, Fraunce also recognizes the poet's (and orator's and historiographer's) resistance to method, or "resistance to theory" as a characteristic of their discourse:[5]

> Historiographers, Poets, Orators, and such other speakers or writers, are not bound to strictly observe the perfection of the first method: but may, according to their matter, meaning, purpose, time, place, persons, wisely observe the best for their intent, altering, hiding, adding, detracting, when and how they list. Poets seeke to please the multitude, a beast of many heades. . . .
>
> This is called the concealed or hidden methode: the method of wit and discretion, for it is rather seene in the provident conceipt of him that writeth or speaketh, then perceived by any rule of art, or precept whatsoever. So it is a good policie, if thy cause be honest and good, to use such *Exordiums* and beginnings, as may make the matter best knowne and understood plainly and simply. (113v–114r)

Fraunce seconds Sidney's claim that the poet "neither [uses] art or imitation rightly," and in so doing, he does grant the poet a stake in the pursuit of wisdom by virtue of a providentially inspired "wit or discretion" borne of providence. Though unperceivable "by any rule of art, or precept whatsoever," Fraunce nevertheless maintains that there is method to the poet's madness, so to speak—albeit concealed or "cryptic," incomprehensibly wise, and providential. Yet whether or not Fraunce assigns what the poet does a method, he and Sidney appear to be talking about the same thing; moreover, with the exception of but one lexical sticking point, they appear to be talking about the same thing in much the same way.

Sidney, however, refuses to critique poetry as a thing; "it" is instead an activity, a discursive making that embodies the genius of humanity's second nature. And in this regard, methods are made too. Fraunce, however, sees poetic invention to be an imitation of the logical process, a thing that follows or is ultimately subject to a particular method.

As a dominant, if not "defining" theme in humanist writings, "rhetoric" is often denoted in modern Renaissance scholarship as a particular thing about which many prominent figures wrote, learned, and taught. In his preface to *William Temple's "Analysis" of Sir Philip Sidney's "Apology for Poetry"* for example, John Webster relies enthythematically on his readers' shared conception of what rhetoric *is* when he notes that Ramistic logic is really more a "rhetorized logic" than a logic proper.[6] Recalling the Ramists' logical yet "unintentionally rhetorical" approach to textual analysis, he notes:

> In its "analytic" mode, [Ramistic] logic is responsible for much of what we would now call "rhetorical analysis," or even "literary criticism." Questions about how ideas are developed, why they are set out as they are, what strategies are employed for what ends—these are all issues to which logic is asked to speak. As a result, the body of Temple's *Analysis* is replete with terms that to modern ears have a distinctly rhetorical cast, but which to Temple are the bread and butter of logic. (25)

"Rhetoric" here, significantly, *is* a field of study that may be denoted by having its own peculiar vocabulary; and the duties performed by that vocabulary are to name "how ideas are developed" (rather than how or why they are invented), to describe formal or organizational aspects of a work, and to identify "strategies" that, on the presumption that the poet's "cause be honest and good," need to be made "knowne and understood plainly and simply." But deploying such a diminished and historically naïve definition of what rhetoric *is* ultimately subordinates the "rhetoric of" a text to the questions asked and answered by a particular mode or method of analysis.

But what Ramistic rhetoric *is* in the schema above, generally speaking, is what rhetoric *became*. More than an early, staid manifestation of a form of rhetorical analysis or literary criticism, Ramism is the earliest of the early modern period's critical or analytic philosophies, philosophies that begat and made "current-traditional rhetoric" traditional. Characteristically, critical philosophies narrow the rhetorical to the strategic, align its ends to deception through pleasure, and variously narrow or expand the domain of poetry by aligning its ends either with the pretty and innocuous verbiage of lyrical toys or a sublime aesthetic. As a quantifiable thing, the "rhetoric of" a text or group of texts is easily separated from the "matter" of a text. Inasmuch as contemporary literary criticism and many histories of rhetoric deploy such a diminished definition of rhetoric as a "subject" in its own right (to be distinguished from the object or matter of critical analysis), it may be said to be consonant with Ramistic rhetoric. If, from the perspective of literary critics, Ramism looks like a "rhetorized logic," then humanist poetry held fast under the glare of such critical philosophies might be described best as a "logicized poetics," for as the art-full accessories to the theoretical matter of analyses, rhetoric and poetics both become subordinate to and knowable by virtue of the critical methodologies imposed on them.

The significance of the Ramist reconfiguration thus lies in the subordination of praxis to gnosis, between language as a form of action and language as the representation of things that, buried under the ornaments and thematic or generic exigencies of a work, might be discovered if only the correct critical method or mode of analysis might be applied. In an analytical mode, the act of judging or critiquing a particular text becomes the primary task because it represents knowing. In a practical mode, knowing how to judge becomes subject to the actions one may (or may not) make or produce regarding present contingencies. For Ramists, however, the matter of knowledge was linked only tenuously and, ultimately, *insubstantially* with the abilities of human kind to perceive and know the world.

A Ramist, for example, would never muse about anyone telling him to look into his heart and write. One preliminary indication of Ramism's detachment of the matter of knowledge from the sensory perceptions is that the matter under investigation is never an action or actions but (and similar to Goeglein's conception of a metaphor) a thing. And it is always the truthfulness or falseness of a thing that is under investigation and waiting to be judged. "Right" and "wrong" action, in other words—or praising the honorable act and censuring the wicked deed—the ancient mainstays of poetry, do not fall into logic's purview.

Placing the "appropriate" yet artificial logical term onto any word or thing (for example, "cause," "subject," "adjunct," etc.), and setting such terms in relationship to others in a phrase or statement constitutes invention in the Ramist system, what Fraunce prefers to call "exposition" or "Genesis" (3r). By "thing," Fraunce also means "argument" or "conceit"; and arguments are defined simply as a "name according to [a thing's] naturall propertie, or by the imposition and fancie of man" (8v); thus "fire" is a thing that qualifies as an argument because its name is "usually knowne" (9r). Any substantive word or noun thus may constitute an argument in the Ramist system. The arguments that are the things in question, furthermore, need not perform the actions of proving or confirming; instead, Fraunce encourages his reader to consider them "more generally" as "declarations" (9v), which require no proof. More particularly, however, the art of logic provides things "an artificiall and secondary name" (9r) or "conceit"; thus fire might be labeled the cause "for that it argueth heate as his effect" (9r). In this "artificall" or art-full yet

eminently logical sense, fire is the argument or conceit toward which reason read-
ily may refer to aver the effect, "heat," or disavow the effect, "wet," for example.
The first book of *The Lawiers Logike* is dedicated to this system of invention, offer-
ing what amounts to a grammar lesson in the new logic by explicating the right
use or identification of an "adjunct," for example, in relationship to other words.
The end of invention is "to expose" the middle term of a syllogism in terms of
logic's artificial rules. If, intuitively, the middle term "bee straightway iudged as true
or false" (7r), then it becomes an axiom or proposition. So, if I were to say, "Fire
causes heat," this phrase would be an axiom of my invention—an invention that
mediates between an "argument of the efficient cause," fire, and an "argument of
the effect," heat. This "axiomaticall" form of invention is, as Fraunce notes, largely
dependent on convention or custom since it presupposes that by the use of the
term "fire," people will know what is meant; as such, the axioms produced by logi-
cal invention are really forms of judgment. Invention in the Ramistic system, that
is, presupposes and is built upon the foundations of the art of logic's "second"
canon, judgment or diposition, since "every axiome and rule of Invention is a part
of Judgement (because it is an axiome, and every axiome is of iudgement). . . . And
so in Invention, every rule is an axiome, [and] every rule doth iudge" (8r).

But, Fraunce continues, invention does not show one *how* to judge, and thus
one needs the second part of logic, judgment, to "dispose" the arguments one has
"invented" in an orderly fashion. Hence the prominence of Ramus's syllogistic
method designed to dispose of all the arguments in a uniform way in order to judge
and so know things as true or false. Fraunce's Ramistic elision of judgment and
disposition is not insignificant, for in a sense it captures the "essence" of the Ramist
system. For Ramists, judgment is largely a product of the methodical, orderly dis-
posing of arguments; judgment, and this diminished conception of invention, that
is, is strictly a matter of *form,* wherein validity trumps goodness.

Consider the example from *The Shepheardes Calender* Fraunce uses to illustrate
the Ramistic doctrine of invention:

> But nothing such thylk sheepheard was
> whome *Ida* hill did beare:
> That, left his flocke to fetch a lasse,
> whose love he bought too deare. (6v)

In order to prove the truthfulness of that which is already known, namely, that
"*Paris* is no good sheepheard," Fraunce notes the presence of two distinct argu-
ments: the first is "Paris," the second is a "good sheepheard" (6v). The verse spoken
by Thomalin in *Julye* offers the middle term, or "Medium"(6v), of the syllogism
"to leave his flocke to fetch a lasse":

1. Paris
2. A good shepheard.
3. To leave his flocks to fetch a lasse
   Whereof it is concluded in this wise syllogistically . . .
   Hee that leaveth his flocke to fetche a lasse, is no good shepheard:
   But Paris did leave his flocks to fetch a lasse,
   Therefore Paris is no good shepheard.
   (7r)

The "rightness" or "wrongness" of Paris's actions, significantly, are not involved in the question Fraunce offers here. What is at stake is the logical validity of the axiom itself, "Paris is no good shepheard," which Fraunce maintains supports this verse logically; as such, it is a thing to be judged. The act Paris takes in leaving his flock is beside the point: that the "lasse" in question happened to be Helen of Troy is insignificant, as is the fact that Paris was Priam's son, as are the consequences of his action and the impossible circumstances occasioning it. Furthermore, *why* Thomalin makes this claim about Paris (or why Immeritô invents a Thomalin to make this claim to Morrell within an eclogue of the *Calender*) does not fall into the purview of Fraunce's logic. Instead, the merit or fault of the verse, indeed the very meaning of the verse, belongs solely to the axiomatical proposition to which, Fraunce claims, it refers.

The truthfulness or falseness of a "thing" will depend on its "essence," on whether or not a thing's essence is perceptible (and so true) or not (thus false). Fraunce tells us that the essence of any thing ultimately depends on its material and formal causes (23v). By the "material," Fraunce appears to be in agreement with the likes of Bryskett and Sidney in observing that the "matter of knowledge" comprises the infinite particulars perceived or sensed by the human body—at least in part. Similarly, Fraunce also seems to be in agreement with the notion that Reason apprehends forms, that is, particulars in a generalizable shape. But Fraunce maintains that Reason's apprehension of forms is constituent to the material of knowledge as well: consequently, the "perception" of knowledge's "matter," "the materiall causes," just like "all other arguments Logicall," need "not to bee tied onely to sensible and bodily matters: but generally to bee applied to any whatsoever, bee it subiect to sence, or conceived of reason" (22r). By "generally," Fraunce means "with reason" in that material causes can be generalized, and reason apprehends generalities. In addition to the sensible matter or feelings the body might perceive singularly, in particulars, the matter of knowledge also comprises *formal* matter conceived by reason.

Fraunce, in short, makes "reason" a sixth sense, a sense that, unlike its physical counterparts, does not experience the world in infinite particulars but apprehends the "essence" of a thing as a form in its entirety, and the parts that comprise that whole are perceived in order; this orderly perception, then, comprises the most reliable apprehension of the matter of knowledge. Using the eminently "true" character of the art of logic as an example, Fraunce notes that one might perceive the material nature of reason just "as, a man conceiveth in his mind or memory the Art of Logike or any other science, the matter whereof is their severall rules and preceptes, the forme, [and] the due diposition of the same" (22r). The sensible perception of matter, furthermore, will always be subordinate to the form of a thing conceived of by reason, as "nether first [the 'sensible'] nor last [that 'conceived of in the mind or memory'] is subiect to sence, but onely understoode by reason," which Fraunce notes is that faculty "imprinted in the inward power of a mans soule" (22r).[7]

That "inward power" apprehends form, which is thought to comprise the material essence of a thing. For the form of a thing, Fraunce writes, "is eyther internall, or externall: Internall which is not perceived by sence. External, which is subiect to sence. External is eyther naturall . . . or Artificiall, which Art hath framed and performed" (22v).[8] Neither "natural" nor "artificiall," the internal essence of thing, which Fraunce admits to "bee hardly either known understoode, or expressed and made plaine" (22v), appears to be either super- or supranatural. And yet, though "hardly knowne . . . or expressed," Fraunce appears to have complete confidence in one's ability to access such essences hidden in the depths and mysteries of "a mans soule." But not everyone's ability. Indeed, this is why Ramus's dialectical method is so important, because the "artificiall [and natural] and externall, is much more easily both conceived in reason, and expressed by woorde" (22v–19r [sic]). Or to put it another way, the artificial and external form is much easier to teach than the internal essence, which, though knowable, is difficult to express. That Fraunce chooses to grant "art" an active role in "framing and performing" the apprehension of the external essence of a thing thus is ultimately based on the artificial form's proximity to the internal essence of a thing—an internal essence that, though "hardley knowne" and difficult to "expresse," does not appear to be completely unknowable. It is on this distinction between the intelligibility of internal and external forms that Fraunce originally distinguishes between "logic" proper and its more customary form, dialectic:

This art may bee called λογική of the internall form, essence, and nature thereof consisting in reason: but διαλεκτική of the externall maner and order of woorking, which is commonly doone by speache and talke, as that woorde importeth. (Bv)

The ultimate aim of the art of logic, thus, is the use of dialectical method to point one in the direction of "the internall form"—in the "polyshing of naturall, as discovering the validitie of euerie reason, bee it necessary, wherof cometh science: or contingent, whence proceedeth opinion" (5r). It is in this respect that Ramism approximates the scholasticism of its medieval predecessors most closely. Though the dialectical process of "discovering" the necessary truths of science aids one in the apprehension of such truths, the apprehension of them, significantly, does not require speech itself. Fraunce declares that "the whole force and vertue of Logike consisteth in reasoning: and . . . reasoning may be without talking, as in solitary mediations and deliberations with a mans selfe" (Br). The "whole force and vertue of Logike," that is, belongs to "contemplation" because it directs "the minde to the view and contemplation of that, which of it selfe it might perceave, if it were turned and framed thereunto" (4v). But because it is easier to teach the external forms through dialectic, talking becomes a necessary evil; because speech involves the natural and external essences of things, it may keep us from perceiving the "true" essence inherent to a thing.

Remarkably, thus, if the internal essence of a thing remains unknowable, it is probably the fault of nature rather than the artifice designed to teach it because it is nature that compels us to sense or feel things. The artifice of logic allows us to circumvent the problem of nature; though "gathered out of divers examples of naturall reason," logic surpasses nature precisely because of its ability go beyond nature—to generalize. "Naturall reason," though an

> ingraven gift and facultie of wit and reason shining in the perticuler discourses of severall men . . . is to no man given in full perfection. . . . And because the true note and token resembling nature must be esteemed by the most excellent nature, therefore the preceptes of artificiall Logike both first were collected out of, and always must be conformable unto those sparkes of naturall reason . . . manifestly appearing in the monumentes and disputations of excellent autors. And then is this Logike of Art more certaine then that of nature, because of many particulars in nature, a generall and unfallible constitution of Logike is put downe in Art. So that, Art, which first was but the scholler of nature, is now become the [master] of nature.[9] (2r)

The presumption at work here is that, by "mastering" nature, one goes beyond the "naturall and externall" essences of things through dialectic to the "internall" essence, "which is not perceived by sense" but by Reason itself. It is precisely this mistrust of nature coupled with this dependence on the artifice of logic that suggests why poetry, which is designed to affect the senses, can *exemplify* logical teachings but will never be able to teach.

How might poetry exemplify the "right use of naturall reason"? Clearly, poetry could never hope to teach one how to invent the matter of knowledge or about judgments that *really* mattered. And even if "sparkling" examples of natural reason can be culled from poetry, they will need to be generalized and methodically disposed in order to be understood properly, and logic, according to Fraunce, not poetry, teaches one the "distinct, firme, constant, and immutable" forms of things. One such sparkling example of natural reason, Thomalin's claim that "Paris is no good shepheard," requires method, not the dynamic, rhetorical world of the poet's making to be understood, according to Fraunce. Yet after proving conclusively that Paris indeed is not a good shepherd, the reader of the poem might well ask, "But why does that matter?"

Sidney's Defence of Ciceronian Rhetoric

When Astrophil, in Sidney's *Astrophil and Stella,* recounts his studies of "inventions fine" by "turning others' leaves," he alludes to the sunburn analogy Antonius offers in *De oratore* in order to "prove" to his auditors that "the activity of the orator has to do with opinion, not knowledge (*scientia*)":[10]

> I sought fit words to paint the blackest face of woe:
> Studying inventions fine, her wits to entertaine,
> Oft turning others' leaves, to see if thence would flow
> Some fresh and fruitfull showers upon my sunne-burn'd braine.
> But words came halting forth, wanting Invention's stay.

As many critics have noted, however, "perusing" books—or "turning other's leaves"—appears to fail Astrophil in his attempts to invent a poem for his beloved; no showers fall upon his "sunne-burn'd braine." Astrophil's failed attempt at Antonian invention, however, does not indicate Sidney's complete rejection of this mode of invention (and so a rejection of the relationship between learning and rhetoric and poetry endorsed by the sunburn analogy), for the poet does not discard or exclude it from this "fained" discussion on invention itself. Sidney, too, emulates the Ciceronian ideal in fashioning his poetic ethos, and he does this by containing both sides of the argument within Astrophil's "internal" dialogue.

For Astrophil comes to realize that poetic invention is not borne of study and "others' leaves," but of "Nature":

> Invention, Nature's child, fled step-dame Studie's blowes,
> And others' feete still seem'd but strangers in my way.
> Thus great with child to speake, and helplesse in my throwes,
> Biting my trewand pen, beating my selfe for spite

"Foole," said my Muse to me, "looke in thy heart and write."
(10–14)

The whole of Sidney's sonnet sequence might be said to begin with the last line of this poem inasmuch as it discloses the moment of discovery that allows him to bring forth his speech into the world, to speak without "halting words," even to invent another self, Astrophil. That moment, significantly, is the recognition of an alternative mode of invention, one that is borne of desire and given its form in language—rather than a mode of invention that apprehends matter already formed in the perusing of old books.

But the recognition of and allegiance to an alternative mode of invention (by looking into one's heart) is not in itself sufficient to facilitate poetic invention, though Astrophil might think so. For in his epiphany, Astrophil neglects to appreciate the process that led him to hear the Muse, the process to which Sidney makes the reader privy. That is, Astrophil's recounting of his failed efforts at Antonian invention is integral to the inventional process rather than prior to the production of not only this poem but also, we may infer, the production of the sonnet sequence that follows.[11] Astrophil, unlike Sidney, appears to be unaware of the role Cicero's invention of Antonius's sunburn analogy plays. Sidney appropriated Cicero's conceit to ornament his poem, and it is precisely that ornament, that figure of speech, that names and orders the relationship between the two parts of the same whole, between perusing "others' leaves" and looking into one's heart. It is not *this* mode of invention or *that* mode of invention, but the realization that one must acknowledge *both* to be necessary to the invention Sidney puts into action in Astrophil's discourse. Looking into one's heart may be the privileged form of invention (just as Crassus is the privileged orator), but because the significance of that looking can not be measured only in terms of what matter one finds therein, it also has to be measured against what it is not. And to understand what can be made of it, one needs to know how things are made, or can be made, in all probability.

Astrophil's "foolishness" stems from the fact that he knew what he should be doing all along. Consider, for example, his rationale for writing in the first place, before the revelation:

Loving in truth, and faine in verse my love to show,
That the deare She might take some pleasure of my paine:
Pleasure might cause her reade, reading might make her know,
Knowledge might pitie winne, and pitie grace obtaine.
(1–4)

Determined "to show" or "prove" his love, Astrophil is beset with the problem of making a verse to accomplish just that. In the lines above, Astrophil describes the learning process he seeks to inculcate in his reader, Stella, in order to persuade her to grant him "grace." That process begins in sensation or feelings (pleasure and pain), moves toward knowledge, and culminates in action. He is a fool because his initial attempts to engender pleasure through study ignore the matters of the heart by referring to "others' leaves." In the study requisite to discovering "inventions fine," he is more likely to move Stella to visit her family library in order appreciate the subtlety of his wit rather than obtain her solicitude. But by looking into his heart, he is more likely to discover the matter for a sensory topos from which words naturally issue in order to "make sense" of the feeling, and from such words a genuine, empathetic, human understanding "might" be possible. That is, conveying or transmitting the sincerity of his own feelings (a romantic notion) is not to be his poetic end; Sidney instead seeks a credibility derived from the sharing of some distinctly human feeling (a credibility that might result in the desired action). Consider the process Astrophil describes:

Pleasure might cause her reade: What is it that his love will be reading? His poem? If that is the case, what provokes the pleasure that might cause her to read the poem to begin with? Pleasure could follow from merely the gift of the poem, from the desire to read the poem for pleasure's sake; but if that is so, curiosity might be just as likely a culprit as pleasure to cause her to read. His pain, that is, would not be as evident to her in receiving the poem as it would be in having read the poem. In any event, pleasure derived from reading the poem cannot cause one to read the poem (unless one studies the poem, and "studying inventions fine," as Astrophil discovers, does not generate knowledge).

But, and for the moment, let us disregard the previous paragraph and suppose that she does read the poem as a result of the pleasure it causes because of, for example, its clever verse or engaging conceits. Having read the poem, then, what might she "know"? His heart? If so, is it really knowledge she gains, or does she simply learn something of the earnest desires of an articulate, sincere, and impassioned gentleman? No, the pleasure of which he speaks is a result of, not the cause of, the poem; the pleasure can only be a result of having read the poem.

Reading might make her know: What Stella "reads," then, will be *her* heart, just as Astrophil discovers that it is his heart that he must look to in order to write. And the knowledge she discovers there will be of her own invention in the sense that it proceeds from her own (aesthetic) experience of another's feelings, the matter of knowledge, embodied in language.

Knowledge might pitie winne: The knowledge produced is inextricable from its aesthetic origins, is fundamentally human (in that "it" can only be shared by humans through language) and rhetorical in the sense that through delight or pain, it teaches, then moves. "Pitie," or empathy or compassion, for another person is part and parcel of the knowledge produced; such knowledge is drawn from a sensory topos that *might* be commonly sensed, and that knowledge then *might* result in a form of action (grace). I have emphasized "might" here because it is repeated four times in the three lines quoted above: as a form of rhetorical action, the poem is ultimately contingent on the actions of another; it might produce the desired end, and it might not.

As words designed to negotiate between the common, communicable sensed experience of the lover and his beloved, the poem Astrophil wants to invent constitutes a form of knowing that grounds itself in the natural processes of human knowing. Between pleasure and knowledge are words that function as both a form of knowing and as an expression of that knowing, though words are never really just an "expression of knowing" in that their expression is rhetorical; they are pointed toward, conditioned by, and subject to the realm of human action. That is to say, then, that words function as both a form of knowing and as an embodiment of knowledge.

Astrophil looks into his heart to write. Sidney looks into his heart as well, but in it he discovers the possibility of humans to make things as they are, and as they are not, discursively—and that includes what humans *might* make of how they know. Astrophil is the conceit or figure that Sidney discovers. To persuade people of a world wherein deliberate and deliberated makings are (humanly) possible, Sidney avers the rhetorical character of making, or *poeisis* itself. And to authorize the rhetorical character of *poeisis*, Sidney allies his "sunne-burn'd braine" with a well-red / read heart that, together, refigure and reenact the idea of Ciceronian rhetoric.

The process Sidney enacts in the above sonnet is described simply in *A Defence of Poetry* in the claim that "the poet . . . doth not learn a conceit out of a matter, but maketh matter for a conceit" (99): Astrophil makes the matter of the heart the matter of poetry by embodying it within a conceit, his "Muse," (as opposed to learning a conceit from someone else's matter, as in Antonius's sunburn analogy); Sidney, however, makes both conceits matter by making them the matter of his own conceit, Astrophil—a speaking figure of speech. This act of making matter for a conceit, then, is the activity proper to what Sidney terms in the *Defence* "indeed right poets" (80). Sidney carefully brings his conception of "indeed right poets" to the fore by comparing them to two other kinds of poets. He notes that, of poets, there have been, historically, "three general kinds" (80), and he defines each on the basis of what matter each imitates. The first type of poets, *vates,* or "prophets," are the "representers" who "imitate the unconceivable excellencies of God" (80); examples include David, Solomon, and Moses as well as Orpheus, Amphion, and Homer (80). Significantly, Sidney is content to leave the vatic or inspired model of poetic imitation in antiquity since he prefers to describe making rather than the representation or "prophesying" of God's "excellencies" as the actions befitting a "right poet." He observes, for example, that of the "divine names" given to the poet by the Romans and Greeks, "the one of prophesying [*vates*], the other of making [*poeta*]," "the name of making is fit" for the kind of poet he is describing (99). In his subsequent critique of Plato, moreover, he notes that the good philosopher "attributeth unto poetry more than myself do, namely, to be a very inspiring of a divine force, far above man's wit" (109). The second category includes the poetic "counterfeiters" (or imitators) of philosophy: moral, natural, astronomical, and historical (for example, Cato, Lucretius, Manilius, and Lucan, respectively; 80). Each in this second group of poets, however, allows his making to be constrained "within the fold of the proposed subject, and takes not the course of his own invention" (80).

Sidney's third category of poet, the group he calls "indeed right poets," "be they which most properly do imitate to teach and delight, and to imitate borrow nothing of what is, hath been, or shall be; but range, only reined with learned discretion, into the divine consideration of what may be, and should be" (80). Unlike historians, geometricians, and philosophers, poets need not be hindered by the "artificial rules, which still are compassed within the circle of a question according to the proposed matter" (78).[12] "Only the poet," he continues,

> disdaining to be tied to any such subjection, lifted up with the vigor of his own invention, doth grow in effect into another Nature, in making things either better than Nature bringeth forth, or, quite anew, forms such as never were in Nature. . . . So (the poet) goeth hand in hand with Nature, not enclosed within the narrow warrant of her gifts, but freely ranging within the zodiac of his own wit. (78)

But what might be "divine" about a "divine consideration" that takes as its subject matter the zodiac of human wit? What might be divine about a creative process that expressly rejects the notion that it can represent the "unconceivable excellencies of God?" Fully aware of the implications of the power he is granting not simply to the poet but also to humankind, Sidney pauses to acknowledge the Maker of both nature and the poet:

> Neither let it be deemed too saucy a comparison to balance the highest point of man's wit with the efficacy of nature; but rather give right honour to the heavenly Maker of that maker, who having made man to His own likeness, set him beyond and over all the works of that second nature: which in nothing he showeth so much as in poetry, when with a divine breath he bringeth things forth surpassing her doings. (81)

The poetic process is itself an imitation of God's generative powers; in a sense, the pious earthly maker imitates the generative Word of the poet's Maker. Though an analogous imitation of God's creative powers, the matter for the poet is always at one human remove from God and God's creation, and is germane to "the second nature" of mankind (all of mankind, not just the poet).[13] Recall Puttenham's claim in *The Arte of English Poesie* (1588): "It is therefore of Poets thus to be conceived, that if they be able to deuise and make all these things of them selues, without any subiect of veritie, that they be (by maner of speech) as creating gods."[14] The distinction Sidney makes between God's nature and humankind's "second nature" parallels the two aspects of Cicero's nature identified by Ernesto Grassi: "[Nature] is in its own way *mirabile,* or hidden, and cannot be known in its most basic reality. . . . The second aspect of nature is that one that is revealed through human activity [*virtus*]."[15] Even if it is assumed that God were knowable through the Nature of His own making as something distinct and separable from human intelligence, Sidney clearly dismisses that potential out of hand for the more attractive possibility of exploring that second nature peculiar to humankind in action, but particularly in rhetorical action. Human beings, or more appropriately, humans becoming thus, are the matter of knowledge; it is in this sense that we might say that Sidney is not a humanist but a humanistic philosopher-poet.

Human action is the stuff of Sidney's humanistic learning, and it is on this basis that he claims "mens manners" to be "the supreme knowledge"(99) and "moral doctrine, the chief of all knowledges" (99). The poet "show[s] doings, some to be liked, some to be misliked" (88); these "doings," furthermore, are not "perfect patterns" (88) but "doings" such as those Cicero figures forth in the persons of Antonius and Crassus—patterns of rhetorical action. (Again, recall Puttenham's rejection of the poet as maker according "to any paterne or mould as the Platonicks with their *Idees* do phantastically suppose.")[16] These less-than-perfect patterns of action, patterns of action that bear endless testimony to humankind's "erected wit . . . and infected will" (79), are precisely *what* Sidney claims "standeth in that idea or fore-conceit of the work, and not in the work itself" (79). Having suffused the "idea or fore-conceit" of the work with the rationale of idealism, critics have used, for the most part, and paradoxically, the work itself as the means to discovering the poet's idea. But Sidney's assertion that the poet offers "what might best be" indicates that probable action, rather than rational certainty, "standeth in that idea or fore-conceit of the work." Patterns of action, that is, *how* humans may act, are Sidney's "fore-conceit"; patterns of action provide the matter from which the poet invents. The "idea or fore-conceit" he refers to is not a mental or ideal image apprehended by reason, not a *what* or a thing, but the "delivering forth" itself, the act of telling as that act is embodied in a tale; it is in the telling, not in what is told, that the reader might "learn aright why and how that maker made" (79). Sidney's subsequent caution "to use the narration" (or the telling) to invent in conjunction with the claim that the main "idea" of the work is not within the work itself points, significantly, more toward the reader's circumstances and abilities than toward the poet's genius. For the poet's invention is not only founded on the contingencies of human action, but as we saw in Astrophil's repeated use of the word "might," the persuasiveness of the poet's invention is always contingent on the reader. In this way, the "speaking picture of poesy" is not valorized for having spoken but for its capacity to continue to speak, and it speaks continually to the reader because of the vivid images that "inhabit the memory and judgment" of the listener. (Again, memory is presented here as a faculty of the sensitive soul containing sensory topoi, not a rational faculty that perceives only forms.)[17]

Perhaps the more appropriate, and less cumbersome, term for the rhetorico-poetic, ethos-based, Ciceronian moral philosophy that poets such as Spenser and Sidney enacted is *topical* philosophy, as opposed to critical or analytical philosophy. The rhetorico-poetic invention Sidney dramatizes in the first sonnet of *Astrophil and Stella* and defends in his *Defence,* and that Spenser "contains" within the covers of *The Shepheardes Calender,* does not aim at "judgment" or "well-knowing" narrowly conceived of as critique borne of analysis but at a judgment subject to action or "well-doing" that is invented and known within rhetorical inquiry, an activity firmly rooted in the drama of human relations and contingent on one's ability to empathize with another. The poet's abilty to persuade the reader toward well-doing ultimately relies on the reader finding the poet's narrative credible with reference to a sensory topic, a feeling common to human experience. Of course, the poet's credibility might rely on the reader's apprehension of the cleverness of his conceit, a conceit borrowed or that can be explained with reference to some thing else in this world. But the poet's credibility might also rely on his ability to move the reader to find the experiential loci or places—the topics—from which the poet both drew the matter of his verse, and upon which he makes his appeal to the reader.

William Temple's *Analysis:*
"Thus Your Proposition Is Wrong"

As John Webster notes in the editorial apparatus to his translation of William Temple's *Analysis,* Temple's willingness "to disagree strongly with his employer— [bears] testimony to Sidney's intellectual generosity as well as to Temple's own critical integrity" (27). Yet Temple's "critical integrity," like E. K.'s, ultimately relies on the presumption that the matter of poetry owes its philosophic vitality to all the matter of learning that is, of necessity, not-poetic. Armed with Ramus's method, Temple is able to analyze and judge with certainty the truthfulness and falseness of every claim, every argument, every assumption—in short, every aspect—of Sidney's *Defence.* In terms of form, Temple's critical integrity is peerless; the moral integrity of Temple's *Analysis,* however, relies on something quite different from "a knowledge of a man's self in his ethic and politic considerations . . . with the ending end of well-doing, not well-knowing only."

The story goes that it was William Temple (1555–1627) who, as Sir Philip Sidney's recently appointed secretary, held the knight-errant in his arms as he died of the thigh wound inflicted some months earlier in Zutphen, Belgium, while fighting the Spaniards. Sidney and Temple appear to have become acquainted after Temple sent him a copy of his *P. Rami dialecticae libri duo* (1584), which he dedicated to Sidney and which Sidney warmly received.[18] Temple had begun to make a name for himself by defending Ramus's method against the attacks of Everard Digby some years earlier.[19] Howell asserts that Temple was, "next to MacIllmaine, the greatest Ramistic logician among sixteenth-century Englishmen" (203). After Sidney's death, he became involved in some minor intellectual and political intrigues, published a Ramistic analysis of twenty psalms, then went on to become the provost of Trinity College in Dublin and a member in the Irish House of Commons for Dublin University. He was knighted in 1622. Whether the relationship between Sidney and Temple was as a patron to his subject, employer to his employee, or based on mutual respect and friendship is impossible to know. What is clear, however, are the acute intellectual differences between them. Temple's dedication of his *Dialecticae* to Sidney, and the latter's warm reception of the same notwithstanding, Temple's *Analysis* of Sidney's *Defence* indicates that, if and when questions regarding the most effective and most virtuous modes of learning were discussed between them, they probably agreed to disagree on the most fundamental matters—such as the matter of knowledge itself.

In all likelihood, Temple had never seen Sidney's *Defence* when he dedicated his *Dialecticae* to him in 1584. And one wonders whether he might have still chosen to do so had he been aware of it, for it is clearly from men like Temple that Sidney defends poetry. For throughout the *Defence,* from his opening remarks on Pugliano's weakness as a "logician" to the characterization of philosophers as method-following "schoolmen," to his facetious use of logic's terminology in his handling of the parts of poetry throughout the *Defence* (for example, parts, whole, specials, etc.), Sidney clearly shows that the scholar's penchant for "order" is detrimental to "freely ranging within the zodiac of his own wit" (*Defence,* 78). When the *Defence* did become known to Temple, he no doubt saw himself in its pages in Sidney's recurring complaints about the "methodical proceeding" (91) of philosophers:

> These men casting largess as they go, of definitions, divisions, and distinctions, with a scornful interrogative do soberly ask whether it be possible to find any path so ready to lead a man to virtue as that which teacheth what virtue is: and teach it not only by delivering forth his very being, his causes and effects, but also making known his enemy, vice, which must be destroyed, and his cumbersome

servant, passion, which must be mastered; by showing the generalities that con-
taineth it, and the specialties that are derived from it; lastly by plain setting down
how it extendeth itself out of the limits of a man's own little world. (83)

Sidney's objections notwithstanding, and secure (or certain) in the power and effi-
cacy of logic to gauge the absolute truthfulness or falseness of Sidney's argument,
Temple proceeds undaunted to define, divide, distinguish, and methodically dis-
pose Sidney's arguments "plainly" according to its generalities, specialities, causes
and effects, and so on.

Consider, for example, the following passage from Temple's *Analysis,* which I
have quoted at length in order to provide a general sense of Temple's Ramistic
interpretation of the *Defence:*

> Your treatise *On Poetry* consists partly in a confirmation of the true nature of
> poetry, partly in a refutation of calumny.
>
> To amplify the praise of poetry, the confirmation of truth is set out through
> several arguments.
>
> The first argument is from adjunct. It is concluded in a full syllogism of the
> second figure:

> In slandering the most ancient discipline and parent of all other disciplines,
> philosophers cannot escape the charge of ungratefullness.
>
> Poetry is the oldest discipline and the parent of all other disciplines.
>
> In slandering poetry, therefore, philosophers cannot escape the charge of un-
> gratefullness.

> Proposition: "And first, truly to al them that professing learning inueigh against
> Poetry, may iustly be obiected, that they goe very neer to vngratefulnes." This is
> illustrated by a double comparison of likes, the first to a hedgehog, the second
> to a viper.
>
> Assumption: partly "who, hauing beene the first of that Country that made
> pens deliuerers of their knowledge to their posterity, may iustly chalenge to bee
> called the Fathers of learning," and partly "for not only in time they had this pri-
> ority (although in it self antiquity be venerable) but went before them, as causes
> to frame with their charming sweetnes the wild vntamed wits to an admiration
> of knowledge."

The first part of this assumption, dealing with antiquity, is confirmed by the induc-
tion of the specials:

> The poetry of Musaeus, Homer, Hesiod, Orpheus, Linus, is older than all dis-
> ciplines.
>
> Poetry, therefore, is the oldest discipline.

> I know that the first term of this last enthymeme has been argued by very
> learned men. Nevertheless, I believe that the discipline of mathematics, which
> the well-nigh most ancient Hebrews inscribed in certain columns, is older than
> the poetry; unless perhaps poets flourished in the times of Noah. (65, 67)[20]

The above passage demonstrates Temple's "invention" of an argument. Having
invented the argument of Sidney's *Defence* according to the rules of logic, and
orderly disposed them thus, Temple judges them. He attempts to undercut the
validity of the whole of Sidney's argument simply on his belief that "mathematics
. . . is older than poetry." Whether these "columns" are older or more venerable
than Scripture (which Sidney cites as the oldest form of learning, noting David's
Psalms, Solomon's Song of Songs, Moses, Deborah, and Job), Temple does not say.
His privileging of mathematics over verbal arts is indicative of the Ramist procliv-
ity to raise forms, numbers, and reason's ability to apprehend such "essences" over
the inherent ambiguity of language (Ramus himself spent the last decade of his life
musing on numbers).[21]

The privileging of forms, numbers, and reason's ability to apprehend such
essences unencumbered by sensory matter, significantly, points to a central issue in
this controversy over learning. As we saw in chapter 3, E. K. could define the poet
as maker only in the sense that the poet makes verses; as a result, the poet is a slave
to poetic forms and genres and more a parasite of true learning than a maker of
knowledge. Temple, similarly, defines the poet as a "fiction-maker" (67) who does
not invent knowledge but creates fictions that imitate "nature":

> And yet truly (most noble Sidney) this argument of yours from effect does not
> make poetry the parent of other arts [that is, poetry is not the efficient cause of
> other arts]. For the admiration of knowledge to which poetry gives birth indi-
> cates that learning had already been created. For how can there be admiration
> of something that does not exist in nature? . . . But the question is really not
> whether poetry should have moved men to study a discipline that had already
> been established (*observatae*), but whether disciplines were first invented as a
> result of poetry. The study of a discipline that has already been established can
> proceed from admiration; but the invention of such disciplines has another
> cause. (67, 69)

Fraunce's exposition of invention (above) will suffice as a general guideline to what
Temple refers to here as "another cause"; specifically, the intuited apprehension of
a form as a material cause "[not] subiect to sence, but onely understoode by reason"
(22r). Temple, in other words, validates what Sidney classified as the second kind
of poets, those who imitate "within the fold of the proposed subject, and takes
not the course of his own invention" (80); and this Temple does by subjecting
humankind to the *observation* and imitation of an objectified nature, a nature that

is understood to operate under rational principles that numbers rather than words best express. In light of the formal essences apprehended in their entirety and Temple's remarks about the primacy of mathematics, Temple attempts to subjugate poetry to *subjects,* that is, to disciplines wherein knowledge might be demonstrated, methodically.

Sidney anticipates this line of argument in the *Defence* when he offers a proof drawn from the "infinite proofs of the strange effects of this poetical invention" (93). Specifically, he recalls the story of Menenius Agrippa, who

> when the whole people of Rome had resolutely divided themselves from the senate, with apparent show of utter ruin, though he were (for that time) an excellent orator, came not among them upon trust of figurative speeches or cunning insinuations, *and much less with far-fet maxims of philosophy, which (especially if they were Platonic) they must have learned geometry before they could well have conceived;* but forsooth he behaves himself like a homely and familiar poet. He telleth them a tale. (93; emphasis added)

Sidney's contrasting of Platonic geometry to tale telling indicates one significant question that arises with the subordination of poetry to imitation and words to ideal forms: Which offers the most effective form of learning? On the basis that "moving is of a higher degree than teaching," Sidney notes that the philosopher's "methodical proceeding" is so obscure and tedious that "no man but to him that will read him, and read him with attentive studious painfulness" can hope to learn from him: "For who will be taught, if he not be moved with desire to be taught?" (*Defence,* 91). Sidney also castigates the method of philosophers when he observes that

> after the philosophers had picked out of the sweet mysteries of poetry the right discerning true points of knowledge, the forthwith putting it in method, and making a school-art of that which the poets did only teach by a divine delightfulness, beginning to spurn at their guides, like ungrateful prentices, were not content to set up shops for themselves, but sought by all means to discredit their masters, the less they could overthrow them, the more they hated them. (107)

Temple's analysis of this particular passage is revealing in that it attempts "to discredit" poets as effective teachers. Indeed, Temple's analysis falls prey to just the problem we confronted in the first sonnet of *Astrophil and Stella.* The question there was, What provokes the pleasure that might cause her to read the poem? How can the pleasure of a text *cause* someone to read if the text is unread? And having read the poem, then, what might she know?

Temple responds to this problem by conceding that though "the cause of teaching is to be valued more highly than teaching itself," he is not willing to "concede the same for the effect of teaching" (115). That is, Temple sees "mouing" to be the effect rather than the cause of learning: "For if we should consider effect only in terms of the relation it holds to cause, then since an effect is itself produced by a cause, it will in fact be either inferior to its cause, or equal at best. Thus your Proposition is wrong" (115).

Significantly, Temple urges Sidney thus to "keep the issue of 'moving' distinct from that of arguments disposed by axiom, syllogism, and method" because "we are only taught by that which brings about some sort of knowledge in the mind; yet this does not happen by any 'moving,' but only by the force of illumination of an argument, ordered through the rules of judgment" (115). This contemplative "force of illumination of an argument" corresponds to Fraunce's apprehension of the "internall forms" or essences of things that are "hardly understoode, and difficult to make plaine by speaking," which, though he termed them the "materiall cause" of knowledge, he made a point of separating from sensory matter. The body, the particulars it senses, the pleasure and pain it feels, and the pity it may show others is severed thus from the matter of knowledge. Poetry, its metaphors, the sensory matter in which metaphors originate and in which poetry persuades the reader to "locate" and draw forth arguments (or actions), are effectively severed thus from the matter of knowledge.

This severance suggests, then, why Temple insists on supplanting Sidney's use of the word "virtue" with "felicity" throughout his *Analysis:* moral action, virtuous action is not the "ending end" of Temple's philosophy, at least not directly. Instead, a more abstract notion of felicity defined primarily as contemplative "well-knowing" is the "ending end" of his pedagogy. For at "the most general level of argument" (137) for Temple, questions about the desire to instruct people in the manners of "right action" in terms of the occasion, people, place, and so on have no significant role. And rhetoric has the unfortunate liability of being contingent and subject to the occasions, people, places, and so on; consequently, the rhetorical arts can reveal "only . . . the image of a thought" (79). As with Fraunce, Ramus's syllogistic method is to be the only arbiter of "truthfulness," which is always presumed to be a good, and falseness, which is always presumed to be an evil. This accounts for why, in closing his *Analysis,* Temple asks his noble reader to "pardon whatever offense" he might have inadvertently raised if he "suggested anything that is less than accurate (*accuratum*)" (175), for *accuracy* can be measured according to the rules and method of logic. The moral import of such an analysis in terms of what consequences it might bear for others, however, remains largely a nonquestion, as it is presumed that truth is formal, categorical, ascertainable, and merely decorated with the "ornaments of rhetoric" rather than probable, contingent, material or sensible, and invented through the processes of rhetoric. As with E. K. and Fraunce, Temple effectively removes poetry from the realm of human learning by subjecting it to the critical glare of reason while simultaneously forgiving it whatever methodological shortcomings it might have by declaring its inexplicability to be the product of a "certain divine and excellent gift" (175).

The late Tudor conversation on the rhyme and reason of poetry is remarkable in that poetry itself plays a defining role in the conversation; yet it is the art of rhetoric, specifically Ciceronian rhetoric, that serves as an ever-present subtext for Bryskett, Spenser, Sidney, Temple, and Fraunce. At issue in the debate is the capacity of poetry to teach, and yet, in order to address this question, all of the above authors appeal to an interpretation of Cicero in their attempts to ornament or order learning. In the *Defence,* Sidney repeatedly associates philosophers with "poet-haters" (88), keenly aware that the philosopher's reordering of humanistic learning subordinates and diminishes poetry and the learning it promises to "methodical proceeding[s]." Though distrustful of poetry, Fraunce and Temple both attempt to circumvent such charges by offering poetry a place "far above man's wit." By redefining poetry as a "divine inspiration," Ramists were able to cede poetry an honorific title as a transmitter of essences. But because these transmissions were obscured by passion and passion's sporadic, "cryptic," "disorderly order[ing]," of reason's rules, they were also able simultaneously to dismiss poetry as a form of learning "of no great weight and importaunce." Consequently, poetry was relegated to exemplifying an "immutable" reason that could only be attained by way of Ramus's syllogistic method.

It is within the context of this controversy, this debate about the matter and form of learning, that Spenser chose to pen a dialogue designed to affect the foreign policy of Her Majesty's government. As a ranking civil servant in his queen's service with vested or propertied interests in his country's foreign policy, Spenser sought to reform Ireland by persuading Elizabeth and her court to enlarge and intensify England's war on the Irish. Contemporary critical narratives on Spenser's dialogue characteristically subordinates this particular poetical effort to the immutable rule of reason dubbed "ideology." Typically, however, rhetoric's capacity to challenge and reform conventional wisdom productively—that is, toward real and practical ends—has not played much of a role in configuring the ideological bubble within which Spenser wrote. But perhaps the dominant ideological configuration of Spenser's views toward Ireland is more telling of the impotence of current critical efforts to affect important and grave public matters than it is of the rationale underpinning Spenser's poetic efforts.

CHAPTER SEVEN

———— ❖ ————

TELLING TALES OUT OF SCHOOL

On Spenser's *View*

*The existence of virtue depends entirely on its use; and its noblest
use is the government of the State.*

—*Cicero,* De re publica

UNTIL STEPHEN GREENBLATT's *Renaissance Self-Fashioning* appeared in 1980,
Edmund Spenser's *A View of the Present State of Ireland* seems to have existed
largely as an embarrassment for lovers of his poetry. The stern, violent, and com-
plete vanquishing of the Irish that the dialogue advocates was granted either brief
mention or complete omission from most previous treatments of Spenser's poetic
vision.[1] Greenblatt, however, refers to the *View* as part of his critical efforts to chal-
lenge what the previous generations of "humanist" critics chose to overlook—or
chose to accept or approve—namely, the ideological origins and political implica-
tions of Spenser's aesthetic. With this shift in critical emphasis toward the ideologi-
cal, away from the sublime, it soon became apparent that whatever moralizing
Spenser hoped to accomplish in his day was no longer tenable for a new genera-
tion of scholars.

A Brief Critical Narrative

Although the evaluative criteria to which Spenser's work is held have undergone
significant revisions in the last decades, the philosophical setting against which the
poet and his aesthetic are set has remained unchanged in the most general sense.
That is, the broader, underlying narrative into which Spenser is placed, and against
which his rhetorical actions are examined—the historical narrative of Renaissance
humanism—has undergone no significant paradigm shift, at least not in terms of
Spenser studies. Specifically, as a humanist, Spenser continues to be understood as

a philosophical idealist, and this premise is granted, in part, as a historical given. Greenblatt, for example, claims that because Spenser's rhetoric always refers to a "reality as given by ideology [that] always lies safely outside the bounds of art, in a different realm, distant, infinitely powerful, perfectly good," his is an art that is "profoundly *undramatic*."[2] Echoing Greenblatt, Patricia Coughlan recasts this sentiment by dubbing Spenser "the most monological of writers," whose authoritarian depiction of his sociopolitical "reality . . . consistently presents physical actuality as inferior, illusory in a Platonic sense, and as the locus of dangerous temptation."[3] It is precisely Spenser's supposed inability to adhere to his idealistic mandate when confronted with the "physical actuality" of the Irish that Annabel Patterson considers to be characteristic of his existential "ambivalence" and that Elizabeth Fowler points toward as evidence for the "failure" of Spenser's moral philosophy.[4]

Consider now Èmile Legouis's 1926 assessment of the poet in light of the *View*:

> That the poets' poet was in many respects a practical man, by no means unable to cope with crabbed and even ugly problems of his day, we have a . . . proof in his *View of the Present State of Ireland*, a pamphlet much in the vein of Machiavelli. . . . Surely, we have here the work of a clear-minded, cool-tempered man of action.
>
> Yet even here the idealist may still be detected. He betrays himself by his very pitilessness; are not often idealists, when they have to deal with human problems, the most unfeeling of men? With their eyes lifted up to the glorious vision that shines in the distance they will run towards it, never caring if they must cut their way through poor suffering human flesh. To purify Ireland from its evils, Spenser would not have hesitated to exterminate the natives. Do not imagine, however, that he utters such ideas with the passion and vehemence of a fanatic. He remains collected and dignified all through. The contrast between the mercilessness of his schemes and the well-bred elegance of his style is perhaps the most characteristic feature of this pamphlet.[5]

This eighty-year-old account offers a figuring of Spenser remarkably similar to the one evident within Greenblatt and others; the major difference is that Spenser has become less of an idealist than a sometimes sycophantic, sometimes temperate ideologue. But the practice of referring and subordinating Spenser's moral compass to a philosophical idealism remains a constant. Though the ends toward which this historical narrative on the ends of Spenser's rhetoric have changed dramatically, the parameters of the history told have not.[6] With the change in critical direction, the *View* is no longer an embarrassment but a remarkably tractable site for the explication and confirmation of the limits, sins, and inherent contradictions of the author's particular brand of idealism.

There are, however, consequences to maintaining this portrait of Spenser as an idealist, regardless of how that idealism is critiqued. One such consequence is that virtue tends to become "de-activated." Historian Nicholas Canny notes that "most historians as well as literary scholars would accept that [Spenser's *View*], like all reform texts of the sixteenth century, had ultimately to be justified on religious grounds."[7] Canny is right: most would agree with him that the dialogue's "greater end" was the "transformation of Ireland into a truly Protestant society." Affixing "morality" to an inflexible religious dogma primarily means that virtue may be referred to certain precepts and so *known;* moral virtue, judgment, and choice thus become less a matter contingent on the probable, practicable realm of human affairs than a facility to adhere to a rigid intellectual schematic regardless of circumstances. With the intellectual landscape of the poet neatly laid out, mapped, and framed, the actions available to the poet's language become significantly diminished. By representing virtue in Spenser's texts as a concept with reference to certain ideals—by subordinating moral philosophy to philosophical idealism as a historical matter of record—criticism all but negates the *drama* of Spenser's work and the historical drama his work participates in. The curtain comes down on Spenserian ethics, as it were, because the (rhetorical) actions of a text are not "substantive" or material but illusory (in a Platonic sense): dependent on, inferior to, and theoretically separable from the constancy or rational consistency of an ideology. With the *idea* of Spenser's world view so firmly fixed in the critic's mind, the great interest in his work, as Coughlan notes, "resides in the appalling difficulty he finds in achieving . . . transcendence, and the complexity with which it is necessary to construct it imaginatively."[8] Why it might be profitable to chart the course of the poet's failed, "ambiguous," and politically undesirable imaginative achievement is itself a question seldom addressed explicitly.

Not only is virtue deactivated, but so is the "rhetoric of" Spenser's texts. Indeed, discussions regarding the rhetoric of Spenser's text are relegated to a similar kind of fate as virtue. "Rhetorical moves," like ethical virtue, become codified as a subset of an ideology. Invariably, discussions concerning the rhetoric of the *View* are accompanied by an articulation of Spenser's real argument—or, at least, an articulation of the philosophical or ideological principles from which his argument is presumed to proceed. Anne Fogarty claims that Spenser's dialogue advertises "the triumph of rhetoric over circumstances" because the rhetoric of the dialogue negotiates, defends and "[indemnifies] the political ideology relayed in the *View*."[9] In the schematic implicit in Fogarty's comment, one may see the diminished moral capacity of rhetorical action: the rhetoric of a text does not owe its vitality to circumstances—to people, places, actions, occasions—but to ideological abstractions. Thus, the moral consequences of the rhetoric of Spenser's texts do not

follow from the poet's involvement in the world but from his attempt to circum-
vent that involvement. The presumed primacy of an ideal and distinctly Protestant
framework governing the choices of Spenser's rhetoric relegates moral philosophy
—ethics and politics—to a cumbersome afterthought subordinate to contempla-
tion of the divine. Less a deliberate choice based on an assessment of the immedi-
ate circumstances than a preprogrammed form of action, the rhetoric of Spenser's
texts becomes an object of cynicism—and ultimately indifference.

With respect to the *View,* Spenser's decision to frame arguments that address
his sovereign's policies regarding the Irish within a dialogue remains a continual
source of dissatisfaction, if not suspicion, for most scholars. As a literary genre, dia-
logues traditionally promise "to teach, move, and delight" through fiction, but
because they exploit the figurative dimension of language, they are prone to digres-
sions (or what appear to be digressions), analogies, and anecdotes, and because
they insist that the reader consider at least two sides of an issue *as that issue devel-
ops,* rhetorically, it seems their informal and variegated method of persuasion is
doomed to be always something less than cogent, at least for the contemporary
critic. Indeed, that persuasion is the aim of Spenser's *View* is often a cause for alarm
in itself: by "seductively" couching or cloaking the "logic" of his "analysis" of the
Irish people, and the English in Ireland, within the fiction of a dialogue, the text
has been described as a "cleverly crafted" attempt to "manipulate" and "dupe" its
original audience into believing or doing something that, if viewed analytically
rather than figuratively (or rhetorically), presumably would appear to be unreason-
able to a rational being.[10] The rhetoric of Spenser's *View,* including its rhetorical
form as a dialogue, skillfully conspires to make palatable the ruthless, virulent, and
bloody imperialism underlying his proposals for the reformation of Ireland, or so
the story goes.

This critical urge to parse out the rhetoric of the *View,* however, is not based
entirely on either the stories told about humanism and Spenser or a cynical atti-
tude toward rhetoric. Nor does license to parse out the rhetoric of texts from their
ideological matter solely rely on the presumed primacy of a Platonic humanism as
a historical given. Reference to the rhetoric of texts also inheres to the *formal*
dimensions of most instances of literary criticism itself, which, significantly, appears
determined to subordinate the rhetoric of its own arguments to the rational con-
sistency of critical methodologies. We have seen one telling consequence of this
already in the observations that Spenser's "cleverly crafted" rhetorical performance
is designed to "manipulate" and "dupe" its original readers into taking action. But
what prevents the contemporary commentator from avoiding the pitfall of suasion?
Plausible responses to the foregoing question may be many and varied, ranging
from a refusal to recognize its legitimacy to the qualified recognition that criti-
cal methods may have a rhetorical force of their own, at least within particular

disciplinary constraints. Another plausible response might arrive in the form of a cynic's resignation, as when Annabel Patterson notes that all of it is "only opinion" anyway.[11]

Sidney and Spenser did not tell tales designed to be told in schools. Whether Spenser, for example, portrays shepherds engaging in civil discourse, or a poet in conversation with his glossarist, whether he attempts to "fashion a gentleman or noble person in vertuous and gentle discipline" or tries to affect his sovereign's policies in Ireland by means of a dialogue, Spenser's rhetorical goals seek to inform and influence the character or ethos of his readers as political animals primarily and explicitly; he wants to teach through delight and move his readers to act in this world. The allegorical indefiniteness of Spenser's "generall end" of *The Faerie Queene* might suggest a movement toward abstraction, but the moral discipline informing Spenser's "fashioning" efforts—that is, the ethical and political "matter" of his work—instead suggests a movement toward civic action. The *View*'s determined involvement with a particular sphere of action indicates both the political origins and aims of Spenser's ethical fashioning.

In the remainder of this chapter, I show how the act of historiography plays a necessary role within Spenser's humanistic moral philosophy, and toward that end, it is helpful to emphasize the inherently, even profoundly, dramatic character of the dialogue, since it is by means of the back and forth of the conversation that qualifications and modifications or amendments are figured or enacted. In the process, the Spenser I create is fundamentally different from the conventional Spenser, but that is because I am bringing a different history into play.

"Matters of Religion Doubtful"

The problem of ruling Ireland effectively was a pressing matter for England at the time of Spenser's writing of the *View* in the summer of 1596. The Irish, though perpetually divided among themselves, had found a quasi-leader in the person of the Hugh O'Neill, Earl of Tyrone, whose threats, appeasements, and rebellion consistently frustrated England's governors and military leaders. Philip II of Spain's repeated pledges of men and financial support to "defend the Catholic religion" loomed over the English, who were again threatened by an Armada in 1597 only to be saved by the weather. The English in Ireland were themselves divided between the "New English" such as Spenser, and the "Old English," who traced their property rights and authority over the Irish back to Henry II's expansion of his rule in Ireland in the twelfth century. Throughout the 1580s and 1590s, furthermore, the English leadership in Ireland was itself less than a model of efficiency.[12] Military and political leaders in Ireland fought among themselves as to the best course of action; corruption, avarice, and cruelty are all hallmarks of English rule in Ireland.

Though there is little question that the "view" advocated by Spenser is a deter-minedly English view of Ireland, there is some question as to whether it is an English view or a Protestant view primarily. The two terms, of course, are not mutually exclusive, but it does matter a great deal as to how one configures this relationship, historically. Is the political character of Spenser's *View* dependent on and a conse-quent of his religious idealism? Or does religion function within the *View* as an aspect or extension of its political aims? Historically, critics have been disinclined to entertain the possibility of the latter on the presumption that the motivating force behind Spenser's body of work derived from a humanist idealism steeped in Protestant doctrine. Though critics may emphasize the "utilitarian" or "pragmatic" dimensions of the *View*, that pragmatism functions as a disconcerting source of "ambivalence" (Patterson), "ambiguity" (Brady and Hadfield), or as an(other) moral failure of Erasmian humanism (Canny, Fowler). There are exceptions, how-ever. Sheila T. Cavanaugh has argued that "as for Aristotle, virtue for Spenser is always essentially an aspect of political life: goodness happens in society; virtuous lives function only in virtuous states" (35).[13] Significantly, however, Cavanaugh does not support this assertion with reference to a moral philosophy of any descrip-tion. The result is that the textual evidence she gathers appears to valorize, and apologize for, a singular, imaginative genius whose "meticulously designed plan for peace . . . emerges as a remarkably calm and objective treatment of a divisive issue" (35). (There is, of course, nothing "objective" about Spenser's *View.*) And William Maley tentatively claims that his "own feeling . . . is that Spenser is a rather reluc-tant royalist; one might even say, an opportunist monarchist" rather than an "unerr-ingly loyal courtier."[14]

Maley's sense of Spenser as a "reluctant royalist" perhaps goes too far. Spenser was no democrat. It might be more appropriate to think of him as a member of "the loyal opposition" regarding his queen's Irish policies. As Brady argues, there may have been nothing original about the course of action Spenser advocates in the *View,* a position Irenius confirms when he says that he offers it not "as a per-fect plot of my own invention . . . but as I have learned and understood the same by the consultations and actions of every wise governor and counselor whom I have sometimes heard treat hereof."[15] But there is little to suggest that Spenser offered an officially sanctioned argument.[16] That Spenser felt compelled to offer the same course of action over two years later in "A Brief Note of Ireland," ad-dressed to "the Queene," suggests that his arguments either were not heeded or contravened official government policy. Furthermore, the fact that Spenser felt compelled to compose this seventy-thousand-word document in order to influ-ence governmental policy suggests that, from his standpoint at least, his audience needed to be persuaded not only that a different course of action was necessary but also that his course of action was the best possible choice given the circumstances—

circumstances he is very careful to portray. The *View* is not an academic exercise in "political thought"; its exigence lies in a state of affairs that directly concerns not only the poet's own well-being and the well-being of England but also, as the *View* vividly shows, the well-being of Ireland under English rule.

In all likelihood, the original or intended audience for the *View* was Queen Elizabeth, her Privy Council, and such nobles and courtiers who might have some influence on the queen's decision-making process. The Privy Council was dominated by the queen's principal, longtime advisor Lord Burghley, William Cecil, and his son, Robert Cecil, whom Burghley was grooming to succeed him. Also on the council was Robert Devereux, earl of Essex. It was Essex who paid for Spenser's funeral in January 1599 in Westminster Abbey, and it is probably Essex to whom Irenius refers when he wishes that a "Lord Lieutenant" be placed in Ireland "such as one I could name, upon whom the eye of all England is fixed and our last hopes now rest" (238).[17] Essex and Cecil do not appear to have been on the best of terms. Whether the *View* fell victim to Burghley's faction within the council, or whether it was involved in a publication-rights controversy, as Jane Brink has argued, is unknown for certain.[18] In any event, when it was entered into the Stationers' Register in April 1598 on the condition that it could be printed on "further authoritie," such authority, whether it was expected to come from Burghley or the author, was not forthcoming.[19] Jonathan Goldberg's contention that the *View* was denied publication because it lays bare the brutality upon which "genuine power" operates "although [speaking] the official language of law and reformation" is provocative, for though the Privy Council may have suppressed the publication of the *View*, it also nominated Spenser to the post of sheriff of County Cork in September 1598.[20]

To be sure, religious concerns were never far removed from the deliberations involved with the affairs of state, and Ireland's dealings with Catholic Spain were no small matter. But it is important to note that, in all probability, Ireland, Spain, and Catholicism in general were not perceived as a threat on the grounds that their faith might prevent English souls from salvation, but that Ireland's "rebellions" and Spain's military force posed a threat to the queen's sovereignty. In his "Brief Note," Spenser reflects this attitude regarding the supportive, subordinate, yet necessary role of religion in civic matters when he states axiomatically that "there can be no conformity of government where [there] is no conformity of religion."[21] In effect, the presumption that Spenser's *View*, as Canny articulated, "had ultimately to be justified on religious grounds" inverts Spenser's axiom, placing "conformitie of religion" in the first position as the primary aim.

Even if one is reluctant to let go of the notion that Spenser was a Protestant first and citizen second, it is difficult to find evidence in the *View* that suggests that he appeals primarily to the religious values of his audience in his efforts to persuade them. Indeed, perhaps the most remarkable quality of the *View* is Spenser's ability to subdue or subsume religious matters to emphasize the political dilemma in-hand. Irenius and Eudoxus agree in the beginning of their dialogue to avoid bas-ing their investigation on the kind of speculation demanded by religion. Though there have been "good plots and wise councils cast already about reformation of that realm," Irenius says that the majority of Englishmen are unwilling to exam-ine the present state of Ireland because

> they say it is the fatal destiny of that land that no purposes whatsoever are meant for her good, will prosper or take good effect, which whether it proceed from the *very Genius* of the soil, or influence of the stars, or that Almighty god hath not yet appointed the time of her reformation or that he reserveth her in this unquiet state still, for some secrete scourge, which shall come by her unto En-gland it is hard to be known yet much to be feared. (43)

Eudoxus, significantly, does not appear to be part of the "they" to which Ire-nius refers, for he is not prepared to accept any of these explanations:

> I would rather think the cause of this evil which hangeth upon the country, to proceed rather of the unsoundness of the councils and plots which you say have been often times laid for her reformation or of faintness in following and effect-ing the same, then of any such fatal course or appointment of god as you mis-deem, but it is the manner of men that when they are fallen into any absurdity or their actions succeed not as they would they are ready always to impute the blame thereof unto the heavens, so to excuse their own follies and imperfec-tions. (44)

This brief exchange is worth considering for several reasons. First, it sets the stage for examining the "manner of men" and their "actions" by resolutely denying the possibility of fate or divine will. The evils are man made, so to speak, and neither blaming them on the heavens nor looking toward the heavens to solve them will help. Second, this exchange points toward the deeply held "fear" of the English motivating this debate; namely, the fear of Spain gaining a foothold on soil so near England. Finally, then, this exchange situates this problem exclusively as an En-glish problem. The character of the Irish present a contingent problem; the pri-mary issue does not rest with them but in the character of the English, whose "unsound" plots consistently fail to bring peace to that land.

Similarly, it is important to note, given Irenius's identification with Spenser's authorial voice, how reluctant Irenius is to discuss "matters of religion doubtful" (138). On both occasions when the topic is raised, religion is mentioned briefly. Irenius excuses himself from delving into it too deeply: "Little have I to say of reli-gion both because the parts thereof be not many, itself being but one, and myself have not much been conversant in that calling, but as lightly passing by I have seen or heard" (136). Though we might be prepared to interpret Irenius's reference to "one" religion as a refusal to accept Roman Catholicism as a possible means for salvation, the conversation that follows does not warrant such an interpretation. For example, Irenius makes a distinction between the doctrine one might profess and the Christian faith in general. Though, initially, the fault Irenius finds in religion in Ireland is that "they are all papists by their profession," their chief fault is their ignorance about religion in general: "Ye would rather think them *Atheists* or infidels but not one amongst a hundred knoweth any ground of religion any article of his faith" (136). As the following passage indicates, neither the papacy nor ignorance of religious matters sits well with Irenius, and yet he is willing to excuse the Irish folk for their misguided ways:

> The general fault cometh not of any late abuse either in the people or their priests who can teach no better then they know nor show no more light then they have seen but in the first institution and planting of religion in all that realm . . . in the time of Pope *Celestine.* . . . In which Pope's time and long before it is certain that religion was generally corrupted with their popish trumpery. Therefore what other could they learn then such trash as was taught them. And drink of that cup of fornification with which the purple harlot had then made all nations drunken. (137)

Eudoxus, however, recoils at such disrespectful talk about "that good pope" since he had brought "such a great people to Christendom. . . . If that were ill," he asks, "what is good?" (137). Irenius must admit then that the "general profession" of Christianity they make will encourage "that mighty Saviour [to] work salvation in many of them" (137). In any event, Irenius finds it easier to blame the ancient Church than to find fault with the current inhabitants of the land. And on the grounds of his admission that perhaps Catholics, too, will be saved, his remark about "one" religion might be based less in the factioning of Christianity than it is an avowal of Christian religion in general.

Eudoxus, however, resists Irenius's attempts to spare the modern Irish of blame for their "defect" in religion. If neither the ignorance of the people nor their priests might be faulted but the "first ordinance and institution" of religion in Ireland, then the fault has not changed "but the fault's master" (138). When presented with this question about who or what is really at fault, Irenius makes an abrupt and surprising observation:

> That which ye blame *Eudox.* is not I suppose any fault of will in these godly fathers which have charge thereof nor any defect of zeal for reformation hereof but [is] in convenience of time and troublous occasions wherewith that wretched realm hath continually been turmoiled. For instruction in religion needeth quiet

times and ere we seek to settle a sound discipline in the clergy we must purchase
peace unto the laity, for it is ill time to preach amongst swords. (138)

At once, the focus of the problem shifts from both the Catholicism and general
ignorance of religion to the ineffectualness of English rule in these "times." Ire-
nius's remarks may be seen as another articulation of Spenser's claim that "there
can be no conformitie of government whereis no conformitie of religion." Eudoxus,
at least, appears to interpret it thus, for he asks whether "the care of the soul
[should be] preferred before the care of the body" (139). Irenius admits that, yes,
the "care of the soul and soul matters is to be preferred" (139), but he also stipu-
lates that "in time of reformation," political circumstances take precedence over
the ecclesiastical matters. The "reformation" Irenius has in mind is a political ref-
ormation in which the reform of "matters of religion doubtful" serves a contin-
gent, convenient, and expedient role. Eudoxus later realizes that the responsibility
for care of both the body and the soul ultimately "lieth upon the Prince" (222),
but the ability of the political body to provide care for the soul is ultimately less
important than the *service* an established, uniform religion may perform for the
state. And that service, Irenius contends, is not to be assessed by the Christian creed
it promulgates (though that creed *must* be Christian) but by the establishment of
a well ordered and peaceful common wealth.

Nor does Irenius appear willing to cede the Church of England—and by impli-
cation, the queen—any moral authority based on doctrine. He brashly notes that
"what ever disorders ye see in the Church of England" can also be found in Ireland.
The second time Irenius discusses religion, again reluctantly, he contradicts—or
qualifies—his previous claim that no "defect of zeal for reformation" lies at the
core of Ireland's Catholic ways. He marvels how so many Catholic priests will
come from Europe to Ireland to bring souls to the church of Rome, "whereas our
idle ministers . . . will neither for [material security] nor for any love of god nor
zeal of religion nor for all the good which they may do by winning of many Souls
to god, be drawn forth from their warm nests, and their sweet loves' side" (222).
Ironically, from England's so-called Protestant poet comes the prediction that the
"good old fathers" of the Catholic Church will "rise up in the day of Judgement
to condemn [such Protestant ministers]" (222). On both occasions, the discussion
on religion ultimately takes refuge not in religious doctrine, but in the law of the
land and the queen and her governors' ability to uphold and enforce that law. And
unlike the political reformation, Irenius insists that religious reformation "be not
sought forcibly to be impressed into them with terror and sharp penalties as now
is the manner, but rather delivered and intimated with mildness and gentleness so
it may not be hated before it is understood" (221).

"The Methode of a Poet Historical"

In *De oratore,* Antonius maintains that he has little use for either philosophers or poets: the former are "so inextricably tangled" in the subtleties of dialectic that he admits to understanding not "a single word"; the latter, he says, speak "altogether a different tongue" (2.14.61). The historian, however, offers the orator a good example to follow, for the historian does not "dare to tell anything but the [whole] truth," is impartial, and employs a method that surveys, chronologically and in a fluent and copious manner, "important affairs worth recording" (2.15.62–63). Why some affairs might be worth recording and others not—that is, who determines, and how, the relative importance of past events—Antonius does not reflect on. Beyond the appealing yet abstract notion that history "bears witness to the passing of the ages, sheds light upon reality (*lux veritatis*), gives life to recollection and guidance to human existence, and brings tidings from ancient days" (2.9.52), Antonius does not consider why or how people might employ or exploit history to guide the ever-present now of human activity this way rather than that.

Cicero himself offers a critique of Antonius's historical method in his *De legibus,* a history of the law. At the beginning of the dialogue, Cicero is referred to neither as an orator nor a statesman but as the poet of the "Marius." Atticus raises a question about parts of the "Marius"—"whether they are fiction or fact"—noting that "certain persons . . . demand that you stick to the truth." Cicero responds, saying that "those 'certain persons' . . . display their ignorance by demanding in such a matter the kind of truthfulness expected of a witness in court rather than of the poet." Quintus then asks whether he is right in drawing from his brother's comments and inquires if "different principles are to be followed in history and in poetry." Cicero offers a qualified response: "Certainly, Quintus; for in history the standard by which everything is judged is the truth, while in poetry it is generally the pleasure one gives; however, in the works of Herodotus, the Father of History, and in those of Theopompus, one finds innumerable fabulous tales." Cicero appears to be reluctant to discount the "kind of truthfulness" poets have to offer, for when the poet of the "Marius" is asked to offer a history on the laws, he is quite willing to follow the traditions and tales of the poet. On the second day of the dialogue, for example, Cicero begins by saying, "With Jupiter the Muses commence their song." When asked, "What is the point of that quotation?" by his brother Quintus, Cicero replies, "That here likewise we must commence our discussion with Jupiter and the other immortal gods" (2.3). The affirmation of a historian's conception of truth as the chronicling of persons and events informs, but it neither provides exigency nor guides the history of the laws he tells; immediate circumstance, good will, and (public) utility do offer exigency and a guiding principle. The "nature of man" from which Cicero extracts the "nature of Justice" is inextricable from the historical integrity of present-day and prospective human action.

In his "Letter to Ralegh" accompanying the publication of the first three books of *The Faerie Queene*, Spenser situates the (projected) first twelve books of his epic in "that part which they in Philosophy call Ethice . . . which if I finde to be well accepted, I may be perhaps encoraged, to frame the other part of polliticke." Just as Sidney compares his poet to those philosophers whose "methodicall proceedings" void "learning" of delight, Spenser anticipates that to "some . . . this Methode will seeme displeasaunt, which had rather haue good discipline deliuered plainly in way of precepts, or sermoned at large, as they use, then thus clowdily enwrapped in Allegorical deuises." More precisely, the method Spenser employs is narrative, namely, a "historicall fiction, the which the most part of men delight to read, rather for variety of matter, then for profite of the ensample." Again, like Sidney and Cicero, Spenser compares his "method" to that of the historian:

> For the Methode of a Poet historical is not such, as of an Historiographer. For as an Historiographer discourseth of affayres orderly as they were donne, accounting as well the times as the actions, but a Poet thrusteth into the middest, euen where it most concerneth him, and there recoursing to thinges forepaste, and diuining of thinges to come, maketh a pleasing Analysis of all.

Within the context of the Ramist stranglehold on the currency of terms such as "method" and "Analysis," Spenser no doubt uses these terms ironically; indeed, as Sidney suggests in the *Defence*, the phrase "pleasing Analysis" constitutes an oxymoron from a poet's perspective on Ramism.[22] The poet's aim is neither chronological nor factual accuracy: as Richard Waswo remarks, it is a "method . . . subordinate [and variable] . . . to the purpose. The meanings pointed at through the story are inscribed within the meaning enacted by the story."[23]

The same grounds and "methode" for argumentation that Spenser uses in his epic appear in the *View*. In their attempts to "devise of those evils by which [Ireland] is held," Eudoxus and Irenius agree that the appropriate area of inquiry their conversation should fathom will have something to do with the "manner[s] of men." At Eudoxus's request, Irenius promises to survey "the evils" plaguing Ireland by selecting from those consequent to the private and public actions (that is, ethical and political action) of those involved in this "wretched case":

> The evils which you desire to be recounted are very many. . . . But since you please I will out of that infinite number, reckon but some that are most capital and commonly occurent both in the liefe and conditions of private men. And also in management and public affairs and policy. (45)

This method of inquiry meets Eudoxus's approval, and he asks Irenius to "tell [those evils] . . . in the same order that you have now rehearsed them," for the "very matter it self" appears to offer "no better method" (45). Irenius chooses to approach this matter, that is, the private and public actions of those involved in present-day Ireland, by discoursing on the laws, the customs, and religion of Ireland, both past and present.

"Two Equal Contraries:
viz. the English and Irish"

Cavanaugh's willingness to accept, however presumptively, that religion ultimately may not furnish the moral foundations (in the form of ideals or precepts) of Spenser's work, and Maley's suspicion that Spenser is not "an unerringly loyal courtier" lead them to consider the rhetorical effect of history in the *View* more fully than most critics.[24] Indeed, Irenius's lengthy discourse on the ancient origins of the Irish and their laws and customs commonly is disregarded as specious or conjectural, derivative, and digressive. Specifically, Cavanaugh and Maley look to the history Spenser tells to qualify and moderate the hard-line position generally attributed to him. The "Methode of a Poet historical" discussed above and the *View*'s insistence on religion to be an institution in service of political power indicates that Spenser's recourse to history is not incidental or digressive but is itself integral to the *View*. For if neither religion nor current policy offer "grounds" for the plan for reformation he proposes, then history might through its examples of past actions. It is a history, furthermore, that has its origins in "the present state of Ireland," that is, it is a history firmly and self-consciously rooted in present-day circumstances, in "what has been done" until the moment of Spenser's writing. It is a history designed to elicit a specific course of action.

And central to the specific course of action Irenius proposes is the recognition that the Irish are not as "other" as his readers might think.[25] As odd as it may at first seem given the harshness of his proposals, Irenius offers an argument that humanizes the Irish people. The history Irenius relates of the Irish people is remarkable in the picture it draws of an ancient people with laws, customs, and a language eminently conducive to "civil conversation." Indeed, he suggests that an "ample discourse" on the origins of their Brehon law and customs "would be most pleasant and profitable" (81–82), and it is just such a discourse Eudoxus requests at the close of the dialogue when he asks Irenius to "declare unto us those your observations which ye have gathered of the antiquities of Ireland" (231). Irenius is quick to point out, furthermore, that the customs he has chosen to discuss are only those "as seem offensive and repugnant to the good government of that realm" (82). Yet even on that basis, he is always careful to qualify his remarks still further.

Though he notes, for example, that the Brehon Law "in many things [repugns] quite to god's law and mans, as for example in the Case of murther," he also remarks that "often times there appeareth great show of equity in determining the right between party and party" (47). Similarly, the basis for Tanistry (the custom whereby a new chief is elected), though admittedly "inconvenient" for the English, is reasonable and, we are led to believe by Eudoxus's comment, "very material to the state of that government" because it originated "specially for the defense and maintenance of their land in their posterity, and for excluding . . . strangers and especially . . . the English" (51). The viability of Irish laws and customs, furthermore, is suggested in Irenius's discussion of the custom of kincongishe, which he notes was probably of English origin and "is now upon advisement made an English Law" (80).[26]

Irenius's brief discourse on the laws and customs of the Irish prompt him to go into the origins of the Irish people, "for it is needful to consider from whence [their customs] first sprung" (82). Though he admits that much of what he has gathered is from chroniclers and Irish bards, whose tales Eudoxus notes, "are fabulous and forged" (84), Irenius (like Cicero at the outset of *De legibus*) is unapologetic. He is not after a historian's truth but "a likelihood of truth, not certainly affirming any thing but . . . a probability of things" (85). Eudoxus (not unlike Antonius), puts his trust in "the verity of things written" (87) and is resistant to giving any credibility to Irish history since they "have always been without letters" (84). It is much to his surprise, then, when Irenius claims that the Irish had letters "very anciently and long before England" (87):

> Eudoxus. Is it possible? how comes it then that they are so barbarous still and so unlearned being so old scholars: for learning, as the Poet sayeth, *Emollit mores nec sinit esse feros* whence then I pray you could they have those letters? (87)

Learning "softens manners nor suffers them to be wild" is the phrase Eudoxus quotes. His surprise is compounded when Irenius, in tracing the origins of the Gaelic tongue, concludes that Gaelic "is the very British the which was generally used here in all Brittany before the coming in of the Saxons" (93). In a complete turnaround from his opening description of Ireland as a "savage nation" (43), Eudoxus must admit after hearing this tale that Irenius has not dishonored the Irish "for you have brought them from very great and ancient nations" (92).

Irenius's history of the Irish "commingling" of the nations that created modern day Ireland culminates with observations on one, remaining conquest, "and that the last and the greatest which was by the English when the Earl of Strongbow having conquered that land delivered up the same into the hands of Henry the Second then king" (96). This last conquest by the English established a "strong colony" that still remains. These Old English, Irenius says, have "grown almost more Irish yea and more malicious to the English then the very Irish themselves"

(96). Eudoxus registers puzzlement at the prospect of Englishmen who were "brought up naturally in such sweet civility as England" could have so "degenerated" (96). Irenius, however, recognizes nothing "natural" in English civility, since "it is but the other day since England grew civil" (118). Characteristically, he points toward the cause of their "degeneration" as "the first evil ordinance and institution of that common wealth" (96). Later in the dialogue, Eudoxus mentions that he has heard that the "Council of England" has considered not reforming Ireland since the newly transplanted English might, like the old, "grow as undutiful as the Irish and become much more dangerous" (210). Irenius rejects such a notion: "Neither is it the nature of the country to alter mens manners, but the bad minds of the man" (211).

One of the assumptions Irenius challenges is the "savage" or "barbarous" nature of the Irish, epithets that Eudoxus uses indiscriminately. Irenius, however, reserves such appellations to describe particular practices, and these practices are always balanced against their relative inconvenience to English law. At one point, for example, Irenius registers his disapproval of the Irish manner of keeping cattle "in summer upon the mountains and living after that savage sort" (217). This custom of "Bolloyinge" (that is, nomadic cattle raising) provides a ready hiding place for thieves away "from danger of the Law." Moreover, he claims, because these people live away from towns, they have the reputation of practicing "villianies . . . either against the government . . . or against private men whom they malign by stealing their goods or murdering [them]" (98). Yet the custom itself, as Eudoxus observes, appears "very behoofull," given the terrain of the country; after Irenius explains the troubles this custom causes in terms of English law, Eudoxus agrees that "more evil come[s] by this use of bollies then good" (99). This habit of Irenius's of measuring Irish customs in terms of English rule is not insignificant as it is the law, then, rather than a vague feeling of superiority, that provides a basis for judgment. It is an English law to be sure, but he is unwilling to admit the absolute justice of English law: "No laws of man, according to the straight rule of right, are just, but as in regard of the evils which they prevent and the safety of the common weal which they provide for" (65).

And English law has not provided for the safety for the common wealth of Ireland. When the presupposition of Spenser as either an ambivalent conformist or a devoted, sycophantic courtier is peeled away, both the tenor and the sheer number of his criticisms on English rule are staggering. His remarks on Irish history begin and end with comments on the negligence of the English to enforce their laws in order to establish peace in that land:

> The Laws Eudoxus. I doe not blame for themselves knowing rightwell that all Laws are ordained for the good of the Common weal and for repressing licentiousness and vice, but it falleth out in Laws no otherwise then it doth in Physic

. . . we often see that either through ignorance of the disease or unseasonable-
ness of the time or other accidents coming between, instead of good it worketh
hurt and out of one evil throweth the patient into many miseries. So the laws
were first intended for the reformation of abuses and peaceable continuance of
the Subject, but are sithence either disanulled or quite prevaricated. (46)

Irenius's use of the term "evil" in the above passage indicates precisely where he be-
lieves the cause for the "evils" of Ireland to be, namely, with the English. And the
list of "evils" Irenius recounts are numerous; not least among them is the attempt
to establish the English Common Law in Ireland: "Though it perhaps fitted well
with the state of England . . . yet with the state of Ireland peradventure it doth not
so well agree" (46). Irenius then catalogues a number of ways in which the English
Common Law has proven counterproductive in Ireland, including the manner it
provides for the jury trials (66), the private rights between parties (67), its treat-
ment of accessories to felonies (70), and "colourable conveyances" (73).

What often goes unnoticed in Spenser's *View* is the thoroughness of his critique
of the ruling English in Ireland, whose offenses range from the brutality and avarice
of the captains to similar faults by the queen's lieutenants in Ireland. When Irenius
implicates the governors in corruption, Eudoxus cautions him: "Is it possible? Take
heed what you say." Irenius feigns a "private" moment: "To you only *Eudox:* I do
tell it and that even with great heart's grief and inward trouble of mind to see her
majesty so abused by some whom they put in special trust of those great affairs"
(143). In addition to his detailed plan for the imposition of force for the reform
of Ireland—a plan that takes into account the cost of his plans, the number of men
it will take county by county, garrison to garrison, how to feed the soldiers, the
best time of year to begin this campaign, how the churches should look, where to
build the schools, and how the English and Irish should be integrated—Irenius's
greatest efforts are given over to the criticism and reform of Ireland's "present state"
under the abuses of English rule. At the end of the dialogue, when Irenius declares
that he has attempted to show Eudoxus "the evil which in my small experience
I have observed to have been the chief hindrance of the reformation" (230), the
specter of the "wild Irish" has been displaced by an image of corrupt and ineffec-
tual rule. Eudoxus confirms this image when he notes that "the whole ordinance
and institution of that realm's government was both at first . . . evil plotted and also
sithens [through] other oversight run more out of square to that disorder which it
is now come unto" (146). The evil he has shown Eudoxus is an English evil.

Spenser was persuaded that peace in Ireland could only come to fruition with
the use of swift, thorough, and ruthless use of force. His plan entails the systema-
tic starvation of the "rebels" in order to simultaneously lessen their numbers
and force them into submission. Yet Spenser, through Irenius, is very careful to
qualify his plan to starve them out. First, he claims that after placing well-fortified

garrisons in strategic locations, a proclamation demanding absolute submission within twenty days should bring in most people, "for that this base sort of people dothe not for the most part rebel of himself having no hart thereunto" (156). Second, he suggests that, given such a threat and faced with the prospect of full-fledged war, the rebels themselves will "turn away all their raskall people whom they think unserviceable as old men, women, children, and [Churles] which would only waste their victuals" (156). Third, he maintains that everyone but the "ringleaders should find grace" (156). And, finally, Irenius qualifies his plan by making it clear that he proposes this course of action well aware of the suffering it will entail. His description of what is likely to happen is drawn from his own experience, and it offers such a striking image that "any stony heart would have rued the same":

> Out of every corner of the woods and glenns they came creeping forth upon their hands, for their legs could not bear them. They looked like anatomies of death, they spake like ghosts crying out of their graves, they did eat the dead carrions, happy where they could find them. Yea and one another soon after, in so much as the very carcasses they spared not to scrape out of their graves. And if they found a plot of water cresses or shamrocks, there they flocked as to a feast for the time. (158)

The thoroughness of Spenser's plan for the reform of Ireland is based on cutting, by the sword, the evils from Ireland. Time and again, the "first cause" and "root" of those evils are not the Irish but the English themselves, whose repeated failures to institute their law effectively and uniformly throughout Ireland has brought this "wretched realm" into its present state. The irony—or tragedy or reality—of Spenser's reliance on legal grounds to realize the goals of his proposal is that it calls up the threat of force upon which law ultimately depends.

What is perhaps most remarkable thus about Irenius's history of the Irish people is that it is less a history of Ireland than it is a history of the English in Ireland. Irenius's account of the "inconveniences in the Law . . . [and] abuses of customs" (81) is subordinate to the main end of his discourse, "the present state of Ireland." And from this perspective, from the perspective of someone engaged in the discourse of current government policy, the inconveniences and abuses of Irish laws and customs are *incidental* to the abuses, mismanagement, and blunders of the English in Ireland, historically speaking.

"Your Wretched Realm of Ireland"

That the Irish were a conquered people who would not suffer conquest was eminently clear to a New English transplant well beyond the Pale such as Spenser. Now, fear and hatred are the only things England and Ireland have in common:

Irenius: The Irish do strongly hate the English by reason that having once been subdued by them they were thrust out of their possessions. So as now they fear that if they were again brought under they should likewise be expelled out of all, which is the cause that they hate the English government according to the saying *Quem metuunt oderunt* (whom they fear, they hate). Therefore the reformation must now be with the strength of great power. (146–47)

The above passage again implies that the Irish, though once conquered, are no longer subdued; thus the hatred bred by conquest is compounded by the fear that they might be "again brought under." Yet Irenius intimates that it is more than just fear of reformation that incites the Irish: if laws are "just" only "in regard of the evils which they prevent and the safety of the common weal which they provide for" (65), then Irish "incivility" may be seen as a direct result of unjust English rule. But the current rebellion in Ireland is a consequence of not only England's past failures but also its all-too-present failures to establish and enforce laws that promote civility. Having lost the opportunity to "apply laws fit to the people as in the first institution of common wealths it ought to be," and having exacerbated the hatred, fear, and rebelliousness of the Irish people through unjust rule, the English must now play the hand they dealt themselves, so to speak, and "apply the people and fit them to the laws as it most conveniently may be" (199).

In "A Brief Note of Ireland," which is believed to have been penned two years after the *View* and just weeks before Spenser's death, Spenser reiterates in both expository and syllogistic form the argument he made for the reformation of Ireland to the queen.[27] His house razed and sacked by the Irish, perhaps impoverished, dislocated, perhaps carrying with him the suffering of a child killed in the raid, perhaps ill, Spenser concludes his letter, which begins, "Out of the ashes and desolation and wasteness of this your wretched realm of Ireland" (236), by suggesting another proposal—if, that is, her government persists in its present course:

But if your Highness will dispose yourself to be inclined to any such milder dealing with [the Irish] or to temporize any longer with pardons and protections as hath been done by your governors here, then we humbly beseech your Majesty to call us your poor subjects altogether away from hence that at least we may die in our country and not see the horrible calamities which thereby will come upon all this land and perhaps further as it may well be thought. (242)

Spenser's suggestion that the queen withdraw her subjects "altogether" from Ireland perhaps is most remarkable because of its very improbability. The English have *never* seriously considered withdrawing from Ireland in eight hundred years. Indeed, Elizabeth's appointment of Essex to be the lord lieutenant in Ireland with the express commission to defeat Tyrone some four months after Spenser's "Brief Note" suggests the implausibility of this proposal at that time. The "calamities which thereby will come upon all this land" will come by way of English rule, through his queen's "mildness" and her governors' reluctance to impose the rule of law, the latter of which Essex again proved. The improbability of Spenser's suggestion emphasizes both the direness or wretchedness of the situation, and the extent to which English rule has paved the way, as it were, for the "horrible calamities" to come to Ireland, and "further" to England "as it may well be thought."

David J. Baker has argued that Spenser could not escape the "official language" of his superiors, the language that provided the "political consensus within which he moved and had his being justified." "Spenser's *View,* then," Baker concludes, "does not 'judge' because Spenser does not have available to him any place outside of justifying beliefs from which he could judge."[28] Aside from the curious assumption that any of us could actually gain access to a place outside of or unrelated to ourselves in order to formulate judgments, what is compelling about Spenser's *View* is that it makes no attempt to locate itself "outside of" its political circumstances. It self-consciously originates in, refers to, critiques, and exploits the circumstances of England's policies in Ireland in order to promote a particular course of action heretofore untried. But an element intrinsic to those circumstances, and in addition to the political rationale available for formulating judgments, is Spenser's personal experience in Ireland. A central part of that experience has included no little time and energy in the study of the Irish people through the history of their ancestry, laws, and customs. Ultimately, it is the sum of that experience that provides the basis for Spenser's argument precisely because it is the dynamic, practical, and probable knowledge of human action within *this* particular set of political circumstances, at *this* particular time, that informs, judges, and is resistant to his government's policies.

In Irenius, whose name plays on "his" Irish experience, the "ire" in which that country is steeped, and his main objective (*iris,* "peace"), Spenser offers a figuration of himself—a New English transplant in Ireland who has had the counsel of "wise governors[s]" and delivers what he knows "both to let you see what [the state of Ireland] now is and also what it may be by good care and amendment" (230). Eudoxus, as Annabel Patterson has argued, is not merely a sounding board; his questions, comments, and reactions are integral to developing the subject in-hand in a thorough manner.[29] Eudoxus, whose name signifies "honorable" or "of good repute," enacts the part of a concerned, intelligent Englishman who, unlike his counterpart Irenius, has had no experience living in Ireland. Eudoxus no doubt figures a likely reader of Spenser's text: he appears to place an unexamined faith in the English model of civility and so is predisposed toward counting the Irish as a "savage nation." He is unfamiliar with the history, laws, and customs of the Irish people, and he appears surprised to learn of the extent to which they rebel against English rule. Or perhaps it would be more accurate to say that Eudoxus is

a figuring for the kind of reader Spenser would like to have or the kind of reader
he would like his actual audience to become; he is inquisitive, sympathetic, and
willing to learn from and be counseled by Irenius. Similarly, Spenser's intended
audience probably saw in Eudoxus a representation of themselves, or how they
might like to think of themselves, for example, intelligent, reasonable, good willed,
and so on. Irenius and Eudoxus are Spenser's (speaking) figures of speech, two fig-
ures that enact a "whole" argument. Spenser's authorial ethos is itself contingent
on not only Irenius's experience, familiarity, and knowledge of England's Irish
affairs but also his ability to appeal to and enact the values, assumptions, and emo-
tions of his readers.

In its grossest formulation, the question why Ireland remained intractable was
referred to staid and unreflective assumptions about English civility and Irish bar-
barism, an attitude usually presented by Eudoxus. And like all such assumptions,
they are founded largely on ignorance. The history Irenius offers appears unwill-
ing to bend to any such assumptions. Indeed, the term Irenius uses most often to
describe the Irish is "rebels," a term that describes the Irish in opposition to his
government's authority (and its inability to establish civil law) rather than by virtue
of any innate characteristic, "savage" or otherwise. In a general sense, "civility" and
"civil conversation" are neither ideals nor a peculiarly English phenomenon but an
as-yet-unrealized practical consequence of political power. In this particular case,
the absence of civility in Ireland represents a political failing, namely, the (histori-
cal) failure to enact and maintain a rule of law.

In a sense, we might think of Spenser's argument as a "constitutional" argument
since it is grounded in an interpretation of the law. Spenser appropriates the sov-
ereignty of English Common Law to resist ineffectual government policy. In this
respect, his authorial ethos is also dependent on establishing credibility with his
audience by appealing to their faith in English law to provide for the common
wealth, and toward that end, his argument is based ultimately on the law's poten-
tial to encourage an ethic of civility wherein the Irish might become participants
rather than an other. This "reasoned" or "formal" dimension of the *View* relies on,
as Elizabeth Fowler rightly notes, jurisprudential reasoning. In fact, it is this reliance
on jurisprudential reasoning that she recognizes to be a move away from (and the
failure of) Spenser's moral philosophy, since it is a move that "[leaves] the scheme
of virtues behind"—ethical "virtues," that is, which she argues Spenser defined in
idealized, individualistic terms separable from the vagaries of the political realm.[30]
In a similar vein, Andrew Hadfield suggests that the "logic" of Spenser's argument
(to be distinguished from its "rhetoric" presumably) adheres to a principle of equity
based on an idealized interpretation of English law qua natural law; a case can be
made that the principle of equity, justice as exception and self-protection, is in-
scribed in the very rhetorical structure of many of the *View*'s most crucial set-pieces,

analogies, and anecdotes, as well as being the logical basis for its formal arguments. This relationship between form and content, rhetoric and logic, suggests that equity, for Spenser, is the "mobile flaw" that enables the political / historical narrative of the *View* to function (Hadfield, "Spenser, Ireland," 13).

Hadfield is right, in a sense, but his reference to "self-protection" suggests Fowler's individualistic schema of virtues separable from the political sphere of human action. As a result, the logic of his argument refers to an idealized conception of law; and perhaps more important, the formal constraints of critical exposition offer him no productive means of discussing the "relationship between form and content, rhetoric and logic."

The relationship Hadfield points to might be described best as analogic or proportional. Rather than working in tandem, in some way, with the "logical basis" of Spenser's formal arguments, the analogic relationship between the formal or reasoned dimension of the text and those rhetorical set-pieces is itself the basis of Spenser's argument. That relationship is dynamic, dramatic, or active, and as such, it can only be perceived in action by the reader. There are no set-pieces in the *View:* each of those pieces to which Hadfield refers are *occasional-pieces.* Specifically, they are pieces occasioned by and understood in terms of what went before and then what comes after. It is only within the dynamic frame of a dialogue that the occasional can be known as such by a reader involved in the action of the dialogue in the here and now. The knowledge this kind of involvement fosters is not logical or certain; it is a probabilistic mode of reasoning that originates in the many different particulars of the occasion, including the sensed or feelable "matter" motivating human action—such as the Irish hatred for the English.

The particulars of a given case, in addition to involving the people, actions, place, and time, also involve this sensed matter of human experience—the emotions and feelings that motivate action and condition reason. Spenser's attempts to humanize the Irish depend on his ability to persuade his readers to empathize with the suffering inflicted on those people and on the English in Ireland in these "troublous times." Thus he invokes pity and horror in the description of the famine; Eudoxus takes "delight" in hearing "of times so remote and customs so ancient" (109); he admires the bravery of the Irish soldier (124); and both interlocutors are (or become) resentful of, if not disgusted by, the practical effects of four hundred years of English rule for producing "licentiousness," "liberty," and hate in the Irish and corruption and an unfeeling attitude in the English, who characteristically disavow responsibility for the moral morass of Ireland by laying the blame at the feet of the wild Irish. In this context, Spenser's plan for civility lays claim to a moral authority based upon its political and ethical dimensions: jurisprudential reasoning provides a reference point for Spenser's argument, but that reasoning is itself framed by the dynamic and eminently changeable political sphere. What the law

might be is ultimately less important that how that law is enforced, or not en-
forced, as the case may be. The all-too-real basis for Spenser's argument, however,
is neither jurisprudential reasoning nor politics but ethics in that it attempts to
have the reader get a better feel for the situation in order to effect a reasonable—
and if not "reasonable," then practical—decision on the basis of both the formal
strictures of law and the obligation one might feel toward other human beings.

The method Irenius and Eudoxus agree on thus recognizes no separation of the
ethical and the political; the evils that plague Ireland are to be found in "both . . .
the liefe [lives] and conditions of private men. And also in the management and
public affairs and policy" (45). If there is one thing that the discourse that follows
shows, it is that the state of the former depends entirely on the state of the latter;
just as the reformation of the lives and conditions of private men is contingent on
the reformation of Her Majesty's management of Ireland, so too is the pitiable,
wretched state of private men contingent of Her Majesty's failed and failing poli-
cies. Because the ethical and political dimensions of human action are two inter-
dependent parts of the same whole, neither can be characterized or defined without
reference to the other. Ethical action refers to the conduct of individuals with re-
spect to one another; political action refers to the conduct of the empowered
with respect to the laws and policies established for the common good. Ethics thus
might be thought of as a potential site of resistance—or compliance. It is the arena
of human action wherein particular acts taken by individuals to promote either
human happiness or suffering might either run afoul of or endorse the established
rules. This relationship between politics and ethics (within moral philosophy)
might be more clearly seen in the analogous relationship in jurisprudence between
justice and equity. "Equity" offers a judge a means to make exceptions, qualify,
amend, or suspend the penalties of law by taking into consideration the particu-
lars of a case. Similarly, ethics is that arena of human action wherein individuals
may resist or oppose political affairs by referring to or drawing upon the particu-
lars inhering to a given "case" rather than blind adherence to the law. In both
moral and jurisprudential considerations, however, the nature of that relationship
between politics and ethics, justice and equity, is dynamic. That is, the nature of
that relationship is itself fundamentally analogic in that it depends on and can
only be "known" or perceived within human action, as human action.

"Civility" and "barbarousness," thus, are terms that cannot be measured on a
one-to-one basis against law, absolute authority, or a transcendent vision. Civility,
for example, accrues what meaning it has within the text by moving between the
wild Irish on the one hand and the absence of and potential for English civility on
the other—as Ireland is "a country of war (as it is handled)" (132). Civility is
understood or "seen" within the drama of the *View* as it moves from the "liberty"
of the Irish and the corruption of the English, the inconvenience of (some) Irish

laws and customs and the English abuse of authority, and the pitiable results required to obtain civility and the pitiable state of Ireland as it now stands under Elizabeth's rule. The ultimate judges for both the political justness and ethical soundness of Spenser's *View* are his intended readers. Spenser knew that. The dialogue form of the *View* both imitates and involves its readers in the practice of decision making by offering a conversation in which questions are raised, historical context is given, assumptions are overturned, qualifications are made, and positions are hedged. The *View* may be seen, then, as a civil conversation designed to exemplify a kind of debate absent from the queen's court. But the *View* also advocates a position, and because persuasion and action are its goals, and the action advocated contravenes current policy, Spenser details the circumstances of "the present state of Ireland," of the "private lives" of the Irish and English in Ireland weighed against the political "management" of the English. Central to that effort is his ability to persuade his audience that the Irish are a part of that common wealth, not simply a colony or foreign outpost or hostile savages. Thus he encourages the notion that the starvation program he poignantly portrays is a lesser evil for Irish people than the recurrent wars plaguing that land and the attitudes that foster them. In this context, Spenser's plan for civility lays claim to a moral authority based upon its political and ethical dimensions: political in that it recognizes the law, ethical in that it promises peace and civil conversation. Toward this end, Spenser enacts a historical fiction wherein the Irish are simultaneously rendered victims and prospective citizens, an ancient people and a conquered people, a licentious, barbarous, and wild people and nation of traditional laws and customs cultivated to promote the common good, a nation of rebels and a nation plagued by wars "as it is handled."

The method Irenius follows is not dissimilar from the "methode of the Poete historicall" Spenser describes in his "Letter to Ralegh." Unlike the historical fiction Spenser tells in *The Faerie Queene,* the story he tells with the *View* has a very particular intention, yet both are designed to inform or modify future action by encouraging the reader to participate in the activity of reading here and now. Both the epic and dialogue may be seen as instances of deliberation that enact and exemplify deliberation, the former aimed at "fashioning" an ethical "gentleman or noble person," the latter an ethical person with respect to government practices in Ireland at *this* time. Both epic and dialogue attempt to encourage in the reader "a knowledge of a mans self in his ethic and politic considerations, with the ending end of well-doing, and not well-knowing only." And what might constitute "well-doing" on any given occasion depends on a variety of circumstances. Virtuous action, for example, might be accounted as such in either its resistance to or compliance with authority. Spenser weighed those circumstances, and based on current policy, the history of England's role in Ireland, the probable (rather than possible) courses of action available to effect peace, and the attitudes and emotions held on both sides of the Irish Sea, he believed "well-doing," that is, virtuous or ethical action, necessarily required force to implement the law. Though we may do well to condemn the particular plan of action Spenser decides on as a result of that deliberation, for whatever such a condemnation might be worth, now, there may be some value to the probabilistic, circumspect, and ethical impulses of the process of deliberation he enacts.

But in order to even approach the notion that there may be some value in the mode or process of deliberation that Spenser enacts, we must recognize that the deliberative standards to which he adheres are not drawn from ideals or ideological absolutes but are rooted in the historical, "sensable," actionable, and terrifyingly contingent—and thus hopeful—realm of human action. Moreover, we must recognize that Spenser's argument is not responsible to a set of deliberative standards that conceives of criticism, literary or otherwise, as an academic exercise or professional virtue, but as a moral or civic duty designed to effect action. Toward that end, telling (hi)stories is an ethical imperative; telling (hi)stories is the quintessential rhetorical act informing the poet's method.

CHAPTER EIGHT

INVENTING CIVIC SELVES IN SPENSER'S "LEGEND OF COURTESIE"

An Ethics of Fashioning Lies

And when one considers the universe as a Making *rather than a* Made,
discussing it from the ethical, creative, poetic point of view, there arises
a similar need to explain a partial event by reference to a total event.

— *Kenneth Burke,* Permanence and Change

THE SCENE IS ATOP MT. ACIDALE IN CANTO 10 of book 6 of *The Faerie Queene,*
"The Legende of S. Calidore Or, of Covrtesie." The drama climaxes when Calidore (and the reader) blunder upon the pastoral figuring of the poet's self, Colin Clout, piping to his love, "a countrey lasse," amid the three Graces and a bevy of naked maidens all dancing about. Calidore, "standing long astonished in spright, / And rapt with pleasaunce," does not know what to make of this sight: "Therefore resoluing, what it was, to know, / Out of the wood he rose, and toward them did go" (10.17).[1] As soon as Calidore steps into the scene, everyone but Colin Clout vanishes, and Colin, "Of that displeasure, broke his bag-pipe quight, / And made great mone for that vnhappy turne" (10.18). Though much irritated, Colin pauses to recount for Calidore the purpose of those vanished figures whom he had gathered with his merry tunes. After an honest apology for having disturbed Colin (to be distinguished from an earlier, disingenuous apology in stanza 19), the knight of courtesy and the poet converse together:

> Long time, as fit occasion forth them led
> With which the Knight him selfe did much content
> And with delight his greedy fancy fed,
> Both of his words, which he with reson red;

And also of the place, whose pleasures rare
With such regard his sence rauished,
That thence he had no will to fare,
But wisht, that with that shepheard he mote dwelling share.
(10.30)

In conversation with the poet, Calidore again experiences the "pleasaunce" he first witnessed, but this time by "reading" Colin's words "with reson." However, abruptly, and in spite of his desire to remain with the poet, Calidore desires to return "to court" his own love, Pastorella, feeling that "enuenimd sting, the which of yore, / His poysnous point deepe fixed in his hart / Had left" (10.31).

A Refiguring

Canto 10 is commonly referred to as the "allegorical core" of *The Faerie Queene* because, atop Mt. Acidale, the poet offers the reader a glimpse into what commonly is regarded to be that private, privileged, autonomous universe of his spiritual self; presumably, it is here in canto 10 that the poet sheds some light on the mysterious "darke conceit" animating the epic. Indeed, the self-reflexive, highly stylized, and personal character of the scene on Acidale has provoked what Robert E. Stillman calls a "rare" degree of "critical uniformity":

> From the formalist critics of the 1970s to the poststructuralist critics of the 1990s, Spenserians have found in Mount Acidale an exemplary display of *la poésie pure,* an autonomous aesthetic environ in which Colin supplies what Angus Fletcher argues Spenser absolutely requires, "a self-reflexive theory of his own poetic process."[2]

Stillman is right. That poets historically staked their claims to authority on the basis of a sublime, divinely inspired, purely contemplative, and transcendent vision of the universe ("as a *Made*") is believed to be a central and defining "fact" of the dominant critical narrative advocating the continued (and thoroughly conventional or disciplined) study of Spenser's work. (Though Derek B. Alwes and Jaqueline T. Miller, whose arguments I address later, offer important qualifications, but not exceptions, to Stillman's observation.) In his own effort to "explain, rather than submit to the idealized autonomy of Spenser's work," Stillman promises to historicize (what is presumed to be) the poet's determined, ahistorical "self-hood."

Perhaps the most disturbing characteristic of this "fact" (if only it is granted as a matter of historical record) is the essentially private nature of such authority. An integral component of the poststructuralist project has been to show that the essentially private, autonomous authority poets laid claim to is a myth—a traditional

or conventional trope that actually is in the service of sociopolitical ends and sub-
ject to historical pressures, whether the poet acknowledges such ends or not. And
. . . behold! The emperor has no clothes.

Well, almost no clothes. For though disrobing the poet of his mantle of author-
ity remains a central strategy for most contemporary criticism, the fact that it is
precisely such a claim to authority that validates the professional study and teach-
ing of literature remains well established within the conventional practice of En-
glish studies.[3] Indeed, the rigor dedicated to disrobing Spenser of (what is presumed
to be) his claim to poetic authority by explicating the philosophic, historical, and
sociopolitical constraints on his art might well be viewed as more an apology than
reproach, more a defense for continuing to quarry poetic texts in spite of them-
selves than any kind of general opprobrium for poetics conceived as an elitist
mode of discourse—more E. K. than Immeritô. For beneath the theory and under
the critique, and in the act of teaching and writing about *this* body of texts as
poetry rather than *that* body of texts as prose (or dialogues, or political treatises,
or histories, etc.) lurks the assumption that the study of literature teaches one
something different from studying—rhetoric, for example. In this sense, retaining
the conception of poetic authority as an essentially private, autonomous thing (if
only as a matter for the historical record) privileges the critic in much the same
way that it was once believed to have privileged the poet. As we shall see, one con-
sequence attendant to preserving the historical validity of the poet's uniqueness,
however obliquely, is that it compels critics to formalize a distinction between
poetic discourse (their particular area of expertise) and other modes of discourse.

I am taking the risk of belaboring this point regarding Spenser's poetic author-
ity and the presumed "otherness" of poetic discourse because the focus of this chap-
ter is very much on Spenser's private self, his particular genius. Furthermore, I
intend to praise him, without the usual apologies.

For what is usually called the "allegorical core" of *The Faerie Queene,* I want to
call the *ethical core* of Spenser's humanistic moral philosophy. If one is willing to
grant that book 6 contains the central installment in what was projected to be
twelve books involved "in that part which they in Philosophy call Ethice, or vertues
of a priuate man" (LR), the scene atop Mt. Acidale in canto 10 is remarkable; for
there, the expansive, outward movement of this ethical inquiry broadly conceived
suddenly contracts, converges, and becomes concentrated on the ethics of *a* pri-
vate man, the poet's self (or, a figuring of the poet's self). Spenser's ethical inquiry,
that is, becomes an inquiry into *his* ethics, into the choices he has made that direct
his actions as an individual making a life for himself as a civic poet. This inquiry
into his private choices, however, is inextricable from his public persona as Colin
Clout, and "who knowes not Colin Clout?" (10.16). Following Burke, we might

say that, while considering the "universe" of faerie land as a making entirely of his own volition, "from the ethical, creative, poetic point of view," Spenser feels "a similar need to explain a partial event," his action, "by reference to a total event"— which "total event" Spenser appears to identify as "Ciuility."

Inventing the Muse

The poet's invocation of the muses in the proem to book 6 and his axiomatic statement that "vertues seat is deep within the mind, / And not in outward shows, but inward thoughts defynd" (Proem. 5), together with his Acidalian piping in canto 10, are tendered as the primary pieces of evidence to legitimate (if only for the historical record) the poet's claim to a sacrosanct, autonomous vision. In the second stanza of the proem, Spenser appeals to "Ye sacred imps, that on *Parnasso* dwell," to

> Guyde ye my footing, and conduct me well
> In these strange waies, where neuer foote did vse,
> Ne none can find, but who was taught them by the Muse.
> (Proem. 2)

Specifically, the poet asks the muses: "Reuele to me the sacred noursery / Of vertue" that lies hidden from "view of men, and wicked worlds disdaine" (Proem. 3). As this revelation appears to originate with and "be taught by" the muses, it depends on inspiration or a "goodly fury" for its transmission, and comes with the promise of a "secret comfort" and "heavenly pleasures" (Proem. 2). Of course, such an appeal to divine forces is presumed usually by critics to have a decidedly Christian (and specifically, a Protestant) character. As Derek Alwes notes, "the fact that the deities on Mount Acidale are pagan does not predetermine the matter, since such displacement was common and entirely conventional."[4]

Though common, and though a poetic convention, eliding Spenser's appeal to the muses into a claim for an evangelical authority ignores the function of the muses within this Proem, within Spenser's work in general, and within poetics more generally. Indeed, such a presumptive "displacement" of Spenser's appeal to the muses into a claim for an evangelical authority is what Spenser complained about in *The Teares of the Muses* (1591). Clio laments that by banishing the praise of noble deeds from the "hight of kingdomes government" (76), the "foes of learning" (64) esteem "all otherwise":

> Of th'heavenly gift of wisdomes influence
> And to be learned it['s] a base thing deemed;
> Base minded they that want intelligence:
> For God himselfe for wisdome most is praised,

And men to God thereby are nighest raised.
(85–90)[5]

Those who praise "God himselfe for wisedome" in order to raise "men" toward Him are the same "foes of learning" (64) who "onely strive to raise themselves through pompous pride, and foolish vanitie" (91–92). Instead of fathoming the unfathomable mind of God, Spenser posits "deeds" as the matter of learning, or knowledge. Calliope, the "nurse of vertue" (457; whom Spenser calls upon at the outset of *The Faerie Queene*), states:

> Due praise, that is the spur of doing well[.]
> For if good were not praised more than ill,
> None would choose goodnes of his owne freewill.
> (454–56)[6]

As the daughters of Mnemosyne (Memory) and Jupiter, the muses inspire the epic poet to remember and recall, or "sing of Knights and Ladies gentle deeds / Whose prayses [have] slept in silence long" (1. Proem. 1). As we saw with reference to Spenser's invention of E. K., Immeritô, and Colin Clout, and to Sidney's *Defence* in previous chapters, poetic invention is essentially a pious, prudential *human invention;* that is, it is a kind of knowing that is based on "discovering" or "inventing" (from *invenire,* to come upon or find) the god*like* ability of humans to make, and make sense of the world by re-membering or re-collecting past actions as a guide to future actions. This inherently contingent and provisional, hence rhetorical character of human learning (or invention), furthermore, is "made sense of" through metaphors. In this respect, the muses are themselves invented metaphors (or "displacements") for human invention, metaphors that embody the ancient conception of wisdom as "knowledge of things human and divine." As the figures for human learning (for example, astronomy, history, rhetoric, dance), the muses embody human knowledge in its several forms; as poetic figures, they are the embodiment of a "divine knowledge"—the knowledge that humans invent their world (as the gods invented the natural world, including humans endowed with the capacity for reason and speech).

When the muses first appear to Hesiod, he says that they "breathed into me a divine voice to celebrate things that shall be and things that were aforetime; and they bade me sing of the race of the blessed gods that are eternally, but ever to sing of themselves both first and last."[7] To always sing of the muses is to always celebrate the godlike power of humans to invent metaphors (such as the muses themselves) and thereby know the world.[8]

In book 6, significantly, the treasures of learning kept, or withheld, or figured by the muses have a distinctly historical, and so human complexion, for the muses "teach" the poet to cast his eye back upon human history. Though virtue in general and courtesy, in particular, were taken from heaven, planted by the gods on earth, and nursed by them "Till it to ripeness grew, and forth to honour burst" (Proem. 3), the poet does not choose to present a speculative argument based on the ethereal composition of those "heauenley seedes" but an argument drawn from a comparison between past and present examples of courtesy. Though courtesy "does plenteous seeme" in this "present age":

> Yet being matcht with plaine Antiquitie,
> Ye will them all but fayned showes esteeme,
> Which carry colours faire, that feeble eies misdeeme.
> (Proem. 4)

The muses "inspire" the poet to remember, or re-collect, a "patterne" of "Princely courtesie" (Proem. 6) by or through similitudes or metaphors—by making a comparison between courtesy as it was, historically, and as it is. (Furthermore, that Spenser chooses to represent virtue in general, and courtesy in particular through the garden metaphor is significant. Though of divine origins, "virtue" is an organic part of the natural world; or, more particularly, "virtue" is an organic part of human nature. It is subject thus to the constancy, and vagaries, of human action—something to be made and remade in their images according to time, place, people, etc.) Argument by comparison thus accounts for how the poet "finds" or invents a pattern of princely courtesy "in all Antiquity" *and* in his present-day queen:

> But where in all Antiquity
> So faire a patterne finde, where may be seene
> The goodly praise of Princely courtesie,
> As in your selfe, O soveraine Lady Queene,
> In whose pure mind, as in a mirrour sheene,
> It showes, and with her brightnesse doth inflame
> The eyes of all, which thereon fixed beene.
> (Proem. 6)

Though it appears otherwise, the court of his queen is the deficient element in this comparison, for the pattern she molds, whereon the "eyes of all . . . fixed beene," exemplifies that courtesy "is now so farre from that, which then it was" (Proem. 5).

The poet contends with the lack of discrimination in the present age, which esteems "all but fayned showes" and which "feeble eies misdeeme." Thus, he proposes a "triall":

> But in the triall of true curtesie,
> Its now so farre from that, which then it was,
> That it indeed is nought but forgerie,

> Fashion'd to please the eies of them, that pas,
> Which see not perfect things but in a glass.
> (Proem. 5)

Yet Spenser is well aware that this legend of courtesy is "nought but forgerie" as well, explicitly "fashioned" to please his readers. In fact, in his "Letter to Ralegh," he defends his choice of allegory "coloured with an historicall fiction" because "these dayes . . . all things [are] accounted by their showes, and nothing esteemed of, that is not delightfull and pleasing to commune sence." The question thus becomes, Which fiction, which forgery, is truer than the other, and why?

One quality of the poet's fiction is that he has chosen to make it. Significantly, Spenser's appeal to the muses to "guyde" his footing through faerie land is preceded by a statement that subordinates this "goodly fury" of the muses to the will of the poet; in the first stanza of the Proem to book 6, it is not the muses, but an "I" that guides his own steps:

> The waies, through which my weary steps I guyde,
> In this delightfull land of Faery,
> Are so exceedingly spacious and wyde,
> And sprinckled with such sweet variety,
> Of all that is pleasant to eare or eye,
> That I nigh rauisht with rare thoughts delight,
> My tedious travell doe forget thereby;
> And when I gin to feele decay of might,
> It strength to me supplies, and chears my dulled spright.
> (Proem. 1)

The agent here is the poet, not the muses. Similarly, it is the poet's "I" that finds (invents or discovers) a pattern in praise of princely courtesy by comparing the current narrative or fiction of courtesy with "Antiquity." It is he who guides his own steps toward the learning kept by the muses. It is his "spright," or spirit, that is strengthened and cheered by the sensory delights of faerie land—sensory delights gained through the "eye or ear" that lead toward "Such secret comfort, and heauenly pleasure" infused into "the mindes of mortall men" (Proem. 2) by the muses.

The "sensed" character of the author's experience here is important because it is indicative of the physical, rather than the metaphysical origins of his "rare thoughts," and the necessity of language in that learning process, especially since it is by appealing to the "sence" he holds in common with his reader that he intends to teach, delight, and move them toward virtuous action. The sensed character of the author's experience by way of language as the origin of thought is important when one considers the statement that "vertues seat is deep within the mind, / And not in outward shows, but inward thoughts defynd." Jaqueline T. Miller observes:

> This definition of courtesy posits a distinction between inner and outer, true
> and false, that as others have noted is problematized as the book unfolds, espe-
> cially by the Blatant beast, whose attacks are directed indiscriminately against
> "good and bad alike" (VI.xii.28). . . . If lying and truth-telling participate
> equally in duplicity and doubleness, the result is the blurring of moral and lin-
> guistic categories. (55–56)[9]

It is important to note, however, that the lines "vertues seat," and so on are not a
"definition of courtesy" but a definition of where virtue sits in this "triall of true
curtesie." And as in any trial, the aim is for one to pass judgment, to choose; choice
itself is the "seat of vertue" (and the absence of discrimination is vice, for example,
the Blattant Beast). Furthermore, the poet's statement about virtue's seat in the
mind in no way diminishes the necessity of "outward shows" within the process of
arriving, or making a sound choice. The separation, albeit blurred, that Miller
posits between moral and linguistic categories is itself premised on the (categori-
cal) separation of thought and deed, thought and word, mind and body, and mind
from mind—on the assumption that "inner" equals true and "outer" equals false.
But the capacity to choose enjoyed by the poet, in his mind, is precisely the same
capacity he shares with all his readers, with all their minds. Furthermore, he at-
tempts to persuade his readers to choose the pattern, the "outward show" of cour-
tesy he "finds" over the pattern found at court, whereof, "it seemes," men Courtesie
doe call" (1.1); and that appeal relies on "commune sence" steeped in a learning
of human action that includes, but is not defined solely by, precepts and contem-
porary mores.

A Burkeian Mystery, Ciceronian Decorum
(Analogical Proofs)

In the appendix to Kenneth Burke's *Permanence and Change,* titled "On Human
Behavior Considered Dramatistically," nestled within a section discussing the "ele-
ment of Mystery arising from a social hierarchy," Burke pauses briefly to recognize
the need for "other mysteries, other orders." Among those other mysteries he
points toward are the "mysteries of adventure and love"; at this point, Burke makes
the rather odd, parenthetical assertion that "love is part natural, part courtesy"
(274).[10]

A "Mystery" for Burke might be considered an expression of a class-based igno-
rance insofar as it communicates the lack of understanding and disconnectedness
one class of people will have with respect to another class, or classes; he defines
"Mystery" as "the obverse expression of the disrelationship among classes" (278).
The element of mystery arising out of the social hierarchy is a direct result "of the
purely *operational* motives binding society" (276): after a people has established

rights, obligations, and the transference of property among themselves, social classes emerge, and the concomitant need to maintain order among them. "Such 'order,'" Burke writes, "is not just 'regularity.' It also involves a distribution of *authority*. And the mutuality of rule and service . . . takes roughly a pyramidal or hierarchical form" (276). Though one social class is entwined within a symbiotic relationship with others, "classes of people become 'mysteries' to one another" because of their "different modes of living and livelihood" (276). Mystery, for Burke, is thus a necessary condition of social life (and all life is social) and "the best way of promoting social cohesion" (276); the question for him is whether the current modes of mystery are "in tune with the times" (277). Significantly, Burke recognizes that the creation of "new modes of Mystery" will require the "unmasking" of others, and that this "unmasking" involves "an element of deception." "While leading you to watch his act of destruction at one point," Burke writes, "the 'unmasker' is always furtively building at another point, and by his prestidigitation he can forestall accurate observation of his own moves" (294).

The prestidigitator can (may) forestall the accurate observation of his own moves, but he may not. For Burke himself is well aware that he, too, is involved in prestidigitation in this "Anatomy of Purpose."[11] While unmasking, or de(con)-structing, the various interpretive strategies or "orientations" dominating the modern age (that is, of magic, religion, and science), Burke is attempting to build a "mode of Mystery" whereby human conduct might be interpreted or critiqued "in dramatistic terms . . . [that] begin in theories of *action* rather than in theories of *knowledge*" (274). A remarkable moment occurs in *Permanence and Change* when Burke departs briefly from his general discourse on human purpose to reflect on his own:

> Every system of exhortation hinges about some definite act of faith, a deliberate selection of alternatives. When this crucial act is not specifically stated, it merely lies hidden beneath the ramifications of the system. I have sought to hunt out this crucial point in my own statements, and I suspect that I have found it in my admission that, when considering war and participation, or war and action, as the two ends of a graded series, I have chosen *action* or *participation* as the word that shall designate the *essence* of this series. Or we might choose such words as *coöperation* and *communication* and note that even in war the coöperative and communicative element is largely present.
>
> Here, in all its nudity, is the Jamesian "will to believe." It amounts in the end to the assumption that good, rather than evil, lies at the heart of human purpose. And as for those who would suggest that this is merely a verbal solution, I would answer that by no other fiction can men truly coöperate in historic processes, hence the fiction itself is universally grounded. (235–36)

Burke's inquiry into human purpose begins with the innocuous sentence "We may begin by noting the fact that all living organisms interpret many of the signs about them" (5) and arrives at the tormenting conclusion that because of "the preposterous fact that both existence and nothingness are equally unthinkable . . . there is no place for purely human boasts of grandeur, or for forgetting that men build their cultures by huddling together, nervously loquacious, at the edge of an abyss" (272). Burke feels compelled to reflect on and articulate *his* purpose, *his* crucial act of faith. Indeed, in a footnote in the "Appendix," Burke conclusively describes *Permanence and Change* as "an individual's approach to motives in terms of the collectivity" (274).

For our purposes here, Burke offers a useful, contemporary patterning of an "ethical, creative, poetic"—or resolutely rhetorical—point of view. It is a view wherein the individual, even the personal, may be considered "dialectics-wise," as he puts it, only within the context of "the collectivity." In fact, Burke cannot consider ethics in general without taking into consideration the personal choices he purposes for himself since, ultimately, the actions of an individual are only knowable insofar as they share or participate with the actions of other individuals; from this "ethical, creative, poetic point of view," Burke feels the need to explain his actions as a partial event by reference to a total event: the actions of others. If the human body is the starting point of all knowledge, then "the ethical bent from which one approaches the universe is itself a part of the universe, and a very important part" (256). Burke chooses to approach the universe as a making, specifically, a human fiction created in language that can only be known historically (without "forgetting") as a natural response to and part of society.

The permanent or "universal" character of Burke's "dramatistic" and utterly humanistic conception of ethics is similar to (that is, analogous with) the Ciceronian moral philosophy informing the rhetorical practices of Spenser's humanistic poetics. In *De officiis,* Cicero discusses the two "characters" (*personis*) of human nature. The first is "universal," or "communal," and it is from this that "all morality and propriety [*honestum decorumque*] are derived," and upon it depends the reasons by which we discover or invent our duties to one another.[12] Cicero is explicit about what this universal nature is, for it is precisely what distinguishes humans from the rest of the animal world, and so constitutes the "first principle" of his moral philosophy. Cicero believes that Nature has endowed humans with reason and speech (*ratio et oratio*) for the purpose of conserving Nature's gifts; it is "the most comprehensive bond that unites together men as men and all to all" (*De officiis* 1.16.51). In this sense, Nature provides the basis or foundation of morality in that it has provided human nature with reason, speech, and a social instinct. Though Nature provides the basis or the tools for morality, it does not provide the *source* for morality: all morality and propriety are derived from and depend on the universal character of human nature, and that nature is, essentially, to reason and speak. Thus "fellowship and society" may be necessary and desirable simultaneously because though a natural occurrence, its development is entirely contingent on human action.

The second persona of human nature "is the one that is assigned to individuals in particular" (1.30.107), and might be described best as "natural ability." The individuated character of human nature partakes of the universal when "by an interchange of acts of kindness, by giving and receiving . . . our skill (*artibus*), our industry, and our talents . . . cement human society more closely together" (1.7.22). One can best contribute to the common weal thus if one makes "a proper estimate of his own natural ability and shows himself a critical judge of his own merits and defects." To the universal and individual characters of human nature, Cicero adds a third and a fourth. Chance or circumstances will impose conditions on the extent to which one may be able to engage one's natural ability productively, including "regal powers and military commands, nobility of birth and political office, wealth and influence, and their opposites." The last kind of character or persona is that "which we assume by our own deliberate choice. . . . And so some turn to philosophy, others to civil law, and still others to oratory" (1.32.115). This fourth kind of character or persona poses "the most difficult problem in the world," for it asks each person to weigh, consider, and choose how their individual talents might best contribute to others.

For having deliberated on the relative merits of one's natural or chosen ability, and subsequently choosing to dedicate that ability to the service of others, and if one leads one's life in a manner consistent with that choice, then one might be said to be "honest," or morally right. Cicero claims that "all that is morally right [*honestum*] rises from some one of four sources" (derived from and dependent on the universal character of humankind):

> It is concerned either with the full perception and intelligent development of the true; or with the conversation of organized society, with rendering to every man his due, and with the faithful discharge of obligations assumed; or with the greatness and strength of a noble and invincible spirit; or with the orderliness and moderation of everything that is said and done, wherein consist temperance and self-control. (1.5.15)

Though these four sources are "closely interwoven," Cicero assigns a particular "office" to each. The virtue associated with the first is wisdom and prudence: of all of the sources, Cicero says this one "touches human nature most closely"; its concomitant vices are treating the "unknown as known and too readily accept[ing] it," and the devotion of "too deep study to matters that are obscure and difficult and useless as well" (1.6.18). Note, also, that this "source" is inherently productive in that it involves the "development of the true." The second virtue has to do with justice and generosity, with kindness—or civility. The first office of justice is to keep "one man from doing harm to another, unless provoked by wrong" (1.7.21) and it is founded upon "good faith, that is truth and fidelity to promises and agreements" (1.7.23). The third point involves courage and fortitude, an indifference to outward circumstances, and recognizes "deeds" as the ending end of moral goodness (1.29.65). Finally, the fourth involves propriety (decorum): "If there is any such thing as propriety at all, it is nothing other than the uniform consistency in the course of our life as a whole and all its individual actions" (1.32.111).

The nature of decorum might be said to have two "characters" as well. One is "proper" to human kind in general and inheres to *honestum* insofar as it is deliberate (or prudent); it inheres to *honestum* in the intelligence, laws, and spirit of human kind in general. The other is "proper" to an individual (with respect to other people); it inheres to individual conduct and is thus "embraced in that science the Greeks called ευταξία . . . by which we understand *orderly conduct.*" Similar to prudence, ethics is the "science of doing the right thing at the right time" (1.40.142), but it differs in its attention to the particular and the occasional, rather than the general. Another way in which Cicero makes the distinction is by noting a general and "another" or "special type" of propriety:

> We assume a general sort of propriety, which is found in moral goodness as a whole; then there is another propriety, subordinate to this which belongs to the several divisions of moral goodness. The former is usually defined somewhat as follows: "Propriety is that which harmonizes with man's superiority in those respects in which his nature differs from that of the rest of the animal creation." And they so define the special type of propriety which is subordinate to the general notion, that they represent it to be that propriety which harmonizes with Nature, in the sense that it manifestly embraces temperance and self-control, together with a certain deportment as becomes a gentleman (*liberali*).
>
> That this is the common acceptation of propriety we may infer from that propriety which poets aim to secure. (1.37.96–28.96–97)

The key distinction Cicero makes here is between the particular genius of human nature in general with respect to the animal world, and in particular with respect to a social nature (hence "harmonizes with Nature," as humans by Nature possess what Cicero calls "a social instinct"). Together, *ratio et oratio* comprise the particular genius of human kind because it is by reason and speech that they *make* the world, continually, according to human needs (as social animals). In this respect, all reason and speech is "proper" in the sense that it is consistent with humankind's universal nature.[13] The "special type of propriety" that "poets aim to secure" relates to "considerateness and the approbation of our fellow-men" (1.40.143), and it "harmonizes with Nature" insofar as it attempts to "secure" an ethic of civility that attends to humans' social nature in its particular manifestation.[14] Of all the social relations possible, the first is the "bond of union . . . between husband and wife; the next between parents and children. . . . And this is the foundation of civil government, the nursery, as it were, of state" (1.17.54). Thus, this "first" bond among humans is in direct support of and material to what Cicero says is the closest, yet most comprehensive social relation possible, "that which links each one of us with our country," for one's "native land embraces all our loves" (1.17.57).

Decorum in the general sense suggests a consistency regardless of circumstances; it is this kind of decorum that wisdom, justice, and fortitude attempt to attain. But Cicero's conception of decorum is not mere consistency regardless of circumstances but a consistency with respect to circumstances, whatever they may be, and it "shows itself in every deed, every word, even in every movement and attitude of the body" (1.35.126). Toward that end, we may infer that poets rely primarily on considerateness, generosity, liberality, and love to persuade, but "of all motives, none is better adapted to secure influence and hold it fast than love" (2.7.23).

In Love on Acidale

For Spenser, the definitive element of the social "Mystery" is love—a love that is part natural, and part courtesy. Of course, "courtesy" for Spenser had all of the connotations of authority and hierarchy Burke associates with social "Mystery," in addition to the romantic connotations Burke seems to have in mind for those involved with "mysteries of adventure and love." For love is "literally" the figurative ground upon which Spenser constructs an ethic of courtesy, an ethic he then patterns or exemplifies in a figuring of himself (as Colin Clout) atop Mt. Acidale, a hill of "matchlesse hight, that seem'd th'earth to disdaine" (10.6), a hill where

> They say that *Venus,* when she did dispose
> Her selfe to pleasaunce, vsed to resort
> Vnto this place, and therein repose
> And rest her selfe, as in a gladsome port,
> Or with the Graces there to play and sport.
> (10.9)

In a more general sense, perhaps it would more appropriate to say that *desire* is the definitive element of Spenser's social mystery, but that he chooses love over the alternatives; or, more appropriate yet, he chooses *a* kind of love over other kinds of loves. As we shall see, Spenser chooses to praise a kind of love that he argues is itself kind or natural, a natural love that proves itself natural to the extent that it promotes civil conversation.

Spenser's "Legend of Courtesie" is strewn with examples of love that do not advance the cause of civil conversation: the pride that characterizes the love between

Briana and Crudor gives rise to "wicked customes" (1.15); the lust and spite that characterize the relationship between Blandina and Turpine effect murder, cowardice, deceit, and flattery, and Calidore's initial lust for Pastorella, when coupled with her general scorn for any who show her affection, leads Calidore to forsake his duty to the Faerie Queene; and Coridon and Pastorella, Aldus and Aladine, Calepine and Serena, Mirabella, Timias, the cannibals—all figure forth a kind of love, or lack of love, that proves to be detrimental to all those personally involved and to most of those who become involved with them.

Just as the various, interpersonal relationships in the previous nine cantos offer differing views on the connection of love and courtesy, so too does canto 10, where atop Mt. Acidale, all eyes are on Colin Clout. Of course, Spenser "authors" all of the perspectives available throughout book 6 on the relationship of love and courtesy, but here, he figures his authority in his pastoral persona, Colin Clout. As a figuration of Spenser, Colin's view, or perspective on the dancing Graces is to be distinguished from the view presented by the narrative voice (which perspective I will refer to as Spenser's own). Another perspective Spenser offers is Calidore's. Calidore, having given up on his quest for the Blattant Beast, now pursues the love of Pastorella; he has chosen to remain "amongst the rusticke sort, / Rather then hunt still after shadowes vaine / Of courtly fauour" (10.2). One day, by chance, Calidore discovers a place, "whose pleasance did appere / To passe all others, on the earth which were" (10.5). He hears a pipe in the distance, "And many feete fast thumping th'hollow ground" (10.10). As he comes closer,

> There he a troupe of Ladies dauncing found
> Full merrily, and making gladfull glee,
> And in the midst a Shepheard piping he did see.
> (10.10)

On still closer inspection, he sees "An hundred naked maiden lilly white" (10.11), in the midst of whom "Three other Ladies did both daunce and sing":

> And in the middest of those same three, was placed
> Another Damzell, as a precious gemme,
> Amidst a ring most richly well enchaced,
> That with her goodly presence all the rest much graced.
> (10.12)

Calidore's point of view is very general, an overview as it were. His response to the scene is great delight, a delight that causes a desire to learn about this dance. At this point, when the reader (or audience) is perhaps as desirous to know what to make of this sight as Calidore, the narrator takes center stage to embellish the scene further.

Where Calidore thought that "grace" goes outward from the fair "Damzell" in the middle, that it is "her presence" that graces the merry company, Spenser's narrative voice observes that it is the other three who graced the fourth, whom "most of all, those three did her with gifts endew" (10.14). Spenser does admit, however, that "she that in the midst of them did stand, / Seem'd all the rest in beauty to excell" (10.14). He further identifies those three maidens as "the Graces, daughters of delight, / Handmaides of *Venus*," and the fourth maiden as the shepherd's love, and he assigns them all a purpose:

> Those three to men all gifts of grace do graunt,
> And all, that *Venus* in her selfe do vaunt,
> Is borrowed of them. But that fair one,
> That in the midst was placed parauaunt,
> Was she to whom that shepheard pypt alone,
> That made him pipe so merrily, as neuer none.
> (10.15)

The narrator subsequently identifies that shepherd as "Poore *Colin Clout*" and heralds the presence of Colin's love as one "aduaunst to be another Grace" (10.16).

As the narrator steps aside, the spotlight on Calidore brightens again to bring the reader's attention to the ravished knight, who "astonished in spright, / And rapt with pleasuance" (10.17) with all that he sees abruptly rises and steps into the scene. As Calidore moves toward them, everyone disappears, except for a very displeased Colin, who breaks his bagpipe and "made great mone for that vnhappy turne" (10.18).

It is then Colin's turn to ornament the scene for Calidore. Colin's interpretation, significantly, remains consistent with and complements the narrator's, though it is more pointed, more detailed:

> These three on men all gracious gifts bestow,
> Which decke the body or adorne the mynde,
> To make them louely or well fauoured show,
> As comely carriage, entertainment kynde,
> Sweete semblaunt, friendly offices that bynde,
> And all the complements of curtesie:
> They teach vs, how to each degree and kynde
> We should our selues demeane, to low, to hie;
> To friends, to foes, which skill men call Ciuility.
> Therefore they alwaies smoothly seeme to smile,
> That we likewise should mylde and gentle be,
> And also naked are, that without guile

Or false dissemblaunce all them plaine may see,
Simple and true from couert malice free.
(10.23–24)

What the narrator simply refers to as "all gifts of grace," Colin describes as "offices"
or duties that "bynde" humans together honestly, that is, "without guile." Further-
more, Colin indicates that the gifts of grace are evident in every attitude of the
body, every word, and every deed.

The consistency between the narrator's and Colin's speech is important because
as a figuring for the poet's self, Colin patterns (or exemplifies or figures forth) the
poet's ethos. In a sense, then, distinguishing between the narrator and Colin is use-
ful if only to note that it is a distinction without a difference. Indeed, that they
are of the same "character" becomes apparent after Colin's lengthy description of
"that fourth Mayd" (10.25). In a jarring move from Acidale to Spenser's present-
time composition of the poem, the narrative voice steps in to offer a stanza to
"Gloriana":

Sunne of the world, great Glory of the sky,
That all the earth doest lighten with thy rayes,
Great Gloriana, greatest Maiesty,
Pardon thy shepheard, mongst so many layes,
As he hath sung of thee in all his dayes,
To make one minime of thy poore handmayd,
And vnderneath thy feete to place her prayse,
That then thy glory shall be farre displayd
To future age of her this mention may be made.
(10.28)

The very next line, "When thus that shepherd ended had his speach" (10.29), fuses
Colin and the narrator. Indeed, this stanza in Spenser's narrative voice enacts pre-
cisely what Colin had been doing in the previous stanzas, though more overtly.
Just as Colin instructs his audience, Calidore, the Faerie Queene's representative
on Acidale, by praising his love, so too does Spenser speak to his (primary) audi-
ence, the queen, in praise of *his* love.

Noting the consistent character of Spenser and his figuring of himself may ap-
pear to be a redundant thing to do. But when we consider Colin as a patterning
of the poet's character or ethos, the question posed the reader is, Is Colin an "hon-
est" figuration of the poet's self? Or does Colin, like Calidore and many of the
other "characters" in book 6, only "seem" genuine, honest, and courteous? These
are moral questions in that they directly address the poet's ethos, his ethics as a
civic poet engaged in the considerable task of fashioning others in "vertuous and

gentle discipline." In other words, these are questions that address the "ethic and politic considerations" of the poet's self.

There are two, perhaps three other sites of instruction in Spenser's legend of courtesy to which we can compare Spenser-Colin's mode of instruction.[15] The first occurs in canto 6, when Arthur, traveling with the Salvage Man, deposits Serena and Timias at the Hermit's cottage. The Hermit rightly determines that the wounds Serena and Timias suffer from their encounters with the Blattant Beast "needed to be disciplinde" with "counsell to the minde" (6.5). Though he accurately predicts that his medical efforts will be in vain because "in your selfe onely helpe doth lie" (6.7), the Hermit fails because he envisions the self as an essentially private and rational thing. Consequently, the Hermit offers precepts designed to abstract or extricate the individual from his or her social being:

> The best (sayd he) that I can you aduize,
> Is to auoide the occasion of the ill:
> For when the cause, whence euill doth arize,
> Remoued is, th'effect surceaseth still.
> Abstaine from pleasure, and restraine your will,
> Subdue desire, and bridle loose delight.
> (6.14)

Of course, the aged Hermit lives by this advice himself; he has removed himself from society, disavowed his knighthood, and from "all this worlds incombraunce did himselfe assoyle" (5.37). Significantly, abstaining from pleasure appears to be synonymous with avoiding the occasion of the ill, and both demand extracting oneself from social intercourse. Similarly, Meliboee in canto 9 tells Calidore that "each vnto himselfe his life may fortunize" (9.30), and having taken that advice to heart, he has removed himself from the larger social world to look after his flock and family in bucolic bliss, content and well satisfied with his choice. Meliboee wears his humility like a badge of honor and speaks disparagingly of the court as full of ambitious, vain, greedy courtiers; he, too, speaks sententiously. The subsequent raid by the Brigants suggests that, in defining himself in terms opposed to and separate from the larger social world, Meliboee has placed too much reliance on one's ability to "fortunize" his life. Indeed, that the Brigants "fortunize" Meliboee's death indicates that he, like the Hermit, has chosen to ignore the inherently social circumstances of each individual life, of each self.

These sites of moral instruction thus are useful to keep in mind when the reader encounters Colin atop Mt. Acidale, for Colin's instruction of Calidore and its relative value or credibility are crucial to Spenser's notion of courtesy. In one respect, Spenser's ethos is analogous with (or, in proportion to) Colin's, as Colin is but a figuration of the poet's self. The kind of proof the figure of Colin thus furnishes of the poet's credibility is analogical or metaphorical. This is an analogy, however, founded on identity rather than difference. Indeed, distinguishing between Spenser's self and his figuring forth of himself is useful only to show (or "prove") that Colin is an honest figuration of the poet's self. In a general sense, then, Colin embodies the poet's chosen way of life; he embodies a choice enlisted in the general employ of disciplining the reader in courtesy, which "of all goodly manners is the ground / And roote of ciuill conuersation" (1.1). That choice points both "inward" toward the maker of that choice and "outward" toward the reader as one who is asked to judge the honesty of the poet's self as it is figured forth by the poet. Colin Clout is a speaking figure of speech: as a figure of speech, he embodies Spenser's decision to be a poet; as a speaking (or dramatic) figure, he communicates or exemplifies (or figures forth) actions consistent with Spenser's own as a civic poet. In this way, Colin is the figuring forth of a knowledge of the poet's self in his "ethic and politic considerations."

But, again, *what* one knows is entirely contingent on *how* one knows, and the fact that Spenser embodies a knowledge of his self figuratively, within a fiction, within speech, points toward a more general principle concerning the nature of knowledge itself. For though it is a knowledge of this particular human's nature, Colin Clout embodies human knowledge more generally. He embodies the quintessential human act of a body making sense of or coming to know the human world in language. It is in this profound yet mundane and essentially human way that Spenser's figuration of Colin Clout substantiates the poet's claim to divine knowledge; in deliberately "coming to know" himself in language, the poet exploits Nature's, or the Maker's, gifts, which separate humans from the rest of natural world. Those gifts, reason and speech, are inherently productive, or generative, in that they are indicative of a distinctly human making as only humans can make and order their world. Those generative gifts are also indicative of the occasion— the circumstances (including historical circumstances), place, time, and people involved in that occasion. Moreover, those generative gifts are indicative of the individual who made (or invented or discovered) those words in order to make sense of and negotiate that occasion. The *arche,* or first principle, of human invention, of human making is this god *like* power to make the world; the poet does this in spades, so to speak, self-consciously, self-reflexively. An integral part of that self-reflexive, self-conscious making is the knowledge that it is human, that it participates in a distinctly human form of action.

Thus we see the more general sort of propriety that Cicero spoke of, the kind "which harmonizes with man's superiority in those respects in which his nature differs from that of the rest of the animal creation." Yet Colin's ethos is also analogous to the characters of every other figuration of courtesy in book 6; "he" plays a part in the "poet's aim to secure" the "special" kind of propriety "which harmonizes with Nature, in the sense that it manifestly embraces temperance and self-control, together with a certain deportment as becomes a gentleman (*liberali*)." This is another kind of proof of Spenser's credibility; it is "decorous" insofar as Colin enacts a pattern of courtesy in proportion to and proper to (or consistent with) the examples of courtesy enacted throughout the legend. What distinguishes Colin's character from every other figure in book 6 (except for Arthur) is that he offers Calidore (as Spenser offers the reader) love as the "grounds" for civil conversation. Specifically, he offers a kind of love for a woman that sees love as both a private and public affair, as both an individual and social act.

The demigod stature of the three Graces, "daughters of delight," serve the divine love as it is figured in Venus. Though divine, Venus is closely associated with the natural world, specifically with Mt. Acidale, where "all that euer was by natures skill / Deuized to work delight, was gatherd there" (10.5). Desire, pleasure, and delight are the attributes that attracted Venus to this natural, earthly hill. Yet the divine is present only in her notable absence from Mt. Acidale; Venus "vsed to resort" (10.9) there. Indeed, whatever one "knows" about Venus and her connection to the pleasures of Nature that characterize Mt. Acidale is from what "They say." What "They" do say about her is figured in the three Graces, who as "Handmaides of *Venus*" embody divine love in a distinctly human way—as the teachers of "Ciuility." For now, the social or moral or distinctly human aspect of Divine-Natural love appears atop Acidale in the figures of the three Graces. It is through, by means of, or "in" the earthly love of a particular woman that the poet sees a "Divine resemblaunce" (10.27). This "Divine resemblaunce" is a perception of the divine by analogy: the poet's love resembles, but is not the divine. Indeed, his love for the "country lass" approaches the divine to the extent that it, in general terms, makes the poet "low to lout" or "demeane" him self to his countrymen. Just as the Graces are the "Handmaides of *Venus*," Colin's love is a "handmayd" to Gloriana; just as the Graces teach one "how to demeane" oneself, Colin's love "made [him] low to lout"; just as the Graces advance Colin's love, Colin's love advances social grace.

As a making, the poet's figure of Colin Clout is a lie, a fiction "invented" and appropriated in order to address the circumstances regarding Spenser's inquiry into courtesy. It is a lie, however, deliberately and "honestly" grounded in an attempt to preserve what makes humans human. Jaqueline T. Miller argues that Spenser anatomizes allegory in book 6 in order to "[investigate] the disturbing affinity between the courtier's mode [of discourse] and his own, which lies precisely in the practice of 'false semblant or dissimulation.'"[16] Similarly, Derek B. Alwes argues that book 6 represents the poet's attempt "to combine two discourses [the poetic

and the political] which were for him commensurate elements in the larger pro-
gram by which civilization is constructed."[17] In both of these arguments, it is pre-
sumed that poetic discourse is representative of "inner" truths (owned exclusively
by the poet) and that political discourse is "outward" and false. But instead of char-
acterizing poetic and political discourses as two, different elements "commensu-
rate" or disturbingly close in the construction of civility, Spenser argues that these
discourses are *identical* in a fundamental sense. The poet shows the reader a uni-
verse of his own making, but the particular genius of the poet's individual nature
is rooted in the "universal nature" of human beings in general, and that universal
nature is inherently social as well as rhetorical in that "all morality and propriety
[*honestum decorumque*]" are derived from and discovered (or invented) in reason
and speech. In patterning a universe of his own making for his readers, the poet
also shows them that *just as* the poet makes his world, *you* (the courtly audience)
have the power to make this world. Again, however, the analogy drawn makes a
distinction without a necessary difference, though there are differences to be made
precisely because the political powers that inform the poet's civil life make the world
without "grounding" courtesy in a love that encompasses all humans, or that is a
love "proper" to humans in the most general sense. Both discourses *could* have as
their end a "civil conversation" that argues for a "gentle discipline"; both *could*
encourage an ethic of civility. The "trick" (in a Burke's sense of "prestidigitation")
is to realize that all ethics of civility are lies, all are necessarily figurings of both a
cives and a civic self. Some lies, however, are more "honest," more moral, than oth-
ers because their tellers know themselves to be social, rhetorical animals—"mere
bellies" who, *like* Hesiod's muses, "know how to speak many false things as though
they were true" and know how, "when they will, to utter true things."

AFTERWORD

INASMUCH AS THE POETIC PRACTICES OF SPENSER are grounded in a Ciceronian moral philosophy that takes as its fundamental principle that human being are, as Kenneth Burke puts it, "Bodies that Learn Language," and inasmuch as the poetic practices of Spenser are determinedly embedded in the life of a polity (or in the stories a polity tells and has told to make sense of its present and guide its future) and inasmuch as his aesthetic functions rhetorically "to teach, move, and delight" his queen and countrymen toward actions deemed virtuous on account of their potential to promote "civility," to effect "what might best be" (rather than because they conform to religious doctrine, policy, or transcendent visions of Beauty), and inasmuch as Spenser affirms an individual's capacity to choose and so to make and remake one's self prudently (that is, with regard to occasion, circumstances, place, history, and the people involved) and inasmuch as his poetry acknowledges and exploits poetry's capacity to shape cultural values and, significantly, to challenge and reform cultural conventions, might we not conclude that his poetic practices are indicative of another sophistic?

In writing this book, I became increasingly cognizant of the truth to Grafton and Jardine's insight on Ramism, that "that *is* the version of liberal arts teaching that 'caught on' and left its indelible trace on western European thought."[1] They are unwilling to critique Ramism too harshly because of this. My argument suggest that the ramifications (or ramistifications?) of Ramism's "indelible trace" obviates ethical and political inquiry that is productive. My use of the term "productive" bears whatever significance it might have by referring to deliberative standards, effects, and audiences *outside* of the narrow confines of Renaissance scholarship in particular or academe in general. The Department of English, my career, this book, your interest (or at least your attention thus far)—all bear witness to Ramism's indelibility. Without the prospect of deliberative standards that inform our civic lives, the guiding motivation for our research and pedagogies assumes narrow, detached, and specialized connotations. Thus communities are defined in terms of disciplinary boundaries, theoretical commitments, historical interests, or they are author- or genre-based: *involvement* or *participation* demands expertise; production is largely a matter of negotiating professional (that is, technical) conventions; and the question "What is to be done?" is seldom referred to outside disciplinary niceties.

With the realm of praxis so abruptly truncated, disciplinary gnosis ("expertise") ascends as the principal aim, and toward that end, methods and language designed to analyze, critique, explicate, objectify, and clarify become the privileged *form* of discourse. It is disciplinary gnosis, consequently, that becomes the matter of learning, the matter of knowledge. And the language best suited to accomplish such goals eschews narrative, figurative speech, and analogies as a matter of form in the effort to mitigate the appearance of persuasion; instead, methodological form, crisp analyses, "transparent" prose, and "logical" support are marshaled toward . . . "well-knowing only"? Robert Young has advanced the argument that contemporary literary theory is not actually "political enough":[2]

> [The formulation of a political literary theory] implies that it is posed from the outside, that the question of politics frames theory with the invocation of more powerful necessities. If the political is invoked as an outside against which theory must be judged, then it is being used in its primary meaning where "the political" describes anything that affects the state or public affairs—something that literature, or literary theory, is not generally noted for doing. ("Politics," 131)

Significantly, Young attributes the nugatory political effects of literary theory largely to critics' allegiance to "traditional models of argument through which we achieve and legitimate knowledge," models that are not grounded in contemporary political practices, but in the mores of a discipline (146). Insofar as these "traditional models [or *forms*] of argument" persist, they are fundamentally at odds with rhetorico-poetic discourse and productive ethical inquiry. There are significant consequences to this state of affairs: cultural and institutional relevance, for example, and funding, or the potential to effect genuine political goals—or simply the wherewithal to fend off indifference.

Elizabeth Fowler encourages Spenserians to accept *The Faerie Queene*'s open invitation "to develop the deliberative standards by which we can measure disciplines and institutions against their own, and our own, ideals" in an argument designed, as the title declares, to illustrate the "Failure of Moral Philosophy in Works of Edmund Spenser."[3] Though Fowler's argument is provocative, well intentioned, and no doubt appealing in its effort to offer a lesson (or moral?) by finding failure in a canonical figure, her insistence on both Spenser's philosophical idealism and the presumption of "our own" idealism suggests a well-disciplined

posture or *attitude* toward Spenser's work, an attitude that epitomizes those "delib-
erative standards"—those rhetorical conventions—she asks her audience to de-
velop. Indeed, it is precisely because deliberative standards are measured principally
in terms of "our" academic "disciplines and institutions," as Fowler indicates, that
a productive ethical inquiry is arrested. This is not to say that literary criticism in
general and Spenser criticism in particular does not produce ethical inquiry (it can
not help but produce a certain habit of doing), nor do I mean to imply that liter-
ary criticism is produced in an unreflective manner, insensitive to the institutional
exigencies of its professional / professorial readers. I simply argue that, within that
well-disciplined sphere of English studies, the relative significance granted to *pub-
lic action* as a necessary and material end to both academic prose and the texts such
prose examines remains elusive.

Of course, the "critical thinking skills" exercised in literature surveys and upper-
level courses always presuppose pragmatic effects (or moral consequences), a use-
fulness beyond the realm of literary analysis. There is that vague, persistent belief
that reading literature will make one a better person. What I find to be the most
troublesome element of this belief is the ineffability of how the process of charac-
ter development (or political consciousness) via "critical thinking skills" applied to
literary texts might actually work. Satisfactory responses are difficult to find to this
query. One compelling characteristic of Bryskett's *Discourse* is that he offers his
readers just such a process, and though optimistic, its probabilistic or skeptical
core contains the possibilities for both success and failure. Most important, Brys-
kett's *Discourse* and Spenser's poetics contain the capacity to challenge and refor-
mulate received ideas and make them anew with respect to deliberative standards
entrenched in our lives as political animals. Rhetoric and poetry are, in the most
general sense, about words, words that empower people to make sense of, guide,
challenge, and transform their experience as individuals indebted to and invested in
the common wealth—or not. "To re-figure rhetorical studies," writes Janet Atwill,
"as an art of intervention and invention is to create a very different classroom."[4]
Re-appropriating Tudor poetic practices into the history of rhetoric might be a
small step toward such a reconfiguration, but it is step toward reconsidering how
we discharge our obligations as scholars and teachers, because how we define "we"
and what "we" do depends largely on the histories we choose to tell and how we
choose to tell them.

NOTES

Chapter One

1. Philip Sidney, *A Defence of Poetry,* in *The Miscellaneous Prose of Sir Philip Sidney,* ed. Katharine Duncan-Jones and Jan van Dorsten (Oxford: Clarendon Press, 1972), 110. All subsequent references to Sidney's *Defence* are quoted from this edition.

2. See, for example, Thomas Wilson's comments on "Digression, or Swerving from the Matter," in *Thomas Wilson: The Art of Rhetoric,* ed. Peter Medine (1560; repr., University Park: Pennsylvania State University Press, 1994), 206–7. Although Sidney explicitly refers to his straying to oratory as a "digression," critics have been unwilling to consider what role either oratory or the status of oratory in England might portend for the argument of the *Defence.* The attention given to rhetoric in the text most frequently is relegated to the observation that it follows, as Duncan-Jones and van Dorsten say, the "compositional rules" prescribed "for this type of oratory" (*Miscellaneous Prose,* 64); thus the editors of the edition I am using furnish an outline separating the body of the text into exordium, narration, proposition, divisions, examination 1, examination 2, refutation, digression (of poetry in England), and peroration. The first modern critic to write on Sidney's *Defence* as a "classical oration" was Kenneth O. Myrick in *Sir Philip Sidney as a Literary Craftsman,* Harvard Studies in England 14 (Cambridge: Harvard University Press, 1935), 46–83.

3. Cicero, *De oratore,* trans. E. W. Sutton, 2 vols., Loeb Classical Library 348/349 (Cambridge: Harvard University Press, 1942), 1.16.69, 3.7.27. All subsequent references are quoted from this edition.

4. Cicero, *Orator,* trans. H. M. Hubbell (Cambridge: Harvard University Press, 1988), 11.37, 13.42.

5. Roger Ascham, *The Schoolmaster,* ed. Lawrence V. Ryan (1570; repr., Ithaca, N.Y.: Cornell University Press, 1967), 150. The epigraph to this introduction may be found on page 119. All quotations from this text are taken from this edition.

6. Francis Bacon, *The Advancement of Learning,* book 1, ed. William A. Armstrong (London: Athlone Press, 1975), 70.

7. Anthony Grafton and Lisa Jardine, *From Humanism to the Humanities: Education and the Liberal Arts in Fifteenth- and Sixteenth-Century Europe* (Cambridge: Harvard University Press, 1986), 218.

8. George A. Kennedy, *Classical Rhetoric and Its Christian and Secular Tradition from Ancient to Modern Times* (Chapel Hill: North Carolina University Press, 1980), 196–97.

9. See chapters 6 and 7 of Grafton and Jardine, *From Humanism to the Humanities.* The authors would not agree, however, with my characterization of humanist ideals being reduced to "pedagogical fodder."

10. Brian Vickers maintains that it is precisely the "increase[d] autonomy of rhetoric" within the halls of academe that demonstrates rhetoric's significance and vitality among humanists. Brian Vickers, *In Defence of Rhetoric* (Oxford. Clarendon Press, 1988), 256.

11. Debora Kuller Shuger, *Habits of Thought in the English Renaissance: Religion, Politics, and the Dominant Culture* (Toronto: University of Toronto Press, 1997), 1. I develop this claim relative to Spenser scholarship in chapters 7 and 8.

12. Ann Moss, "Commonplace-Rhetoric and Thought-Patterns in Early Modern Culture," in *Renaissance Rhetoric,* ed. Peter Mack (New York: St. Martin's Press, 1994), 55.

13. See Timothy J. Reiss, *Knowledge, Discovery and Imagination in Early Modern Europe: The Rise of Aesthetic Rationalism* (Cambridge: Cambridge University Press, 1997), as well as Timothy J. Reiss, *The Meaning of Literature* (Ithaca, N.Y.: Cornell University Press, 1992).

14. William Temple, *William Temple's "Analysis" of Sir Philip Sidney's "Apology for Poetry,"* ed. and trans. John Webster, Medieval and Renaissance Texts and Studies 32 (Binghamton, N.Y.: Medieval & Renaissance Texts & Studies, 1984), 163.

15. For a contemporary's view on poetry as the "nurse of abuse" to the common weal, see Stephen Gosson's work "The Schoole of Abuse," in *English Reprints,* vol. 1, "carefully edited by" Edward Arber (1579; repr., New York: AMS Press, 1966).

16. Patricia Coughlan refers to Spenser as "the most monological of writers" in "'Some Secret Scourge Which Shall by Her Come unto England': Ireland and Incivility in Spenser," in *Spenser and Ireland: An Interdisciplinary Perspective,* ed. Patricia Coughlan (Cork: Cork University Press, 1989), 62. Bruce Avery similarly notes (with respect to Spenser's *View of the Present State of Ireland*) that though the "most intriguing aspect" of the text is its "polyvocality," the text "is essentially monovocal" (Bruce Avery, "Mapping the Irish Other: Spenser's *A View of the Present State of Ireland,*" *English Literary History* 57 [1990]: 264). See also Stephen Greenblatt, *Renaissance Self-Fashioning: From More to Shakespeare* (Chicago: University of Chicago Press, 1980), 192. A more sophisticated and insightful understanding of Spenser's rhetoric, albeit firmly entrenched within Spenser studies in the sense that it avers Spenser's Platonism and has little real interest in developing the historical currencies of rhetoric available in Tudor England, is Michael F. N. Dixon's *Polliticke Courtier: Spenser's "The Faerie Queene" as a Rhetoric of Justice* (Montreal: McGill-Queen's University Press, 1996). Also worth noting here is that although the dominance of Protestant doctrine and Neoplatonic thought in Spenser's work serves as a critical commonplace, such has not always been the case. See, for example, C. S. Lewis's review essay of Robert Ellrodt's *Neoplatonism in the Poetry of Edmund Spenser* (Geneva: Librarie E. Droz, 1960) in the same-titled essay in *Studies in Medieval and Renaissance Literature* (Cambridge:

Cambridge University Press, 1966), 149–63. This review is reprinted from *Etudes Anglaises* 14, no. 2 (1961).

17. See Thomas O. Sloane, *On the Contrary: The Protocol of Traditional Rhetoric* (Washington, D.C.: Catholic University of America Press, 1997). Sloane rightly observes the long-recognized yet persistent "neglect of rhetoric as an intellectual pursuit" (10).

18. Thomas O. Sloane, *Donne, Milton, and the End of Humanist Rhetoric* (Berkeley and Los Angeles: University of California Press, 1985); Sloane, *On the Contrary;* Victoria Kahn, *Rhetoric, Prudence, and Skepticism in the Renaissance* (Ithaca, N.Y.: Cornell University Press, 1985); Shuger, *Habits of Thought;* Ernesto Grassi, *Renaissance Humanism: Studies in Philosophy and Poetics,* trans. Walter F. Veit, Medieval and Renaissance Texts and Studies 51 (Binghamton, N.Y.: Medieval & Renaissance Texts & Studies, 1988); Ernesto Grassi, *Rhetoric as Philosophy* (University Park: Pennsylvania State University Press, 1980); Richard Waswo, *Language and Meaning in the Renaissance* (Princeton, N.J.: Princeton University Press, 1987); Wayne A. Rebhorn, *The Emperor of Men's Minds: Literature and Renaissance Discourse on Rhetoric* (Ithaca, N.Y.: Cornell University Press, 1995); and Nancy S. Struever, *Theory as Practice: Ethical Inquiry in the Renaissance* (Chicago: University of Chicago Press, 1992).

19. Jeffrey Walker, *Rhetoric and Poetics in Antiquity* (Oxford: Oxford University Press, 2000), ix.

20. Paul Ricoeur, *The Rule of Metaphor: Multi-disciplinary Studies of the Creation of Meaning in Language,* trans. Robert Czerny (Toronto: University of Toronto Press, 1977), 3.

21. Ascham, *Schoolmaster,* 107.

22. All quotations of Sidney's poetry are taken from Philip Sidney, *The Poems of Sir Philip Sidney,* ed. William A. Ringler Jr. (Oxford: Clarendon Press, 1962).

23. Kenneth Burke, *Permanence and Change: An Anatomy of Purpose* (1935; repr., Berkeley and Los Angeles: University of California Press, 1984), 260. Burke's influence permeates this inquiry.

24. James Berlin, "Revisionary Histories of Rhetoric," in *Writing Histories of Rhetoric,* ed. Victor J. Vitanza (Carbondale: Southern Illinois University Press, 1994), 112–27. Nevertheless, I think that inasmuch as this study is a "limited and localized" attempt to "address features of experience that grand narratives exclude" (Berlin, "Revisionary Histories of Rhetoric," 123), it complies in an odd, perhaps unanticipated way with Berlin's theoretical goals.

Chapter Two

1. Lodowick Bryskett, *"A Discourse of Civill Life": The Literary Works of Lodowick Bryskett,* ed. J. H. P. Pafford (Westmead, Hants: Gregg International, 1972). All quotations are taken from this edition, which is a reprint of the 1606 text "Printed for William Aspley." Another 1606 edition is identical to the Aspley printing except for the imprint "Printed for Edward Blovnt." A modern spelling edition is also available: *Lodowick Bryskett: "A Discourse of Civill Life",* ed. Thomas E. Wright, San Fernando Valley State College Renaissance Editions 4 (Northridge, Calif.: San Fernando State College, 1970).

2. Bryskett and the *Discourse* have been cited most frequently by Spenser scholars in relationship to Spenser's life in Ireland and as a means for chronicling the composition of *The Faerie Queene*. See Henry R. Plomer and Thomas Peete Cross, *The Life and Correspondence of Lodowick Bryskett* (Chicago: University of Chicago Press, 1927); Josephine Waters Bennett, *The Evolution of "The Faerie Queene"* (Chicago: University of Chicago Press, 1942); Edmund Spenser, vol. 10 of *The Works of Edmund Spenser: A Variorum Edition,* gen. ed. Edward Greenlaw, spec. ed. Rudolf Gottfried (Baltimore: Johns Hopkins University Press, 1949); Deborah Jones, "Lodowick Bryskett and His Family," in *Thomas Lodge and Other Elizabethans,* ed. Charles Sisson (New York: Octagon Books, 1966), 243–362; and Thomas Wright's entry on Bryskett in *The Spenser Encyclopedia,* gen. ed. A. C. Hamilton (Toronto: University of Toronto Press, 1990), 119. For a discussion of Bryskett in reference to his translation of Guazzo's *La Civile Conversatione,* see John L. Lievsay, *Stefano Guazzo and the English Renaissance, 1575–1675* (Chapel Hill: University of North Carolina Press, 1961). For a very good discussion of humanists' use of the dialogue genre, see David Marsh, *The Quattrocento Dialogue: Classical Tradition and Humanist Motivation* (Cambridge: Harvard University Press, 1980).

3. Sean Kane, *Spenser's Moral Allegory* (Toronto: University of Toronto Press, 1989), 1–6.

4. See David L. Miller, "Aesthetic Theology," in *The Poem's Two Bodies: The Poetics of the 1590 "Faerie Queene,"* by David L. Miller (Princeton, N.J.: Princeton University Press, 1988), 68–82.

5. Edmund Spenser, "A Letter of the Authors," in *The Faerie Queene,* ed. A. C. Hamilton (New York: Longman, 1977), 737–38. All subsequent references to Spenser's "Letter to Ralegh" ("A Letter of the Authors") will be noted parenthetically as "LR" (no pagination). Hamilton's edition retains the "u" for "v" and "i" for "j."

6. Drummond reports in his *Notes of Conversations with Ben Jonson* that Jonson had said that "the Irish having Robd Spensers goods & burnt his house & a little child new born, he and his wife escaped, & after he died for lake of bread in King Street." William Drummond, *Notes of Conversations with Ben Jonson,* in *Ben Jonson: Discoveries 1641, Conversations with William Drummond of Hawthornden 1619,* ed. G. B. Harrison (1619; repr., Edinburgh: Edinburgh University Press, 1966), 8–9.

7. In the "Letter to Ralegh," one instance of where Spenser eschews the idealism commonly associated with Renaissance Neoplatonism occurs when he opts for the temporal, more practically minded, civic-oriented example of Xenophon, who, he says, is to be "preferred before Plato, for that the one . . . formed a Commune welth such as it should be, but the other in the person of Cyrus and the Persians fashioned a gouernement such as might best be."

8. See Roland MacIlmaine, trans., *The Logike of the Moste Excellent Philosopher P. Ramus Martyr,* ed. Catherine M. Dunn, San Fernando Valley State College Renaissance Editions 3 (Northridge, Calif.: San Fernando State College, 1969), and Roland MacIlmaine, trans., *Peter Ramus: The Logike, 1574* (Leeds: Scolar Press, 1966). For the spread of Ramism in England, see Walter J. Ong, S.J., "The Diffusion of Ramism," in *Ramus, Method, and the Decay of Dialogue* (Cambridge: Harvard University Press, 1958), 295–318; Walter J. Ong, S.J., "Tudor Writings on Rhetoric," *Studies in the*

Renaissance 15 (1968): 39–69; and W. S. Howell, "Ramus and English Rhetoric: 1574–1681," *Quarterly Journal of Speech* 37 (1951): 299–310. For a discussion of Ramism's effects on English humanism, see Thomas O. Sloane's chapter "A History of English Humanist Rhetorical Theory," in Sloane, *End of Humanist Rhetoric,* 130–44.

9. Victoria Kahn, "Humanism and the Resistance to Theory," in *Literary Theory / Renaissance Texts,* ed. Patricia Parker and David Quint (Baltimore: Johns Hopkins University Press, 1986), 384.

10. Notably, Bryskett's discussion of logic and rhetoric does not engage in any of the sectarian Catholic bashing characteristic of Ramist handbooks; if virtuous actions are engendered by virtuous learning, Bryskett rejects this opportunity to wed virtue to a particular religious doctrine.

11. Aristotle, *Nicomachean Ethics,* trans. Martin Oswald (New York: Macmillan, 1962). All references to Aristotle's *Ethics* are taken from this translation; parenthetical citations use the abbreviation *NE.*

12. Cicero himself described *De oratore* as an imitation of Aristotle's dialogues; in *Epistulae ad Familiares,* he says that it was "written . . . on the model of Aristotle . . . [and is] three books in the form of a discussion and dialogue" (1.9.23). See Cicero, *Letters to His Friends,* trans. W. Glynn Williams, Loeb Classical Library (Cambridge: Harvard University Press, 1958), 1:83. Of course, humanist authors had no recourse to Aristotle's dialogues.

13. Kahn, *Rhetoric, Prudence, and Skepticism,* 30. Earlier in this century, arguments regarding the civic nature of quattrocento humanism were cogently put forth by Hans Baron; see, for example, "Cicero and Roman Civic Spirit in the Middle Ages and the Early Renaissance," *Bulletin of the John Rylands Library* 22 (1938): 72–97. Of further interest will be an exchange between Baron and Jerrold Seigel, especially since the latter's monograph, *Rhetoric and Philosophy in Renaissance Humanism: The Union of Eloquence and Wisdom, Petrarch to Valla* (Princeton, N.J.: Princeton University Press, 1968), is still an often-referred-to text. See Jerrold Seigel's "'Civic Humanism' or Ciceronian Rhetoric?" *Past and Present* 34 (1966): 3–48, and Hans Baron's reply, "Leonardo Bruni: 'Professional Rhetorician' or Civic Humanist?" *Past and Present* 36 (1967): 21–37.

14. Sloane, *End of Humanist Rhetoric,* 95, 92.

15. In general terms, Bryskett's Aristotelian analysis of the "morall vertues," their connection with the senses, their role in learning, and their relationship with the intellectual virtue of *phronesis* resonates with modern scholarship on Aristotle's ethics. Particularly instructive is Amelie Oksenberg Rorty, ed., *Essays on Aristotle's Ethics* (Berkeley and Los Angeles: University of California Press, 1980). See M. F. Burnyeat, "Aristotle on Learning to Be Good" (69–92); L. A. Kosman, "Being Properly Affected: Virtues and Feelings in Aristotle's *Ethics*" (103–16); J. O. Urmsen, "Aristotle's Doctrine of the Mean" (157–70); and Julia Annas, "Aristotle on Pleasure and Goodness" (285–99). See also Sarah Broadie, *Ethics with Aristotle* (Oxford: Oxford University Press, 1991), and Mary Sim, ed., *The Crossroads of Norm and Nature: Essays on Aristotle's "Ethics" and "Metaphysics"* (New York: Rowman and Littlefield, 1995).

16. Kenneth Burke offers an outline of "metabiology" or "metabolism" that is conceptually similar to the one presented by Bryskett in *Permanence and Change,* 232–36;

of course, both Burke and Bryskett were steeped in Aristotle's works. This study of Bryskett owes its general framework to three key ideas articulated by Burke: Burke, like Bryskett, stipulates that "man is essentially a *participant*" (235) in all living things, and thus "inactivity is categorically an evil, since it is not possible to the biologic process" (236); Burke also notes that "man lives by purpose—and purpose is basically *preference*" (235); and preference for Burke appears to be a mode of choosing that is something less than rational or deliberate, that is, purposeful.

17. On one level, thus, the *sensus communis* is the faculty that permits each person to develop a sense of his or her own self as a distinct entity because it harbors those sensations that tell individuals that they are, at the very least, physically separate from other selves. On another level, however, this faculty is also a unifying force in that it is a "sense common to all."

18. The term "imaginative universals" has been taken from Donald Phillip Verene, whose *Vico's Science of the Imagination* (Ithaca, N.Y.: Cornell University Press, 1981) offers a more comprehensive account of the relationship among imagination, memory, science, poetry, and rhetoric in the (late) humanism of Giambattista Vico. Vico himself referred to the *universale fantastico* as sensory topoi, which Verene argues formed "the basis of speech itself" (172) in Vico's thought.

19. Philosophical knowledge is thus inductive in that it originates with the body's physical presence in the world; this is perhaps what Aristotle means when he says that "the fundamental principles of philosophy and natural science come from experience" (*NE* 1142b; 1139b). Aristotle also takes up the necessity of the senses and sensory experience to speculative or theoretic wisdom in the opening pages of his *Metaphysics*.

20. Aristotle says of metaphor in his *On the Art of Poetry*, ed. and trans. Ingram Bywater (Oxford: Clarendon Press, 1909), 63: "The greatest thing by far is to be a master of metaphor. It is the one thing that cannot be learnt from others; and it is also a sign of genius, since a good metaphor implies an intuitive perception of the similarity in dissimilars." Similarly, Cicero notes in *De officiis,* trans. Walter Miller, Loeb Classical Library (Cambridge: Harvard University Press, 1913), that it is the power to draw analogies (*similitudenes comparat rebusque*) together with the power of reason that allows humans to survey "the course of his whole life and [make] the necessary preparations for his conduct" (1.4.11). Ernesto Grassi explores the formative power of fantasy, or what he calls (following Vico) *ingenium,* in humanist philosophy in *Renaissance Humanism.*

21. See Thomas M. Tuozzo, "Conceptualized and Unconceptualized Desire in Aristotle," *Journal of the History of Philosophy* 32 (1995): 525–49. Tuozzo discusses the differences between sense perception and a "mental experience" in Aristotle and offers an example similar to the one I have offered here to distinguish between the two (though I composed the above before discovering Tuozzo's). Significantly, Tuozzo argues that "though Aristotle is not explicit on this point," the sense perceptions's apprehension of a thing might be termed a "phantasma [which] for Aristotle is not an experiencing, but rather something that occasions a mental activity" (529).

22. Though both Bryskett and Spenser claim to derive twelve moral virtues from Aristotle, it is unclear on what basis their reckoning proceeds. In any case, the twelve private moral virtues Bryskett offers are the principal virtues of Fortitude, Temperance,

Justice, and Prudence, from which are derived Liberality, Magnificence, Magnanimity, Mansuetude ("being a meane betweene wrathfulnesse with desire for reuenge . . . and coldnesse or lacke of feeling of wrongs" [240]), Desire for Honor, Verity, Affability, and, finally, Urbanity (*Discourse*, 214–16).

23. This claim, which for some humanists education served as a moral imperative incumbent on human beings as political humans, is meant to contribute to an abiding principle that explains the humanists' peculiar tendency to conflate pedagogy with philosophy; and it is meant to modify the widely held thesis, put forward by Paul Oskar Kristeller, for example, that humanists were professional, itinerant pedagogues bent on spreading an elitist, philologic enterprise throughout medieval Europe to effect political and religious reform and enhance personal fortunes by imposing (ancient) standards of culture, beauty, and good Latin. See Paul Oskar Kristeller, *Renaissance Thought I: The Classic, Scholastic, and Humanist Strains* (New York: Harper, 1961).

24. In the Loeb translation, *cordis* in the following passage is translated as "brain": "Hinc discidium illud exstitit quasi linguae atque cordis, absurdum sane et inutile et reprehendum, ut alii nos sapere, alii dicere docerunt." *Cordis* can mean "brain" or "mind" in a very general sense; etymologically and in a technical sense, however, it usually denotes "heart." I have chosen the latter because, within the context of Cicero's critique of Plato and Aristotle, it seems more appropriate. In any event, there appears to be an inherent ambiguity between "heart" and "mind" similar to the kind that persists in English in the expression "You know in your heart . . ." or when people might preface a claim with "I feel" instead of "I think."

25. Though he does not acknowledge Cicero's *sermo*, or "conversation" (in conjunction with *contentione*, or "oratory"), in his discussion on the relationship of rhetoric and ethics, Thomas S. Frentz has made a similar argument regarding the role of speech in ethical instruction in "Rhetorical Conversation, Time, and Moral Action," *Quarterly Journal of Speech* 71 (1985): 1–18. Specifically, Frentz argues that "rhetorical conversation" is a vital means of coming to know the world, and one's relationship with that world insofar as conversations subsume personal narratives within larger myths about the world.

26. See Hannah Gray, "Renaissance Humanism: The Pursuit of Eloquence," *Journal of the History of Ideas* 24 (1963): 497–514.

27. "Virtutis enim laus omnis in actione consistit" (Cicero, *De officiis* 1.6.19).

Chapter Three

1. Edmund Spenser, *The Yale Edition of the Shorter Poems of Edmund Spenser*, ed. William A. Oram, Einar Bjorvand, Ronald Bond, Thomas H. Cain, Alexander Dunlap, and Richard Schell (New Haven, Conn.: Yale University Press, 1989), 213. All quotations from the *Calender* are taken from this edition.

2. Ricoeur, *Rule of Metaphor*, 3.

3. See Ong, *Decay of Dialogue*, 301–7, and W. S. Howell, *Logic and Rhetoric in England 1500–1700* (Princeton, N.J.: Princeton University Press, 1956). Ong notes that although "Bacon spoke accurately for the learned tradition in England when he judged that Ramism was already over with in his day," Ramism found an easy welcome in England and quickly became part of the intellectual fabric. Both Ong and Howell indicate that Ramism was largely a young man's vice, owing in no small part to the

rash of Ramist logics printed in England between 1574 and 1632 designed specifically for young scholars.

4. See Gabriel Harvey, *Ciceronianus,* trans. Clarence A. Forbes. and ed. Harold S. Wilson, Studies in the Humanities 4 (Lincoln: University of Nebraska Press, 1945).

5. Though the influence of Ramism in England at the time of Spenser's composition of the *Calender,* then *Faerie Queene,* is often noted by critics, especially because of his relationship with Harvey, critics on the whole have been reluctant to examine the possible relationship between Ramism and Spenser's poetry. Two exceptions to this rule are John Webster, "'The Methode of a Poete': An Inquiry into Tudor Conceptions of Poetic Sequence," *English Literary Renaissance* 11 (1981): 22–43, and Tamara A. Goeglein, "Utterance of the Protestant Soul in *The Faerie Queene:* The Allegory of Holiness and the Humanist Discourse of Reason," *Criticism* 36 (1994): 1–19. Both Webster and Goeglein characterize Spenser as being favorably disposed toward appropriating the Ramist method on the common critical assumptions that the formal conventions of poetry (Webster) and the rigors of Protestant doctrine (Goeglein) guided Spenser's poetic efforts rather than the principles of a humanistic or rhetorical moral philosophy.

6. For surveys of the criticism regarding E. K.'s identity, see Louise Schleiner, "Spenser's 'E. K.' as Edmund Kent (Kenned / Of Kent): Kyth (Couth), Kissed, and Kunning, Conning," *English Literary Renaissance* 20 (1990): 374–407, and Louis Waldman, "Spenser's Pseudonym 'E. K.' and Humanist Self-Naming," *Spenser Studies* 9 (1991): 21–31.

7. Michael McCanles, "*The Shepheardes Calender* as Document and Monument," *Studies in English Literature 1500–1900* 22 (1982): 5–6. Relying on Foucault, McCanles demonstrates how E. K. forces the reader to constantly question and reinterpret the eclogues in terms of their historicity. McCanles does not recognize any philosophical distinction between the poet and his glossarist—at least not in the broad terms I outline in the following argument. Two works that make a distinction between the poet and E. K. on doctrinal and political grounds are Robert Lane, *Shepheards Devises: Edmund Spenser's "Shepheardes Calender" and the Institutions of Elizabethean Society* (Athens: University of Georgia Press, 1993), and Dominic Delli Carpini, "Rewriting Holiness in the Age of Mechanical Reproduction: Cultural and Theological Contexts of Spenserian Allegory" (Ph.D. diss., Pennsylvania State University, 1995), 43–90.

8. This is not to say that Immeritô does not exploit, allude to, or emulate a rich poetic tradition of poetry in a self-conscious manner. My argument only questions the assumptions that seem to underlie E. K.'s reasons for placing Immeritô within this rather narrow critical context *primarily.*

9. Another example of E. K.'s narrow conception of the poet's moral obligations occurs in his gloss to the *Julye* eclogue wherein he notes that Thomalin refers to Aaron, the brother of Moses, at line 161. E. K.'s gloss reads: "He meaneth Aaron: whose name for more Decorum, the shephearde sayeth he hath forgot, lest his remembraunce and skill in antiquitie of holy writ should seeme to exceed the meanenesse of the Person" (*Shepheardes Calender,* 133).

10. The ridiculousness of Cuddie as "the perfect paterne of a Poete" is underscored in his equation of poetic inspiration with out-and-out drunkenness:

> And when with Wine the braine begins to sweate,
> The nombers flowe as fast as spring doth ryse.
> Thou kenst not *Percie* howe the ryme should rage.
> O if my temples were distaind with wine . . .
> (*Shepheardes Calender,* 107–10)

E. K., unphased, glosses the last line quoted above as follows: "He seemeth here to be ravished with a Poeticall furie. For (if one rightly mark) the nomber rise so ful, and verse groweth so big, that it seemeth he hath forgot the meanesesse of a shepheards state and stile" (182).

11. Ut, cum in sole ambulem, etiamsi aliam ob causam ambulem, fieri natura tamen, ut colorer: sic, cum istos libros ad Misenum (nam Romê vix licet) studiosius legerim, sentio illorum tactu orationem meam quasi colorari (*De oratore* 2.14.60).

12. The orator thus is proscribed to the documenting of actual events and persons —of "not only . . . what was said or done, but also of the manner of doing and saying it" (*De oratore* 2.15.63).

13. E. K. makes a similar distinction in the "Epistle to Harvey," when he commends Harvey for his "Latin Poemes, which in my opinion both for invention and Elocution are very delicate, and superexcellent" (*Shepheardes Calender,* 21).

14. To "separate words from thought as one might sever body from mind" prefigures Crassus's defining criticism of Socrates (which is intended explicitly then to indict Socrates' disciples, Plato's Academicians, and Aristotle's Peripatetics), when later he says that Socrates introduced that "absurd and unprofitable and reprehensible severance between the tongue and the heart," which leads "us to our having one set of professors to teach us to think and another to teach us to speak" (*De oratore* 3.16.61). Cicero articulates a similar complaint in his opening remarks to Quintus at 1.6.23.

15. Struever, *Theory as Practice,* 3–56, 134–42; Kahn, *Rhetoric, Prudence, and Skepticism,* 19–54; Sloane, *End of Humanist Rhetoric,* 69–99, 112–29; and Grassi, *Renaissance Humanism,* 80–82, 111–25.

16. See Lane's *Shepheards Devises* and Delli Carpini's "Rewriting Holiness" for analogous developments of this argument.

17. George Puttenham, *The Arte of Englishe Poesie* (1589; repr., Kent, Ohio: Kent State University Press, 1970), 53.

Chapter Four

1. Describing Spenser's posture toward the affairs of human kind as "ambivalent" has not been problematic for most critics, historically. Anthea Hume noted that "Spenser's characteristic stance as a pastoral poet is thought to be one of 'balance' or 'ambivalence' in relation to the opposing views put forward in the eclogues" in *Edmund Spenser: Protestant Poet* (Cambridge: Cambridge University Press, 1984), 13. Hume efficiently cites in support of her claim William Nelson's *Poetry of Edmund Spenser* (New York: Columbia University Press, 1963), 46; Patrick Cullen's *Spenser, Marvell, and Renaissance Pastoral* (Cambridge: Harvard University Press, 1970); and Nancy Jo Hoffman's *Spenser's Pastorals: "The Shepheardes Calender" and "Colin Clout"* (Baltimore: Johns Hopkins University Press, 1977), 118. Hume's own attempt to amend this view of the poet as "ambivalent" by aligning Spenser with Protestant dogma has proven to be influential, though in an indirect way. By either overlooking

or complicating the salient political concerns Hume focuses on, critics typically cast the poet's lot in with the spiritual as the poet's a priori claim to "poetic authority," thus rendering the rhetorical work of the poem an (arhetorical) demonstration or the mere "expression of" the poet's "vatic" ambition. Others who have noted the poet's "ambivalence" to be a prominent character trait include Harry Berger Jr., "Afterword," in *Revisionary Play,* by Harry Berger Jr. (Berkeley and Los Angeles: University of California Press, 1988), 468; Roland Greene, "*The Shepheardes Calender,* Dialogue, and Periphrasis," *Spenser Studies* 8 (1987): 1–33; Kane, *Spenser's Moral Allegory,* 11–15 (Kane describes Spenser's use of metaphor as a "tactic" of "eqivalent opposition" that allows one "to draw an imaginary line through complexity" [12–13]); and David Shore, *Spenser and the Poetics of Pastoral: A Study of the World of Colin Clout* (Kingston: McGill-Queen's University Press, 1985), 4. As a consistent element that traverses not only generations of Spenser criticism but also across many and various critical theories current today, citing the poet's "ambivalence" is perhaps indicative of the general consistency inhering in the philosophical frame that defines the discipline of "English literature" apart from the rhetorical tradition.

Two works that examine and develop the socially active or *interested* role Spenser intends for the *Calender* on grounds associated with a benevolent and patriarchal nationalism are Lynn Stanley Johnson, *"The Shepheardes Calender": An Introduction* (University Park: Pennsylvania State University Press, 1990), and Lane, *Shepheardes Devises.*

2. McCanles, "*Shepheardes Calender* as Document and Monument," 9.

3. Louis Adrian Montrose, "'The Perfect Paterne of a Poete': The Poetics of Courtship in *The Shepheardes Calender,*" *Texas Studies in Literature and Language* 21 (1978): 34–67. Montrose's cursory yet obligatory nod toward the "artistic and ethical idealism of Renaissance humanism" is indicative of the enthythematic (or putative) role the principles of humanist moral philosophy play within Spenser criticism.

4. Cicero avers the same dictum for the orator, of course; Horace, however, is cited more frequently in connection with Spenser's poetry by critics.

5. Montrose, "'Perfect Paterne of a Poete,'" 35.

6. Greene, "*Shepheardes Calender,* Dialogue, and Periphrasis," 9.

7. S. K. Heninger, introduction to *The Shepheardes Calender,* Scholar's Facsimiles and Reprints 328 (1579; repr., Delmar, N.Y.: Scholar's Facsimiles and Reprints, 1979), xiv.

8. See Waswo's compelling (and much too brief) discussion of Sidney and Spenser in *Language and Meaning,* 230–31.

9. Richard McKeon matter-of-factly states that the architectonic function of rhetoric-poetry in Renaissance humanism owed its vitality to Cicero. See Richard McKeon, "The Use of Rhetoric in a Technological Age: Architectonic Productive Arts," in *Rhetoric: Essays in Invention and Discovery,* ed. Mark Backman (Woodbridge, Conn.: Ox Bow Press, 1987), 5–11.

10. See Kahn, *Rhetoric, Prudence, and Skepticism,* 38–41; Sloane, *End of Humanist Rhetoric;* Thomas O. Sloane, "Rhetorical Education and Two-Sided Argument," in *Renaissance-Rhetorik / Renaissance Rhetoric,* ed. Heinrich F. Plett (Berlin: Walter de Gruyter, 1993), 163–78; and Waswo, *Language and Meaning,* 213–59.

11. In addition to previously cited works, see Thomas O. Sloane, "Reinventing *inventio*," *College English* 51, no. 5 (1989): 461–73, and Thomas O. Sloane, "Schoolbooks and Rhetoric: Erasmus's *Copia*," *Rhetorica* 9, no. 2 (1991): 113–29.

12. Burke, *Permanence and Change*, 235.

13. Grassi discusses the indicative character of metaphors in *Rhetoric as Philosophy*, 18–34.

14. A. Leigh DeNeef, *Spenser and the Motives of Metaphor* (Durham, N.C.: Duke University Press, 1982).

15. See David L. Miller, *The Poem's Two Bodies: The Poetics of the 1590 "Faerie Queene"* (Princeton, N.J.: Princeton University Press, 1988). Miller's conception of Spenser's metaphor also refers to a "body"; significantly, however, this "'body' is an ideological formation derived from the religious myth of the *corpus mysticum*, and its imperial counterpart, the notion of the monarch as incarnating an ideal and unchanging political body" (4).

16. Harry Berger Jr., *Revisionary Play* (Berkeley and Los Angeles: University of California Press, 1988), 468.

17. For the pervasiveness of Cicero's authority as *the* moral philosopher of Tudor humanism, see T. W. Baldwin, *William Shakspere's Small Latine and Lesse Greeke*, 2 vols. (Urbana: University of Illinois Press, 1944), 2:578–616.

18. Colin's immaturity, similar to E. K.'s editorial comments and glosses, commonly serves as a point worth noting when convenient or unavoidable.

19. Sloane, "Rhetorical Education," 165–66. A more in-depth consideration of human/social concord occurs in my chapter 8 when Colin reappears to enact the virtue of courtesy, which virtue Spenser says is the "root" of civil conversation.

20. Ben Jonson puts it another way when he says, "Language most shewes a man: speake that I may see thee," in *Timbers: Or, Discoveries*, in Drummond, *Ben Jonson: Discoveries 1641*, 78.

21. The proclivity to deny the rhetorical work of Spenser's poetry as evidence of a moral character can be seen more readily in critical work on *The Faerie Queene*. Harry Berger Jr., for example, insists on calling "the Spenserian narrator an *it*, not a *he*" because "it" is "a function and not a figure, an act and not an agent" (10), in "Narrative as Rhetoric in *The Faerie Queene*," *English Literary Renaissance* 21 (1991): 3–48. For similar approaches to the poet's voided *ethos*, see Paul Alpers, *The Poetry of "The Faerie Queene"* (Princeton, N.J.: Princeton University Press, 1967), and Paul Alpers, "Narration in *The Faerie Queene*," *English Literary History* 44 (1977): 22–48.

22. Grassi, *Rhetoric as Philosophy*, 33. Pertinent to my study, Grassi's "some authors" could include Tamara Goeglein, whose semiotic analysis of the uses of poetry in English Ramist manuals effectively levels all metaphor to the theoretic or "literary" level Grassi alludes to, emptying metaphor thus of its moral content. See Tamara A. Goeglein, "'Wherein Hath Ramus Been So Offensious?': Poetic Examples in the English Ramist Logic Manuals (1574–1672)," *Rhetorica* 14, no. 1 (1996): 73–101.

23. The Ramist implications of E. K.'s turn to cognitive topics void of "knowledge-by sound" (*Shepheardes Calender*, 110) may be seen in Ong's account of Ramus's "topical logic" in *Decay of Dialogue*, 104–12.

24. Crassus terms the metaphorical process as the mode (or "method") of trans-
ferring words (*modus transferendi verbi*); he refers to the metaphor most often as a
"translation" (*translatio*) that conveys the sense of an activity, and considerably less
often as a *similitudo*, or "resemblance." Grassi notes in *Rhetoric as Philosophy*, "We also
must not forget that the term 'metaphor' is itself a metaphor; it is derived from the
verb *metapherein* 'to transfer' which originally described a concrete activity (Herodotus
1.64.2)" (33).

25. Ernesto Grassi, *The Primordial Metaphor*, trans. Laura Pietropaolo and Manuela
Scarci, Medieval and Renaissance Texts and Studies 121 (Binghamton, N.Y.: Medieval
& Renaissance Texts & Studies, 1994), ix. Grassi identifies "wonder" "(Gk. *thau-
mazein*)" as the "expression of astonishment and estrangement" (7) of one's experience
in the world that animates the making of metaphors. In concluding his introductory
chapter, Grassi states, "Teaching must be based on a sense of wonder, or the emotion
awakened by the text to be studied. It is a wonder which is nourished by experiencing
the changes of meaning of the words in the [reader's] act of interpretation" (14).

26. Mark Johnson, *The Body in the Mind, the Bodily Basis of Meaning, Imagination,
and Reason* (Chicago: University of Chicago Press, 1987), xv.

27. I have borrowed the term and the notion of sensory topoi from Verene's discus-
sion of the same in *Vico's Science of the Imagination*, 159–92. Vico was a consummate
Ciceronian, of course, and Verene discusses this notion of sensory topoi in his chapter
on Vico's rhetoric. For a superb discussion of Cicero's *ars topica* concomitant with the
one Verene ascribes Vico, see Michael C. Leff, "The Topics of Argumentative Inven-
tion in Latin Rhetorical Theory from Cicero to Boethius," *Rhetorica* 1, no. 1 (1983):
23–45. Leff's conclusion that Cicero's "theory of invention . . . was not divisible on
either material [or active] or inferential criteria, and it emerged as a single, unified the-
ory" (31), especially to Renaissance humanists, is persuasive.

This notion of drawing from the "commonplaces" of sensed experience in which
the sensed matter of *a* body's feelings may be "felt" by others can be found in Brys-
kett's discussion of the *sensus communis* in the *Discourse*, 123.

Chapter Five

1. "Dicendi autem omnis ratio in medio posita, communi quodam in usu, atque
in hominum more et sermone versatur."

2. Cicero, *De partitione oratoria*, in *De Oratore*, trans. H. Rackham, Loeb Classical
Library 349 (Cambridge: Harvard University Press, 1960).

3. Grassi, *Rhetoric as Philosophy*, 91. Also drawing on Grassi, James Robert Goetsch
Jr. notes the connection between *ornatus* and *kosmos* in *Vico's Axioms: The Geometry of
the Human World* (New Haven, Conn.: Yale University Press, 1995), 11.

4. In his introductory comments to book 3 to his brother Quintus, Cicero encour-
ages future readers to "form a mental picture of Lucius Crassus on a larger scale than
the sketch I shall draw" not unlike the picture of Socrates one imagines while read-
ing Plato (*De oratore* 3.4.15). In *Brutus*, furthermore, Cicero notes that "some crit-
ics maintain that Antonius and Crassus were speakers of equal ability," but he adds,
"It is my reasonable judgment that Crassus was the embodiment of consummate
perfection." Cicero, *Brutus*, trans. Hubert M. Poteat (Chicago: University of Chicago
Press, 1950), 111.

5. Cicero, *De oratore* 1.4.14–15.

6. Antonius's technically oriented and theoretically narrow approach to oratory need not be detrimental to an orator's character and effectiveness (as is evident by Antonius's own integrity), but Crassus notes in book 3 that "if we bestow fluency of speech on persons devoid of [integrity and wisdom], we shall have put weapons into the hands of madmen" (*De oratore* 3.14.55).

It is worth noting that there is evidence to suggest that Antonius is not committed to the version of rhetoric he offers in book 2. When Crassus chides Antonius for leaving "little or nothing to me" after having "finally unmasked and stripped [off] the veil of your pretended ignorance" by making himself known "as a master of the theory [of rhetoric]," Antonius replies: "Oh, as for that . . . the amount I shall have left you will be for you to decide; if you want complete candour, what I leave to you is the whole subject, but if you want me to keep up the pretence, it is for you to consider how you may satisfy our friends here" (*De oratore* 2.86.350–51).

7. See William Rueckert, "Both/And: The Aesthetic of *Counter-Statement*," in *Kenneth Burke and the Drama of Human Relations*, by William Rueckert, 2nd ed. (1963; repr., Berkeley and Los Angeles: University of California Press, 1982), 8–33. An implicit formulation of "both/and" is also evident in Kenneth Burke, "Poetic and Semantic Meaning," in *The Philosophy of Literary Form*, 3rd ed. (1941; repr., Berkeley and Los Angeles: University of California Press, 1967), 138–67.

8. For an excellent account of the centrality of *narration* to Cicero's rhetorical philosophy, see John D. O'Banion, "Cicero and Narration as the Art of Establishing Significance," in *Reorienting Rhetoric: The Dialectic of List and Story*, by John D. O'Banion (University Park: Pennsylvania State University Press, 1991), 57–75.

9. Protagoras, "Truth or Refutations," in *The Older Sophists*, trans. Michael J. O'Brien and ed. Rosamond Kent Sprague (Columbia: University of South Carolina Press, 1972), 18.

10. Burke, *Philosophy of Literary Form*, 25–26. Burke goes on to say that he has become "convinced that this [the synecdoche] is the 'basic' figure of speech, and that it occurs in many modes beside the formal trope" (26).

11. As Sloane notes, "Cicero's preferred rhetoric, in sum, is ethos-centered." *End of Humanist Rhetoric*, 128.

12. Cicero recalls the metaphor of Zeno's hand to Torquatus (an Epicurean) at 2.6.17 in *Finibus bonorum et malorum*, trans. H. Rackham, Loeb Classical Library 40 (New York: G. P. Putnam's Sons, 1931), 99.

13. Howell, *Logic and Rhetoric in England*, 4.

14. Howell, in *Logic and Rhetoric in England*, insists that the "poetic" remained the "one important aspect of communication . . . which logic and rhetoric did not seek fully to explain or to teach during the sixteenth and seventeenth centuries" (4). In parceling poetry out of "communication theory," he hands Renaissance rhetoric and logic over to humanist scholars, thus reaffirming a persistent disciplinary and critical convention exploited by both literary critics and some historians of rhetoric. Howell's use of Zeno's metaphor thus represents what Grassi calls a "literary metaphor." It is a "borrowing" which relies on available or known fields of reference for meaning or significance and lends itself to being explained in rational or formal terms. To get a fuller

sense of the particular relationship Howell's use of the metaphor names, we would have to situate Howell's understanding of rhetoric, logic, and poetry with his contemporary Kenneth Burke, whose debates with Howell exemplify or disclose a fuller sense of the "whole."

15. Antonius speaks about metaphors (similitudes, analogies) under the category of "witticisms" and "jests" (2.61–72); they are devices useful for provoking laughter thus gaining the favor of one's audience.

16. See Izadora Scott, *Controversies Over the Imitation of Cicero in the Renaissance* (1910; repr., Davis, Calif.: Hermagoras Press, 1991); John O. Ward, "Renaissance Commentators on Ciceronian Rhetoric," in *Renaissance Eloquence: Studies in the Theory and Practice of Renaissance Rhetoric,* ed. James J. Murphy (Berkeley and Los Angeles: University of California Press, 1983), 126–73; and Wayne A. Rebhorn, *Renaissance Controversies on Rhetoric* (Ithaca, N.Y.: Cornell University Press, 2000), 1–13.

17. Vives, however, was not mentioned until the second edition of Erasmus's *Ciceronianus* after being omitted from the first. See Betty I. Knott, "Introductory Note" to *The Ciceronian,* in *The Collected Works of Erasmus* (Toronto: University of Toronto Press, 1986), 21:324–36.

18. Scott offers a partial translation of an oration on Ciceronianism that an Italian named M. Antoine Muret (Muretus) published in 1572; Muretus appears to have carried Erasmus's critique of the zealous imitators of Cicero (such as Nizzolius) into the latter half of the century, see Scott, *Controversies Over the Imitation of Cicero,* 106–11.

19. See James D. Tracey, *The Politics of Erasmus: A Pacifist Intellectual and His Political Milieu* (Toronto: University of Toronto Press, 1978), and Lisa Jardine, *Erasmus, Man of Letters* (Princeton, N.J.: Princeton University Press, 1993).

20. Ong, *Decay of Dialogue,* 145–46. Also, Howell translates the following passage by John Prideaux, an Oxford scholar, whose *Notes on Logic* (*Hypomnemata Logica,* c. 1650) suggests that Ramus's scholasticism was evident at least to the next generation of English logicians:

> Q: Is it true that scholastic and Ramistic methods of breaking a subject down insist too much at various times upon trifles?
> A: Yes.
> Q: Are the Aristotelian and the Ramistic methods one and the same?
> A: Yes. (313)

21. Ong, *Decay of Dialogue,* 28.

22. Bruce A. Kimball, *Orators and Philosophers: A History of the Idea of Liberal Education* (New York: Teachers College, Columbia University, 1986), 87.

23. Struever, *Theory as Practice,* 52.

24. Kahn, *Rhetoric, Prudence, and Skepticism;* Sloane, *End of Humanist Rhetoric;* Waswo, *Language and Meaning.* Also see Charles B. Schmitt, *Cicero Scepticus: A Study of the Influence of the Academica in the Renaissance,* International Archives of the History of Ideas 52 (The Hague: Martinus Nijhoff, 1972).

25. See Struever, *Theory as Practice.* Struever's interest in Italian authors of the Renaissance somewhat prejudices her view of the northern humanism; much of what she says

regarding "theory as practice" in the Renaissance is, as Kahn shows in her chapter on Erasmus in *Rhetoric, Prudence, and Skepticism,* applicable to Erasmus as well.

26. Erasmus, *The Tongue,* ed. Elaine Fantham and Erika Rummel, trans. Elaine Fantham, vol. 29 of *Collected Works of Erasmus* (Toronto: University of Toronto Press, 1986), 383. Though Fantham's choice to render *De lingua* as *The Tongue* places emphasis on the physicality of the tongue, I have chosen to refer to the text as *On the Tongue* for reasons that will become apparent.

27. Margaret Mann Phillips, *Erasmus and the Northern Renaissance* (1949; repr., London: English Universities Press, 1984), 114. Also see Laurel Carrington, "Erasmus' *Lingua:* The Double-Edged Tongue," *Erasmus of Rotterdam Society Yearbook* 9 (1989): 106–18.

28. See Fantham's "Introductory Note," in Erasmus, *Tongue,* 250–56, note 56.

29. For a thorough and insightful study of Erasmus's "attitude" toward language, see Marjorie O'Rourke Boyle's *Erasmus on Language and Method in Theology* (Toronto: University of Toronto Press, 1977). See her discussion on "The Scope of Theology," 72–81, for references to Luther. Her first chapter, "Sermo," is particularly instructive; in it, she discusses Erasmus's use of the word *sermo* rather than *verbum* to refer to the speech of Christ in his Latin translation of the New Testament from the Greek: "Erasmus's appropriation of *sermo* emphasized the speaking activity of the *Logos* as the Father's revelation to the form of creation" (22).

30. Erasmus, *De ratione studii,* trans. and ed. Brian McGregor, vol. 24 of *Collected Works of Erasmus* (Toronto: University of Toronto Press, 1978), 666.

31. Richard J. Schoeck notes the uselessness "to speak dismissingly of Erasmus' as being a merely literary rhetoric" (45) in "Going for the Throat: Erasmus' Rhetorical Theory and Practice," in *Renaissance-Rhetorik / Renaissance Rhetoric,* ed. Heirich F. Plett (Berlin: Walter de Gruyter, 1993), 43–58.

32. Walter Ong, S. J., *Ramus and Talon Inventory* (Cambridge: Harvard University Press, 1958), 37–45. Ramus's collaborator, Omer Talon, contributed another five "explications" of Cicero's work in this time period.

33. "Vereor ne tantae rerum tenebrae perinde percipiantur ab aliis, atque animo pervideo." Peter Ramus, *Peter Ramus's Attack on Cicero: Text and Translation of Ramus's "Brutinae Quaestiones,"* trans. Carole E. Newlands and ed. James J. Murphy (Davis, Calif.: Hermagoras Press, 1992), 72. Murphy's editorial apparatus is especially useful; the bibliography provides an excellent list of both primary and secondary texts.

34. Cf. Peter Mack seems to aver the usefulness of Ramistic dialectic when he claims that "Ramus ensures that rhetoric and dialectic work together by clarifying the division between the two subjects." Peter Mack, *Renaissance Argument: Valla and Agricola in the Traditions of Rhetoric and Dialectic,* Brill's Studies in Intellectual History 43 (Leiden: E. J. Brill, 1993), 353. Similarly, Brian Vickers speaks of the "great contribution" Ramus, his cohort Talon, and their followers made "in their systematic development of *elocutio,* and their espousal of the vernaculars," claiming that the Ramists "had a beneficial influence in applying rhetoric to literature." Vickers, *In Defence of Rhetoric,* 209. (Both Mack and Vickers offer a useful bibliography regarding contemporary studies of Ramus in Europe.) In a different vein, it is the practicality of Ramism (by

virtue of its pedagogical impetus) that Victoria Kahn sees to be elemental to the end of humanist rhetoric. See Kahn, "Humanism and the Resistance to Theory," 393.

35. Ong, *Decay of Dialogue,* 177.

36. Ramus had been jailed earlier in the decade and his books banned.

37. Memory for Ramus appears to be a purely rational faculty; see Ong, *Decay of Dialogue,* 226–27, 280.

38. See Peter Ramus, *Arguments in Rhetoric Against Quintillian,* trans. Carole Newlands (Dekalb: Northern Illinois University Press, 1986). Here Ramus declares that "prudence is not a moral virtue but a virtue of the intelligence and mind." Similarly, and although he claims that "rhetoric is a virtue," he says that "it is a virtue of the mind and the intelligence, as in all the true liberal arts. Nor is rhetoric a moral virtue" (87).

39. For the point I am making here, it is irrelevant whether E. K. is accurate in defining "forswonk and forswatt" as "overlaboured and sunneburnt" (questions of his lexical accuracy have dominated discussion on these lines). What is important is that Antonius's analogy again rears its head at a crucial moment in the text as Colin ponders his poetic resources; E. K. appears to be completely unaware of the relationship his "sunneburnt" gloss might have to Calliope as "the honor of all Poeticall Invention" or as the "Goddesse of Rhetorick" (*Shepheardes Calender,* 81).

40. In chapter 4, you will recall, I cited the verse Colin "invents" upon being "inspired" by Calliope ("Bring Coronations, and Sops in wine," followed by a listing of flowers) in order to show that Colin considers such facile, ephemeral, and technically proficient exercise in *copia* to pass for poetic invention. Sidney disdains such versifying; he dismisses all "herbarists" (collections of plants) as "rifled up" and asserts that such are "certainly as absurd a surfeit to the ears as possible" (*Defence of Poetry,* 118).

41. See my third chapter, "E. K.'s Antonian Sunburn."

Chapter Six

1. Abraham Fraunce, *The Lawyer's Logic,* English Linguistics 1500–1800 174, ed. R. C. Alston (1588; repr., Menston, Yorks.: Scolar Press, 1969), ¶v–¶2r. This is "A Scholar Press Facsimile" of *The Lawiers Logike.* All references to *The Lawiers Logike* are taken from this facsimile edition; the pagination is inconsistent throughout this edition.

2. See Sister Mary Martin McCormick, P.B.V.M., ed., "A Critical Edition of Abraham Fraunce's *The Sheapheardes Logike* and *Twooe General Discourses*" (Ph.D. diss., St. Louis University, 1968).

3. See Goeglein, "Wherein Hath Ramus Been So Offensious?" 73–101.

4. See Goeglein, "Utterance of the Protestant Soul," 1–19.

5. Again, the phrase "resistance to theory" is developed by Kahn in "Humanism and the Resistance to Theory."

6. Temple, *William Temple's "Analysis,"* 25. I believe Webster is referring here to Ong's description of Ramism as a "rhetorized logic." But as what follows shows, and in spite of Webster's acknowledgment to Ong for his help on this work, Webster and Ong appear to have very different ideas about what is rhetorical about Ramistic logic.

7. Note that Fraunce divorces memory from the sensitive soul here, making it simply a facet of the rational faculty that apprehends forms rather than a faculty from which speech, then reason, is born (as in Bryskett's *Discourse*).

8. Note that it is "art" rather than a person who frames and performs the action here; the method does the work of judging for the individual. This is characteristic of the Ramists. The unquestioning faith in axioms derived from convention and syllogisms condemns Ramists to imitate the world; it is their reliance on their one, true method that absolves them from taking responsibility for the actions their imitations make.

9. Thus Fraunce echoes E. K.'s claim regarding "monuments of Poetry" (*SC,* 212), and to similar effect, as having gathered those "sparkes of naturall reason" from "excellent autors," they may be promptly subjugated to the "artificiall rules" generalized therefrom.

10. W. L. Godschalk's note titled "Cicero, Sidney, and the 'Sunne-Burn'd Braine,'" *Notes and Queries* 27 (1980): 139–40, correctly identifies Sidney's allusion to be from Cicero's *De oratore* (2.14.60). Godschalk also reminds us of E. K.'s use of this reference in his prefatory epistle, and Thomas Wilson's use of it in *The Art of Rhetorique* (1560), as well as George Gascoigne's use of it in "A Discourse of the Adventures passed by Master F. J.," in *A Hundred Sundrie Flowers* (1573).

11. My emphasis on a process of invention in which both the intellectual process of "turning others' leaves" and "looking into one's heart" are integral elements to poetic invention is meant to address the common critical practice of privileging the latter over the former by dismissing the intellective element as being antipoetic. For example, Mary Thomas Crane's analysis of this sonnet in *Framing Authority: Sayings, Self, and Society in Sixteenth-Century England* (Princeton, N.J.: Princeton University Press, 1993) identifies what I call the "Antonian" kind of invention alluded to as typical of humanist practices which she narrowly defines in terms of the "composition . . . taught in school" (192). Crane, consequently, describes the alternative mode of invention that I argue to be deeply Ciceronian as "antihumanistic." Without this Ciceronian tradition, Crane's analysis must return thus to the familiar, romantic portrait of Sidney as an artist who does not want to create a "moral argument" (193) but as one who seeks to establish a "myth of a 'whole' essential self that is sufficient even in its natural state to see its situation clearly and speak its own desires, if not persuasively, then ironically" (195).

12. Crassus, while developing the "very near" relationship of the poet and orator, recognizes that "something like identity exists" between the orator and the poet because the poet, too, "sets no boundaries or limits to his claim, such as would prevent him from ranging whither he will with the same freedom and license as the other" (*De oratore* 1.16.70). In his *Orator,* Cicero discusses difference between the poet and the orator; see 19.66–22.73.

13. For a parable or *fabula* involving the generative powers of this "second nature," see Giambattista Vico's narrative of the first mens' invention of Jove in his *New Science,* 3rd ed., trans. Thomas Goddard Bergin and Max Harold Fisch (1744; repr., Ithaca, N.Y.: Cornell University Press, 1968), ¶374–¶384 (pp. 116–20), and Verene's discussion of the same in *Vico's Science of the Imagination,* 173–77.

14. Puttenham, *Arte of Englishe Poesie,* 20.

15. Grassi, *Rhetoric as Philosophy,* 8.

16. Puttenham, *Arte of Englishe Poesie,* 19.

17. In *De partitione oratoria,* Cicero describes memory as "the twin sister of written script . . . very similar to it [but] in a dissimilar field. For just as script consists of marks indicating letters and of the material on which those marks are imprinted, so the stucture of memory, like a wax tablet, employs topics (*locis*) and in these stores images which correspond to the letters in written script" (7.26). See also Francis Yates, *The Art of Memory* (Chicago: University of Chicago Press, 1966), and Sharon Crowley, *Ancient Rhetorics for Contemporary Students* (Boston: Allyn and Bacon, 1994), 221–26.

18. Howell offers a transcription of the letter Sidney wrote to Temple thanking him for the gift of his book in *Logic and Rhetoric in England,* 205; Webster does the same in Temple, *William Temple's "Analysis,"* 38–39 (see note 6 above).

19. For a good account of the Temple-Digby debate, see Lisa Jardine's *Francis Bacon and the Art of Discourse* (London: Cambridge University Press, 1974), 59–65.

20. In quoting from Sidney, Webster uses G. Gregory Smith's edition of *An Apology for Poetry* in *Elizabethan Critical Essays* (Oxford: Clarendon Press, 1904), 150–207; this edition does not have modernized spelling (as does the Duncan-Jones edition I use throughout this study). Webster also expands Temple's references to the *Apology* "since the sense of his analysis is often incomplete without the full passage in the *Apology* to which he refers" (*William Temple's "Analysis,"* 43).

21. My focus on the Ramists' privileging of mathematics over the verbal arts is but one way to identify a fundamental difference in how a rational idealist such as Temple and a Ciceronian such as Sidney would see the role of language in the world. In a sense, the Ramist view may be seen as a secularization of what Grassi calls the "Problem of the Word" (*Renaissance Humanism,* 1–5); the mathematical, of course, became preeminent in the development of the sciences in the seventeenth century. Johannes Kepler, for example, appends a letter "to Ramus" at the beginning of *The New Astronomy* (1609), wherein he praises Ramus for asking the "assistance of Logic and Mathematics for the noblest art [philosophy]." Also, Kepler offers a "Synopsis of the Whole Work" with Ramist-like tables or graphs that lay out the "arguments" of his work through the repeated division of Astronomy's parts. See Johannes Kepler, *The New Astronomy,* trans. William H. Donahue (Cambridge: Cambridge University Press, 1992), 28–34. Of course, the Ramists view of language also had far-reaching implications for biblical hermeneutics, and so the religio-political turmoil of the Reformation. For an excellent discussion of "the problem of the word" with regard to Augustine, Erasmus, Luther, and "the Augustinian Reaction" (including Calvin and English Protestants), see Waswo's *Literature and Meaning.*

Chapter Seven

1. Nicholas Canny makes a similar observation in his introduction to *Spenser and Ireland: An Interdisciplinary Perspective,* ed. Patricia Coughlan (Cork: Cork University Press, 1989), 9.

2. Greenblatt, *Renaissance Self-Fashioning,* 192.

3. Coughlan, "Some Secret Scourge," 62.

4. Annabel Patterson, "The Egalitarian Giant: Representations of Justice in History/Literature," *Journal of British Studies* 31 (1992): 97–132. Elizabeth Fowler, "The Failure of Moral Philosophy in the Work of Edmund Spenser," *Representations* 51 (1995): 47–76.

5. Quoted in Edmund Spenser, *A View of the Present State of Ireland,* vol. 10 of *The Works of Edmund Spenser: A Variorum Edition,* gen. ed. Edwin Greenlaw, spec. ed. Rudolf Gottfried (Baltimore: Johns Hopkins University Press, 1949), 499. The text from which this passage is drawn is Émile Legouis's *Spenser* (New York: E. P. Dutton, 1926). Concrete examples of this practice of appropriating a portrait of Spenser painted by previous generations without question may be seen in David J. Baker's "'Some Quirk, Some Subtle Evasion': Legal Subversion in Spenser's *A View of the Present State of Ireland,*" *Spenser Studies* 6 (1986): 147–63; Baker offers a sketch of the poet drawn directly from W. B. Yeats's characterization of Spenser as "the first of many Englishmen to see nothing but what he was desired to see [by the state]" (149).

6. Paul Lauter has argued that within the discipline of English, "we may find ourselves perpetuating habitual assumptions that work against our goals [as teachers]"; see Lauter, "Teach/Discipline," *English as a Discipline; or, Is There a Plot in This Play?* ed. James C. Raymond (Tuscaloosa: University of Alabama Press, 1996), 30. This presumptive appropriation of what "humanism is" is one such assumption habitually perpetuated. Also, see David Hill Radcliffe's *Edmund Spenser: A Reception History,* Literary Criticism in Perspective series (Columbia, S.C.: Camden House, 1996). There is an eerie consistency to the "Spenser" that appears throughout Radcliffe's historical survey of Spenser criticism. Significantly, the notion that contemporary Spenser criticism is done by people who, in all probablitlity, spend most of their professional time in the business of *teaching* is not considered. Thus when Radcliffe writes that "Spenser criticism bears witness to the idea that classics are constantly being rewritten within a tradition that believes in classics" (197), it is fair to say that the tradition of which he speaks involves, primarily, the perpetuation of a discipline which measures itself through the production of literary criticism and "students of literature."

7. Canny, *Spenser and Ireland,* 14. There is a considerable range for critics regarding the extent to which Spenser averred Protestant doctrine, ranging from zealot to moderate; my point is that "ultimately" critics point to Protestant doctrine as the basis or source for his political thought.

8. Patricia Coughlan, ed., *Spenser and Ireland: An Interdisciplinary Perspective* (Cork: Cork University Press, 1989), 62.

9. Anne Fogarty, "The Colonization of Language: Narrative Strategy in *A View of the Present State of Ireland* and *The Faerie Queene,* Book VI," in *Spenser in Ireland,* ed. Coughlan, 82. Though I disagree with Fogarty's conclusions, her starting premise is compelling. She notes that "all of Spenser's work evinces a passionate concern with the mediatory function of language and with the shaping and thereby political forces of rhetoric. For him writing is, in Foucault's phrase, 'the prose of the world'" (77). To be fair, both Coughlan and Fogarty arrive at a point where they claim that the "rhetoric of" of the *View* cannot be easily separated from its "content." They arrive at that point, however, by parsing out the "rhetoric of" the text from its "real," ideological matter.

10. Examples are numerous, and the following are intended to be indicative, not comprehensive. In Ciaran Brady's "Reply" within "Debate, Spenser's Irish Crisis: Humanism and Experience in the 1590s," *Past and Present* 120 (1988): 210–15, Brady characterizes Spenser's rhetorical efforts in the *View* as a "dissimulation" designed to "dupe" his readers by taking them through "a dense thicket of ambiguity" constructed

out of "all the rhetorical devices at his disposal"; "Spenser strains logic, language and image until at length his thought collapses into the moral and linguistic abyss of 'that evil that is of itself evil'" (214–15); Andrew Hadfield distinguishes between the "rhetoric and the logic . . . the form and the content" of the *View* in "Spenser, Ireland, and Sixteenth-Century Political Theory," *Modern Language Review* 89 (1994): 1–18; and, finally, Richard M. McCabe characterizes Spenser's rhetorical practices as an exercise in "wish-fulfilment if not self-delusion"; through analogies and historiography, Spenser attempts to reconcile "moral and political necessity . . . calculated to appeal only to like-minded theorists" (123). See "The Fate of Irena: Spenser and Political Violence," in *Spenser and Ireland,* ed. Coughlan, 109–25.

11. Patterson, "Egalitarian Giant," 102.

12. Steven G. Ellis writes in *Tudor Ireland: Crown, Community and the Conflict of Cultures, 1470–1603* (New York: Longman, 1985), that Tudor policies in Ireland were "erratic" and full of "frequent reversals of policy"; "Tudor policies . . . failed because they were not given the chance to succeed."

13. Sheila T. Cavanaugh, "'Such was Irena's Countenance': Ireland in Spenser's Prose and Poetry," *Texas Studies in Language and Literature* 28 (1986): 24–50.

14. Willy Maley, "How Milton and Some Contemporaries read Spenser's *View*," in *Representing Ireland,* ed. Brendan Bradshaw, Andrew Hadfield, and Willy Maley (Cambridge: Cambridge University Press, 1993), 201.

15. Spenser, *View of the Present State of Ireland,* 230. All quotations are taken from this edition. I have modernized most of the spelling and capitalization, with the exception of verbs that are formed with "-eth" and some archaic words.

16. Brady, "Debate, Spenser's Irish Crisis."

17. Essex demanded and received from the queen the lord lieutenancy in March 1599, against her better judgment. Going against her orders, Essex did not confront Tyrone immediately; after wasting time, men, and money, he finally reached a truce with Tyrone, then left Ireland without the queen's permission in September of that same year. For his defiance, he was jailed; for the very real threat he posed to the queen's authority, he was convicted of treason and put to death in 1601.

18. Jane Brink, "Constructing the *View of the Present State of Ireland*," *Spenser Studies* 11 (1990): 203–28.

19. Lisa Hopkins, *Elizabeth I and Her Court* (New York: St. Martin's Press, 1990). Essex saw his new command as a means to cultivate a loyal following by bestowing honors and titles on his friends; the queen instructed Essex, Hopkins writes, "to give knighthoods only to men who had shown exceptional valour in battle. . . . These orders Essex disobeyed" (100–101).

20. Jonathan Goldberg, *Endlesse Worke: Spenser and the Structures of Discourses* (Baltimore: Johns Hopkins University Press, 1981), 9. For an opposing view, see Baker, "'Some Quirk,'" 147–63. Baker maintains that Spenser intended the *View* as a vindication of Elizabeth's colonialist policy: "He misjudged the effect his text would have on its intended readers—and those readers, for their part, misread (or disregarded) his intent" (150).

21. *Varorium,* 10:244.

22. E. K. employs the term "analysis," albeit in the Greek, in his lengthy and misguided attempts to ascertain the reason motivating Immeritô's decision to use the spelling "Æglogues" rather than "eclogues" in his opening epistle in *The Shepheardes Calender.*

23. Waswo, *Language and Meaning,* 230.

24. In addition to the texts by Maley and Cavanaugh already cited, see Sheila T. Cavanaugh's "The Fatal Destiny of That Land": Elizabethan View of Ireland," in *Representing Ireland,* ed. Brendan Bradshaw, Andrew Hadfield, and Willy Maley (Cambridge: Cambridge University Press, 1993), 116–31, and Maley, *A Spenser Chronology* (Lanham, Md.: Barnes & Noble Books, 1994).

25. That Spenser attempts to portray the Irish as a cultural "other," innately inferior to the English, is a commonplace within Spenser criticism.

26. Irenius defines kincongishe as a custom that requires "every head of every sept, and every chief of every kindred or family . . . to be answerable and bound to bring forth every one of his kindred or sept under him at all times to be justified when he should be required or charged with any treason, felony, or other heinous crime" (Spenscr, *View,* 80).

27. See "Appendix IV" of the *Varorium,* 10:533.

28. Baker "'Some Quirk,'" 148.

29. Annabel Patterson, *Reading Between the Lines* (Madison: University of Wisconsin Press, 1993), 80–115.

30. Fowler, "Failure of Moral Philosophy," 47.

Chapter Eight

1. I have dispensed with the conventional manner for citing material from *The Faerie Queene* (e.g., 6.x.17) because with few exceptions, all material is from book 6. Unless a different book number is given in the first position within the parenthetical reference, you thus may assume that the canto and stanza numbers referred to are from book 6.

2. Robert E. Stillman, "Spenserian Autonomy and the Trial of New Historicism: Book Six of *The Faerie Queene," English Literary Renaissance* 22, no. 4 (1993): 299–314. The work by Angus Fletcher referred to is *The Prophetic Moment: An Essay on Spenser* (Chicago: University of Chicago Press, 1971), 93. Among the works that alternately explain or submit to "the idealized autonomy of Spenser's work" (Stillman, "Spenserian Autonomy," 301) that have been useful in developing the argument for this chapter are Mark Archer, "The Meaning of 'Grace' and 'Courtesy': Book VI of *The Faerie Queene," English Literary Renaissance* 17 (1987): 156–71; Goldberg, *Endlesse Worke;* David L. Miller, "Abandoning the Quest," *English Literary History* 46 (1979): 173–92; Richard Neuse, "Book VI as Conclusion to *The Faerie Queene," English Literary History* 35 (1968): 329–53; Dewitt. T. Starnes, "Spenser and the Muses," *Texas Studies in Language and Literature* 10 (1942): 31–58; and Humphrey Tonkin's *Spenser's Courteous Pastoral: Book Six of "The Faerie Queene"* (Oxford: Clarendon, 1972).

3. Stillman, for example, offers as his reason for historicizing book 6 the notion that "Renaissance culture" offers new historicism "peculiar challenges" ("Spenserian Autonomy," 314). See note 2 above.

4. Derek B. Alwes, "'Who Knowes Not Colin Clout': Spenser's Self-Advertisement in *The Faerie Queene,* Book 6," *Modern Philology* 88 (1990): 26–42; see p. 31.

5. Edmund Spenser, "The Teares of the Muses" (1591) from *The Yale Edition of the Shorter Poems of Edmund Spenser,* ed. William A. Oram, Einar Bjorvand, Ronald Bond, Thomas H. Cain, Alexander Dunlop, and Richard Schell (New Haven, Conn.: Yale University Press, 1989).

6. As Hamilton notes, however, there is some question as to whether Spenser calls upon Calliope or Clio (see note 1 to stanza 2 for the Proem to book 1); Spenser appears to conflate the two muses in terms of what they do.

7. Hesiod, *Theogony,* in *The Homeric Hymns and Homerica,* trans. Hugh G. Evelyn-White (Cambridge: Harvard University Press, 1914), 81.

8. This interpretation of the muses is derived from Donald Phillip Verene, *The New Art of Autobiography: An Essay on the "Life of Giambattista Vico Written by Himself"* (Oxford: Clarendon Press, 1991), 157, 211, 216; and Verene, *Vico's Science of the Imagination.*

9. Jaqueline T. Miller, "The Courtly Figure: Spenser's Anatomy of Allegory," *Studies in English Literature 1500–1900* 31 (1991): 51–68.

10. Cf. Dixon, *Polliticke Courtier,* 10. Dixon appropriates Kenneth Burke's discussions of courtship with regard to Castiglione's *Book of the Courtier* from Burke's text *A Rhetoric of Motives* (Berkeley and Los Angeles: University of California Press, 1969).

11. For the self-conscious fictivity of Burke's own work, see Tilly Warnock, "Making Do, Making Believe, and Making Sense: Burkeian Magic and the Essence of English Departments," in *English as a Discipline; or, Is There a Plot in This Play?* ed. James C. Raymond (Tuscaloosa: University of Alabama Press, 1996), 143–59.

12. Cicero, *De officiis* 1.30.107.

13. By this definition, *honestum* remains a very general notion: an organized crime boss could be "honest" if he has determined that his particular genius is killing or stealing in the service of others, his "family" perhaps; and if he remains true to that character, then he has led a "proper" life. In this case, *honestum* and *decorum* are determined by the mores of organized crime.

14. Cicero is well aware, however, that the distinction between the two proprieties is a distinction without a difference since any individual is but part of a larger whole; see 1.27.95. Cicero, *De officiis,* 1.27.95.

15. The third site of instruction may be inferred from Prince Arthur's actions in book 6.

16. Miller, "Courtly Figure," 55–56.

17. Alwes, "'Who Knowes Not Colin Clout?'" 29.

Afterword

1. Grafton and Jardine, *From Humanism to the Humanities,* 162.

2. Robert Young, "The Politics of 'The Politics of Literary Theory,'" *Oxford Literary Review* 11 (1989): 131–57. The "politics of literary theory," Young argues, produces theoretical differences which "constitute[s] the very mode of thinking that produces theoretical insight. . . . From this perspective, English Studies itself constitutes nothing other than a practice of crisis management" (146–47). Jonathan Culler

offers a similar critique in "Criticism and Institutions," in *Post-structuralism and the Question of History,* ed. Derek Attridge, Geoff Bennington, and Robert Young (Cambridge: Cambridge University Press, 1987), 82–98. Culler writes, "If, as Gramsci says, intellectuals in the capitalist state function as 'experts in legitimation,' then theoretical criticism might be deemed the place where critiques of legitimacy are continually being carried out—in a quarter where they may seem to pose the least direct threat to social and political institutions" (96).

3. Fowler, "Failure of Moral Philosophy," 71.

4. Janet Atwill, *Rhetoric Reclaimed: Aristotle and the Liberal Arts Tradition* (Ithaca, N.Y.: Cornell University Press, 1998), 210.

BIBLIOGRAPHY

Alpers, Paul. "Narration in *The Faerie Queene*." *English Literary History* 44 (1977): 22–48.

———. *The Poetry of "The Faerie Queene."* Princeton, N.J.: Princeton University Press, 1967.

Alwes, Derek B. "'Who Knowes Not Colin Clout?': Spenser's Self-Advertisement in *The Faerie Queene,* Book 6." *Modern Philology* 88 (1990): 26–42.

Archer, Mark. "The Meaning of 'Grace' and 'Courtesy': Book VI of *The Faerie Queene*." *English Literary Renaissance* 17 (1987): 156–71.

Aristotle. *Nicomachean Ethics.* Translated by Martin Oswald. New York: Macmillan, 1962.

———. *On the Art of Poetry.* Translated and edited by Ingram Bywater. Oxford: Clarendon Press, 1909.

Ascham, Roger. *The Schoolmaster.* Edited by Lawrence V. Ryan. 1570. Reprint, Ithaca, N.Y.: Cornell University Press, 1967.

Attridge, Derek, Geoff Bennington, and Robert Young, eds. *Post-structuralism and the Question of History.* Cambridge: Cambridge University Press, 1987.

Atwill, Janet M. *Rhetoric Reclaimed: Aristotle and the Liberal Arts Tradition.* Ithaca, N.Y.: Cornell University Press, 1998.

Avery, Bruce. "Mapping the Irish Other: Spenser's *A View of the Present State of Ireland*." *English Literary History* 57 (1990): 263–79.

Bacon, Francis. *The Advancement of Learning.* Book 1. Edited by William A. Armstrong. London: Athlone Press, 1975.

———. *The Masculine Birth of Time.* Edited and translated by Benjamin Farrington. In *The Philosophy of Francis Bacon,* 59–72. Liverpool: Liverpool University Press, 1964.

Baker, David J. "'Some Quirk, Some Subtle Evasion': Legal Subversion in Spenser's *A View of the Present State of Ireland*." *Spenser Studies* 6 (1986): 147–63.

Baldwin, Thomas W. *William Shakspere's Small Latine and Lesse Greeke.* 2 vols. Urbana: University of Illinois Press, 1944.

Baron, Hans. "Cicero and Roman Civic Spirit in the Middle Ages and the Early Renaissance." *Bulletin of the John Rylands Library* 22 (1938): 72–97.

————. "Leonardo Bruni: 'Professional Rhetorician' or Civic Humanist?" *Past and Present* 36 (1967): 21–37.

Bennet, Josephine Waters. *The Evolution of "The Faerie Queene."* Chicago: University of Chicago Press, 1942.

Berger, Harry, Jr. "Narrative as Rhetoric in *The Faerie Queene.*" *English Literary Renaissance* 21 (1991): 3–48.

————. *Revisionary Play: Studies in the Spenserian Dynamics.* Berkeley and Los Angeles: University of California Press, 1988.

Berlin, James A. "Rhetoric, Poetics, and Culture: Contested Boundaries in English Studies." In *The Politics of Writing Instruction: Postsecondary,* edited by Richard Bullock and John Trimbur, 23–38. Portsmouth, N.H.: Boynton/Cook, 1991.

————. *Rhetoric and Reality: Writing Instruction in American Colleges, 1900–1985.* Carbondale: Southern Illinois University Press, 1987.

Boyle, Marjorie O'Rourke. *Erasmus on Language and Method in Theology.* Toronto: University of Toronto Press, 1977.

Bradshaw, Brendan, Andrew Hadfield, and Willy Maley, eds. *Representing Ireland.* Cambridge: Cambridge University Press, 1993.

Brady, Ciaran. "Reply" within "Debate, Spenser's Irish Crisis: Humanism and Experience in the 1590s." *Past and Present* 120 (1988): 210–15.

————. "Spenser's Irish Crisis: Humanism and Experience in the 1590s." *Past and Present* 111 (1986): 17–49.

Brink, Jane. "Constructing the *View of the Present State of Ireland.*" *Spenser Studies* 11 (1990): 203–28.

Broadie, Sarah. *Ethics with Aristotle.* Oxford: Oxford University Press, 1991.

Bryskett, Lodowick. "A Discourse of Civill Life." In *Lodowick Bryskett: "A Discourse of Civill Life."* Edited by Thomas E. Wright. San Fernando Valley State College Renaissance Editions 4. Northridge, Calif.: San Fernando State College, 1970.

————. *"A Discourse of Civill Life": The Literary Works of Lodowick Bryskett.* Edited by J. H. P. Pafford. Westmead, Hants.: Gregg International, 1972.

Burke, Kenneth. *Attitudes toward History.* New Republic Series. New York: New Republic, 1937.

————. *Permanence and Change: An Anatomy of Purpose.* 1935. Reprint, Berkeley and Los Angeles: University of California Press, 1984.

————. *The Philosophy of Literary Form.* 1941. Reprint, Berkeley and Los Angeles: University of California Press, 1967.

Carrington, Laurel. "Erasmus' *Lingua:* The Double-Edged Tongue." *Erasmus of Rotterdam Society Yearbook* 9 (1989): 106–18.

Cavanaugh, Sheila T. "'Such was Irena's Countenance': Ireland in Spenser's Prose and Poetry." *Texas Studies in Language and Literature* 28 (1986): 24–50.

Cicero, Marcus Tullius. *Brutus.* Translated by Hubert M. Poteat. Chicago: University of Chicago Press, 1950.

———. *De natura deorum.* Translated by H. Rackham. Loeb Classical Library 268. New York: G. P. Putnam's Sons, 1933.

———. *De officiis.* Translated by Walter Miller. Loeb Classical Library. Cambridge: Harvard University Press, 1913.

———. *De oratore.* Translated by E. W. Sutton. 2 vols. Loeb Classical Library 348/ 349. Cambridge: Harvard University Press, 1942.

———. *De re publica / De legibus.* Translated by Clinton Walker Keyes. Loeb Classical Library 213. Cambridge: Harvard University Press, 1966.

———. *Finibus bonorum et malorum.* Translated by H. Rackham. Loeb Classical Library 40. New York: G. P. Putnam's Sons, 1931.

———. *Letters to His Friends.* Vol. 1. Translated by W. Glynn Williams. Loeb Classical Library. Cambridge: Harvard University Press, 1958.

Coughlan, Patricia, ed. *Spenser and Ireland: An Interdisciplinary Perspective.* Cork: Cork University Press, 1989.

Crane, Mary Thomas. *Framing Authority: Sayings, Self, and Society in Sixteenth-Century England.* Princeton, N.J.: Princeton University Press, 1993.

Crowley, Sharon. *Ancient Rhetorics for Contemporary Students.* Boston: Allyn and Bacon, 1994.

———. *The Methodical Memory: Invention in Current-Traditional Rhetoric.* Carbondale: Southern Illinois University Press, 1990.

———. "Writing and Writing." In *Writing and Reading Differently: Deconstruction and the Teaching of Composition and Literature,* edited by G. Douglas Atkins and Michael L. Johnson, 93–100. Lawrence: University of Kansas Press, 1985.

Cullen, Patrick. *Spenser, Marvell, and Renaissance Pastoral.* Cambridge: Harvard University Press, 1970.

Delli Carpini, Dominic. "Rewriting Holiness in the Age of Mechanical Reproduction: Cultural and Theological Contexts of Spenserian Allegory." Ph.D. diss., Pennsylvania State University, 1995.

DeNeef, A. Leigh. *Spenser and the Motives of Metaphor.* Durham, N.C.: Duke University Press, 1982.

Dixon, Michael F. N. *The Polliticke Courtier: Spenser's "The Faerie Queene" as a Rhetoric of Justice.* Montreal: McGill-Queen's University Press, 1996.

Drummond, William. *Notes of Conversations with Ben Jonson.* In *Ben Jonson: Discoveries 1641, Conversations with William Drummond of Hawthornden 1619,* edited by G. B. Harrison. 1619. Reprint, Edinburgh: Edinburgh University Press, 1966.

Ellis, Steven G. *Tudor Ireland: Crown, Community and the Conflict of Cultures, 1470–1603.* New York: Longman, 1985.

Erasmus, Desiderius. *De ratione studii.* Translated and edited by Brian McGregor. Vol. 24 of *Collected Works of Erasmus.* Toronto: University of Toronto Press, 1978.

———. *Dialogus Ciceronianus.* Edited and translated by Betty I. Knott. Vol. 27. Toronto: University of Toronto Press, 1986.

————. *The Tongue.* Translated by Elaine Fantham and edited by Elaine Fantham and Erika Rummel. Vol. 29 of *Collected Works of Erasmus.* Toronto: University of Toronto Press, 1986.

Fletcher, Angus. *The Prophetic Moment: An Essay on Spenser.* Chicago: University of Chicago Press, 1971.

Fowler, Elizabeth. "The Failure of Moral Philosophy in the Work of Edmund Spenser." *Representations* 51 (1995): 47–76.

Fraunce, Abraham. *The Lawyer's Logic.* Edited by R. C. Alston. English Linguistics 1500–1800 174. 1588. Reprint, Menston, Yorks.: Scolar Press, 1969.

Frentz, Thomas S. "Rhetorical Conversation, Time, and Moral Action." *Quarterly Journal of Speech* 71 (1985): 1–18.

Godschalk, W. L. "Cicero, Sidney, and the 'Sunne-Burn'd Braine.'" *Notes and Queries* 27 (1980): 139–40.

Goeglein, Tamara A. "Utterance of the Protestant Soul in *The Faerie Queene:* The Allegory of Holiness and the Humanist Discourse of Reason." *Criticism* 36 (1994): 1–19.

————. "'Wherein Hath Ramus Been So Offensious?': Poetic Examples in the English Ramist Logic Manuals (1574–1672)." *Rhetorica* 14, no. 1 (1996): 73–101.

Goetsch, James Robert, Jr. *Vico's Axioms: The Geometry of the Human World.* New Haven, Conn.: Yale University Press, 1995.

Goldberg, Jonathan. *Endlesse Worke: Spenser and the Structures of Discourses.* Baltimore: Johns Hopkins University Press, 1981.

Graff, Gerald, and Michael Warner, eds. *The Origins of Literary Studies in America.* New York: Routledge, 1989.

Grafton, Anthony, and Lisa Jardine. *From Humanism to the Humanities: Education and the Liberal Arts in Fifteenth- and Sixteenth-Century Europe.* Cambridge: Harvard University Press, 1986.

Grassi, Ernesto. *The Primordial Metaphor.* Translated by Laura Pietropaolo and Manuela Scarci. Medieval and Renaissance Texts and Studies 121. Binghamton, N.Y.: Medieval & Renaissance Texts & Studies, 1994.

————. *Renaissance Humanism: Studies in Philosophy and Poetics.* Translated by Walter F. Veit. Medieval and Renaissance Texts and Studies 51. Binghamton, N.Y.: Medieval & Renaissance Texts & Studies, 1988.

————. *Rhetoric as Philosophy.* University Park: Pennsylvania State University Press, 1980.

Gray, Hannah. "Renaissance Humanism: The Pursuit of Eloquence." *Journal of the History of Ideas* 24 (1963): 497–514.

Greenblatt, Stephen. *Renaissance Self-Fashioning: From More to Shakespeare.* Chicago: University of Chicago Press, 1980.

Greene, Roland. "*The Shepheardes Calender,* Dialogue, and Periphrasis." *Spenser Studies* 8 (1987): 1–33.

Hadfield, Andrew. "Spenser, Ireland, and Sixteenth-Century Political Theory." *Modern Language Review* 89 (1994): 1–18.

Harvey, Gabriel. *Ciceronianus.* Translated by Clarence A. Forbes and edited by Harold
    S. Wilson. Studies in the Humanities 4. Lincoln: University of Nebraska Press,
    1945.

Heninger, S. K. Introduction to *The Shepheardes Calender.* Scholar's Facsimiles and
    Reprints 328. 1579. Reprint, Delmar, N.Y.: Scholar's Facsimiles & Reprints, 1979.

Hesiod. *Theogony.* In *The Homeric Hymns and Homerica,* translated by Hugh G. Eve-
    lyn-White. Cambridge: Harvard University Press, 1914.

Hoffman, Nancy Jo. *Spenser's Pastorals: "The Shepheardes Calender" and "Colin Clout."*
    Baltimore: Johns Hopkins University Press, 1977.

Hopkins, Lisa. *Elizabeth I and Her Court.* New York: St. Martin's Press, 1990.

Howell, W[ilbur] S[amuel]. *Logic and Rhetoric in England 1500–1700.* Princeton, N.J.:
    Princeton University Press, 1956.

———. "Ramus and English Rhetoric: 1574–1681." *Quarterly Journal of Speech* 37
    (1951): 299–310.

Hume, Anthea. *Edmund Spenser: Protestant Poet.* Cambridge: Cambridge University
    Press, 1984.

Jardine, Lisa. *Erasmus, Man of Letters.* Princeton, N.J.: Princeton University Press, 1993.

———. *Francis Bacon and the Art of Discourse.* London: Cambridge University Press,
    1974.

Johnson, Lynn Stanley. *"The Shepheardes Calender": An Introduction.* University Park:
    Pennsylvania State University Press, 1990.

Johnson, Mark. *The Body in the Mind, the Bodily Basis of Meaning, Imagination, and
    Reason.* Chicago: University of Chicago Press, 1987.

Jones, Deborah. "Lodowick Bryskett and His Family." In *Thomas Lodge and Other Eliz-
    abethans,* edited by Charles Sisson, 243–362. New York: Octagon Books, 1966.

Kahn, Victoria. "Humanism and the Resistance to Theory." In *Literary Theory /
    Renaissance Texts,* edited by Patricia Parker and David Quint, 373–96. Baltimore:
    Johns Hopkins University Press, 1986.

———. *Rhetoric, Prudence, and Skepticism in the Renaissance.* Ithaca, N.Y.: Cornell
    University Press, 1985.

Kane, Sean. *Spenser's Moral Allegory.* Toronto: University of Toronto Press, 1989.

Kepler, Johannes. *The New Astronomy.* Translated by William H. Donahue. Cambridge:
    Cambridge University Press, 1992.

Kimball, Bruce A. *Orators and Philosophers: A History of the Idea of Liberal Education.*
    New York: Teachers College, Columbia University, 1986.

Kinney, Arthur. *Humanist Poetics: Thought, Rhetoric, and Fiction in Sixteenth-Century
    England.* Amherst: University of Massachusetts Press, 1986.

Kristeller, Paul Oskar. *Renaissance Thought I: The Classic, Scholastic, and Humanist
    Strains.* New York: Harper, 1961.

Lane, Robert. *Shepheards Devises: Edmund Spenser's "Shepheardes Calender" and the
    Institutions of Elizabethan Society.* Athens: University of Georgia Press, 1993.

Leff, Michael C. "The Topics of Argumentative Invention in Latin Rhetorical Theory
    from Cicero to Boethius." *Rhetorica* 1, no. 1 (1983): 23–45.

Legouis, Émile. *Spenser.* New York: E. P. Dutton, 1926.

Lewis, C. S. *Studies in Medieval and Renaissance Literature.* Cambridge: Cambridge University Press, 1966.

Lievsay, John L. *Stefano Guazzo and the English Renaissance, 1575–1675.* Chapel Hill: University of North Carolina Press, 1961.

Logan, Marie Rose. "The Renaissance: Foucault's Lost Chance?" In *After Foucault: Humanistic Knowledge, Postmodern Challenges,* edited by Jonathan Arac. 97–109. New Brunswick, N.J.: Rutgers University Press, 1988.

Lyotard, Jean-François. "Time Today." *Oxford Literary Review* 11 (1989): 3–20.

MacIlmaine, Roland, trans. *The Logike of the Moste Excellent Philosopher P. Ramus Martyr.* Edited by Catherine M. Dunn. San Fernando Valley State College Renaissance Editions 3. Northridge, Calif.: San Fernando State College, 1969.

———, trans. *Peter Ramus: The Logike, 1574.* Leeds: Scolar Press, 1966.

Mack, Peter. *Renaissance Argument: Valla and Agricola in the Traditions of Rhetoric and Dialectic.* Brill's Studies in Intellectual History 43. Leiden: E. J. Brill, 1993.

Maley, Willy. *A Spenser Chronology.* Lanham, Md.: Barnes & Noble Books, 1994.

Marsh, David, *The Quattrocento Dialogue: Classical Tradition and Humanist Innovation.* Cambridge: Harvard University Press, 1980.

McCanles, Michael. "*The Shepheardes Calender* as Document and Monument." *Studies in English Literature 1500–1900* 22 (1982): 5–19.

McCormick, Sister Mary Martin, P.B.V.M., ed. "A Critical Edition of Abraham Fraunce's *The Sheapheardes Logike* and *Twooe General Discourses.*" Ph.D. diss., St. Louis University, 1968.

McKeon, Richard. "The Use of Rhetoric in a Technological Age: Architectonic Productive Arts." *Rhetoric: Essays in Invention and Discovery.* Edited by Mark Backman. Woodbridge, Conn.: Ox Bow Press, 1987.

Miller, David L. "Abandoning the Quest." *English Literary History* 46 (1979): 173–92.

———. *The Poem's Two Bodies: The Poetics of the 1590 "Faerie Queene."* Princeton, N.J.: Princeton University Press, 1988.

Miller, Jaqueline T. "The Courtly Figure: Spenser's Anatomy of Allegory." *Studies in English Literature 1500–1900* 31 (1991): 51–68.

Montrose, Louis Adrian. "'The Perfect Paterne of a Poete': The Poetics of Courtship in *The Shepheardes Calender.*" *Texas Studies in Literature and Language* 21 (1978): 34–67.

Moss, Ann. "Commonplace-Rhetoric and Thought-Patterns in Early Modern Culture." In *The Recovery of Rhetoric,* edited by R. Roberts and J. Good. 49–60. Bristol: Duckworth, 1993.

Murphy, James J., ed. *Renaissance Eloquence: Studies in the Theory and Practice of Renaissance Rhetoric.* Berkeley and Los Angeles: University of California Press, 1983.

Myrick, Kenneth O. *Sir Philip Sidney as a Literary Craftsman.* Harvard Studies in English 14. Cambridge: Harvard University Press, 1935.

Nelson, William. *The Poetry of Edmund Spenser.* New York: Columbia University Press, 1963.

Neuse, Richard. "Book VI as Conclusion to *The Faerie Queene.*" *English Literary History* 35 (1968): 329–53.

O'Banion, John D. *Reorienting Rhetoric: The Dialectic of List and Story.* University Park: Pennsylvania State University Press, 1991.

Ong, Walter J., S.J. *Ramus, Method, and the Decay of Dialogue.* Cambridge: Harvard University Press, 1958.

———. *Ramus and Talon Inventory.* Cambridge: Harvard University Press, 1958.

———. "Tudor Writings on Rhetoric." *Studies in the Renaissance* 15 (1968): 39–69.

Patterson, Annabel. "The Egalitarian Giant: Representations of Justice in History/Literature." *Journal of British Studies* 31 (1992): 97–132.

———. *Reading between the Lines.* Madison: University of Wisconsin Press, 1993.

Phillips, Margaret Mann. *Erasmus and the Northern Renaissance.* 1949. Reprint, London: English Universities Press, 1984.

Plett, Heinrich F., ed. *Renaissance-Rhetorik / Renaissance Rhetoric.* Berlin: Walter de Gruyter, 1993.

Plomer, Henry R., and Thomas Peete Cross. *The Life and Correspondence of Lodowick Bryskett.* Chicago: University of Chicago Press, 1927.

Poulakos, Takis, ed. *Rethinking the History of Rhetoric: Multidisciplinary Essays on the Rhetorical Tradition.* Polemic Series. Boulder, Colo.: Westview Press, 1993.

Protagoras. "Truth or Refutations." In *The Older Sophists,* translated by Michael J. O'Brien and edited by Rosamond Kent Sprague. Columbia: University of South Carolina Press, 1972.

Puttenham, George. *The Arte of English Poesie.* Kent English Reprints, the Renaissance. 1589. Reprint, Kent, Ohio: Kent State University Press, 1970.

Radcliffe, David Hill. *Edmund Spenser: A Reception History.* Literary Criticism in Perspective. Columbia, S.C.: Camden House, 1996.

Ramus, Peter. *Arguments in Rhetoric Against Quintilian.* Translated by Carole Newlands. Dekalb: Northern Illinois University Press, 1986.

———. *Peter Ramus's Attack on Cicero: Text and Translation of Ramus's "Brutinae Quaestiones."* Translated by Carole E. Newlands and edited by James J. Murphy. Davis, Calif.: Hermagoras Press, 1992.

Raymond, James C., ed. *English as a Discipline; or, Is There a Plot in This Play?* Tuscaloosa: University of Alabama Press, 1996.

Rebhorn, Wayne A. *The Emperor of Men's Minds: Literature and the Renaissance Discourse of Rhetoric.* Ithaca, N.Y.: Cornell University Press, 1995.

———. *Renaissance Controversies on Rhetoric.* Ithaca, N.Y.: Cornell University Press, 2000.

Reiss, Timothy J. *Knowledge, Discovery and Imagination in Early Modern Europe: The Rise of Aesthetic Rationalism.* Cambridge: Cambridge University Press, 1997.

———. *The Meaning of Literature.* Ithaca, N.Y.: Cornell University Press, 1992.

Ricoeur, Paul. *The Rule of Metaphor: Multi-disciplinary Studies of the Creation of Meaning in Language.* Translated by Robert Czerny. Toronto: University of Toronto Press, 1977.

Rorty, Amelie Oksenberg, ed. *Essays on Aristotle's Ethics.* Berkeley and Los Angeles: University of California Press, 1980.

Rueckert, William. *Kenneth Burke and the Drama of Human Relations.* 1963. Reprint, Berkeley and Los Angeles: University of California Press, 1982.

Rummel, Erika. *The Humanist-Scholastic Debate in the Renaissance and Reformation.* Cambridge: Harvard University Press, 1995.

Schilb, John. *Between the Lines: Relating Composition Theory and Literary Theory.* Portsmouth, N.H.: Boynton/Cook, 1996.

Schleiner, Louise. "Spenser's 'E. K.' as Edmund Kent (Kenned / Of Kent): Kyth (Couth), Kissed, and Kunning, Conning." *English Literary Renaissance* 20 (1990): 374–407.

Schmitt, Charles B. *Cicero Scepticus: A Study of the Influence of the "Academica" in the Renaissance.* International Archives of the History of Ideas 52. The Hague: Martinus Nijhoff, 1972.

Schoeck, Richard J. "Going for the Throat: Erasmus' Rhetorical Theory and Practice." In *Renaissance-Rhetorik / Renaissance Rhetoric,* edited by Heirich F. Plett, 43–58. Berlin: Walter de Gruyter, 1993.

Scott, Izadora. *Controversies Over the Imitation of Cicero in the Renaissance.* 1910. Reprint, Davis, Calif.: Hermagoras Press, 1991.

Seigel, Jerrold. "'Civic Humanism' or Ciceronian Rhetoric?" *Past and Present* 34 (1966): 3–48.

———. *Rhetoric and Philosophy in Renaissance Humanism: The Union of Eloquence and Wisdom, Petrarch to Valla.* Princeton, N.J.: Princeton University Press, 1968.

Shore, David. *Spenser and the Poetics of Pastoral: A Study of the World of Colin Clout.* Kingston: McGill-Queen's University Press, 1985.

Shuger, Debora Kuller. *Habits of Thought in the English Renaissance: Religion, Politics, and the Dominant Culture.* Renaissance Society of America Reprint Texts 6. Toronto: University of Toronto Press, 1997.

Sidney, Philip. *An Apology for Poetry.* In *Elizabethan Critical Essays,* edited by G. Gregory Smith, 150–207. Oxford: Clarendon Press, 1904.

———. "Astrophil and Stella." In *The Poems of Sir Philip Sidney,* edited by William A. Ringler Jr. Oxford: Clarendon Press, 1962.

———. *A Defence of Poetry.* In *Miscellaneous Prose of Sir Philip Sidney,* edited by Katharine Duncan-Jones and Jan Van Dorsten. 73–121. Oxford: Clarendon Press, 1972.

———. *The Poems of Sir Philip Sidney.* Edited by William A. Ringler Jr. Oxford: Clarendon Press, 1962.

Sim, Mary, ed. *The Crossroads of Norm and Nature: Essays on Aristotle's Ethics and Metaphysics.* New York: Rowman and Littlefield, 1995.

Sloane, Thomas O. *Donne, Milton, and the End of Humanist Rhetoric.* Berkeley and Los Angeles: University of California Press, 1985.

————. "The Most Significant Passage on Rhetoric in the Works of Francis Bacon." *Rhetoric Society Quarterly* 26, no. 3 (1996): 46–49.

————. *On the Contrary: The Protocol of Traditional Rhetoric.* Washington, D.C.: Catholic University of America Press, 1997.

————. "Reinventing *Inventio.*" *College English* 51 (1989): 461–73.

————. "Rhetorical Education and Two-Sided Argument." In *Renaissance-Rhetorik / Renaissance Rhetoric,* edited by Heirich F. Plett, 163–78. Berlin: Walter de Gruyter, 1993.

————. "Schoolbooks and Rhetoric: Erasmus's *Copia.*" *Rhetorica* 9, no. 2 (1991): 113–29.

Spenser, Edmund. *The Faerie Queene.* Edited by A. C. Hamilton. London: Longman, 1977.

————. *A View of the Present State of Ireland.* Vol. 10 of *The Works of Edmund Spenser: A Variorum Edition.* Edited by Edwin Greenlaw, special editor Rudolf Gottfried. Baltimore: Johns Hopkins University Press, 1949.

————. *The Yale Edition of the Shorter Poems of Edmund Spenser.* Edited by William A. Oram, Einar Bjorvand, Ronald Bond, Thomas H. Cain, Alexander Dunlop, and Richard Schell. New Haven, Conn.: Yale University Press, 1989.

Starnes, Dewitt. T. "Spenser and the Muses." *Texas Studies in English* 10 (1942): 31–58.

Stillman, Robert E. "Spenserian Autonomy and the Trial of New Historicism: Book Six of *The Faerie Queene.*" *English Literary Renaissance* 22, no. 4 (1993): 299–314.

Struever, Nancy S. *Theory as Practice: Ethical Inquiry in the Renaissance.* Chicago: University of Chicago Press, 1992.

Temple, William. *William Temple's "Analysis" of Sir Philip Sidney's "Apology for Poetry."* Translated and edited by John Webster. Medieval and Renaissance Texts and Studies 32. Binghamton, N.Y.: Medieval & Renaissance Texts & Studies, 1984.

Tonkin, Humphrey. *Spenser's Courteous Pastoral: Book Six of "The Faerie Queene."* Oxford: Clarendon, 1972.

Tracey, James D. *The Politics of Erasmus: A Pacifist Intellectual and His Political Milieu.* Toronto: Toronto University Press, 1978.

Tuozzo, Thomas M. "Conceptualized and Unconceptualized Desire in Aristotle." *Journal of the History of Philosophy* 32 (1995): 525–49.

Verene, Donald Phillip. *The New Art of Autobiography: An Essay on the* Life of Giambattista Vico Written by Himself. Oxford: Clarendon Press, 1991.

————. *Vico's Science of the Imagination.* Ithaca, N.Y.: Cornell University Press, 1981.

Vickers, Brian. *In Defence of Rhetoric.* Oxford: Clarendon Press, 1988.

Vico, Giambattista. *New Science.* Translated by Thomas Goddard Bergin and Max Harold Fisch. 1744. Reprint, Ithaca, N.Y.: Cornell University Press, 1968.

Vitanza, Victor J., ed. *Writing Histories of Rhetoric.* Carbondale: Southern Illinois University Press, 1994.

Waldman, Louis. "Spenser's Pseudonym 'E. K.' and Humanist Self-Naming." *Spenser Studies* 9 (1991): 21–31.

Walker, Jeffrey. *Rhetoric and Poetics in Antiquity.* Oxford: Oxford University Press, 2000.

Waswo, Richard. *Language and Meaning in the Renaissance.* Princeton, N.J.: Princeton University Press, 1987.

Webster, John. "'The Methode of a Poete': An Inquiry into Tudor Conceptions of Poetic Sequence." *English Literary Renaissance* 11 (1981): 22–43.

White, Hayden. "Foucault's Discourse: The Historiography of Anti-Humanism." In *The Content of Form: Narrative Discourse and Historical Representation.* Baltimore: Johns Hopkins University Press, 1987.

Wilson, Thomas. *Thomas Wilson: The Art of Rhetoric.* Edited by Peter E. Medine. 1560. Reprint, University Park: Pennsylvania State University Press, 1994.

Wright, Thomas. "Lodowick Bryskett." In *The Spenser Encyclopedia.* General editor A. C. Hamilton. Toronto: University of Toronto Press, 1990.

Yates, Francis. *The Art of Memory.* Chicago: University of Chicago Press, 1966.

Young, Robert. "The Politics of 'The Politics of Literary Theory.'" *Oxford Literary Review* 11 (1989): 131–57.

INDEX